W9-CTW-395

DATE DUE

DEMCO 38-296

THE ELECTIONS
OF 1996

R

THE ELECTIONS OF 1996

Edited by

Michael Nelson
Rhodes College

A Division of Congressional Quarterly Inc.
Washington, D.C.

Riverside Community College
Library
4800 Magnolia Avenue
Riverside, CA 92506

JK1968 1996
The elections of 1996

.

Copyright © 1997 Congressional Quarterly Inc.
1414 22nd Street, N.W., Washington, D.C. 20037

All rights reserved. No part of this publication may be reproduced or transmitted in any form
or by any means, electronic or mechanical, including photocopy, recording, or any information storage and retrieval system, without permission in writing from the publisher.

Printed and bound in the United States of America

Cover design: Paula Anderson

The paper used in this publication meets the minimum requirements of the American National
Standard for Information Sciences—Permanence of Paper for Printed Library Materials,
ANSI Z39.48-1984.

Library of Congress Cataloging-in-Publication Data

The elections of 1996 / edited by Michael Nelson.
p.   cm.
Includes bibliographical references and index.
ISBN 1-56802-247-6 (hard). — ISBN 1-56802-219-0 (paper)
1. United States.   Congress—Elections, 1996.   2. Presidents—
United States—Election—1996.   3. Elections—United States.
I. Nelson, Michael, 1949– .
JK1968 1996
324.973'0929—dc21   97-2059

Contents

Preface

The extraordinary thing about elections in the United States is that they are so ordinary. No one woke up on November 5, 1996, wondering whether the elections would be held or canceled that day. No one doubted on December 16 that the electors would be permitted to assemble in their various state capitals and cast the votes that officially elect the president and vice president, or that Congress would gather on January 6, 1997, for the counting of the electoral votes and the vice president's announcement of the winners, or that the newly elected Congress would actually be sworn in on January 7. Similarly, the suspense on inauguration day, January 20, was not whether President Bill Clinton would be allowed to take the oath of office but whether he would play the saxophone at any of the fifteen inaugural balls being held in Washington that night. (He did not.)

Even in the midst of the Civil War, elections went on as scheduled in the United States—the midterm congressional election of 1862 and the presidential and congressional elections of 1864. In August 1864, facing the "exceedingly probable" prospect that "this Administration will not be reelected" and that an opponent whose policies he deplored would be chosen instead, President Abraham Lincoln nonetheless instructed his cabinet to sign a pledge to cooperate in the transfer of power to the new president. Lincoln was a better candidate than prognosticator—he won the election—but his actions laid to final rest the long dormant fears of the Antifederalist opponents of the Constitution that the president, as head of the army, would use any pretext to cancel elections and hold on to power illegitimately. Elections went on as scheduled—and with no doubt in any quarter that they would do so—during World War I, the Great Depression, World War II, the Korean War, and the Vietnam War.

Perhaps the sheer "givenness," the "of course" quality, of American elections explains why sometimes, as in 1996, they seem dull to many voters and pundits. They should not. Blessings that we take for granted are no less thrilling for that. A remarkable, two centuries–old phenomenon is, if anything, made even more remarkable by the fact that we can take it for granted.

In any event, however uninteresting the elections of 1996 may have seemed to some while they were happening, they lend themselves to fascinating study and analysis. Consider, for example, the political setting in which they occurred. In the three consecutive midterm and presidential elections that took place in 1990, 1992, and 1994, the American people tried out nearly every possible partisan combination of presidents and Congresses. In 1990 they reaffirmed the pattern that had prevailed since 1968: President George Bush, at the time the fourth president of the last five to be a Republican, was given a Democratic Congress (the norm since the 1930s) to work with. In 1992, after flirting for much of the year with the possibility of electing a third-party candidate, Ross Perot, as president, the voters chose a Democratic president, Clinton, to work with the again Democratic Congress. Two years later, with Clinton still in the White House, they elected a Republican Congress for the first time since 1952. In the aftermath of that election, many pundits confidently predicted that in 1996 a Republican president would be elected along with a Republican Congress, completing the sequence of ever-changing partisan combinations.

The pundits were, of course, wrong: Clinton was reelected, comfortably if not overwhelmingly. They were wrong again when, after Clinton's lead became apparent during the summer and fall of 1996, they began predicting the election of a Democratic Congress.

The Elections of 1996 goes a long way toward explaining what happened in 1996 and why. Like its predecessor volumes, beginning with *The Elections of 1984*, it also does more than that. All eight of the book's chapters, each of them written with care by an outstanding political scientist and carefully edited for clarity and felicity, look back in time to set the events of 1996 in historical context and look forward to assess the elections' implications for the future of American politics.

My thanks go to those contributors—both familiar names from earlier books in this series such as John J. DiIulio Jr., Jean Bethke Elshtain, Gary C. Jacobson, and Paul J. Quirk, and new members of the team, including Christopher Beem, Matthew Robert Kerbel, Sean Matheson, and Harold W. Stanley. Thanks, too, to the outstanding editorial and production team at CQ Press for the assurance, skill, and warmth with which they have treated this book: acquisitions editor Brenda Carter, senior managing editor Ann Davies, chapter editors Carolyn Goldinger and Jerry Orvedahl, and project editor Chris Karlsten. L. Pilar Wyman wrote the index. Aware of the quadrennial crunch that the writing and editing of these books impose on family life, Linda E. Nelson, my wife, and Michael C. L. Nelson Jr. and Samuel M. L. Nelson, our sons, were patient, loving, and supportive, as ever. The help through the years of authors, editors, and family members such as these, like the regularity of American elections, is something I celebrate even as I take it for granted.

Michael Nelson

Contributors

Christopher Beem is director of the Council on Civil Society, a project of the University of Chicago Divinity School and the Institute for American Values. His writings have appeared in the *Journal of Religious Ethics,* the *Responsive Community,* and the *Los Angeles Times,* among others. He received his Ph.D. in ethics and society in 1994 from the University of Chicago Divinity School. He is currently working on a book on the concept of civil society.

John J. DiIulio Jr. is professor of politics and public affairs at the Woodrow Wilson School, Princeton University. He is director of the Partnership for Research on Religion and At-Risk Youth at Public/Private Ventures, Douglas Dillon Fellow at the Brookings Institution, and a contributing editor of the *Weekly Standard.* He is coauthor (with James Q. Wilson) of *American Government* (6th ed., 1995) and (with William J. Bennett) of *Body Count: Moral Poverty—and How to Win America's War Against Crime and Drugs* (1996).

Jean Bethke Elshtain is Laura Spelman Rockefeller Chair of Political and Social Ethics at the University of Chicago. She is most recently the author of *Democracy on Trial* (1995) and *Augustine and the Limits of Politics* (1995). She also has two books currently in press: *Real Politics: Politics and Everyday Life* and *New Wine and Old Bottles: International Politics at Century's End.* She is a regular columnist on political issues for the *New Republic.*

Gary C. Jacobson is professor of political science at the University of California, San Diego. He is the coauthor of *Strategy and Choice in Congressional Elections* (2d ed., 1983) and the author of *Money in Congressional Elections* (1980), *The Electoral Origins of Divided Government* (1990), and *The Politics of Congressional Elections* (4th ed., 1997).

Matthew Robert Kerbel is associate professor of political science at Villanova University, where he specializes in media politics. He is the author of three books and numerous articles about the media, campaigns, and the presidency, including *Edited for Television: CNN, ABC and the 1992 Presiden-*

tial Campaign (1994) and *Remote and Controlled: Media Politics in a Cynical Age* (1995). His interest in media politics derives from his previous work as a television newswriter for public broadcasting in New York and as a radio news reporter.

Sean Matheson is a doctoral candidate in political science at the University of Illinois at Urbana—Champaign. He has published or presented research on electoral politics and American foreign policy. His dissertation examines children's images of the presidency.

Michael Nelson is professor of political science at Rhodes College. A former editor of the *Washington Monthly*, he has written articles that have appeared in numerous scholarly publications and popular magazines. He is the author, coauthor, or editor of several books on the presidency, including *Presidents, Politics, and Policy* with Erwin C. Hargrove (1984), *The Elections of 1984* (1985), *The Elections of 1988* (1989), *The Elections of 1992* (1993), *The Presidency and the Political System* (4th ed., 1994), and *The American Presidency: Origins and Development, 1776–1993* with Sidney M. Milkis (1993), which won the Benjamin Franklin Award for History, Politics, and Philosophy. His most recent book is *Celebrating the Humanities: A Half-Century of the Search Course at Rhodes College* (1996).

Paul J. Quirk is professor of political science at the University of Illinois at Urbana—Champaign. He is the author of *Industry Influence in Federal Regulatory Agencies* (1981) and *The Politics of Deregulation* (1985), along with numerous articles and essays on the presidency, presidential elections, public policymaking, and American politics. He has served on the editorial boards of several leading journals, including the *American Political Science Review*. He is currently doing research on the president's role in public policymaking.

Harold W. Stanley is associate professor and chairman of political science at the University of Rochester. He is the author of articles on voting, political parties, and elections and *Senate vs. Governor, Alabama 1971: Referents for Opposition in a One-Party Legislature* (1975) and *Voter Mobilization and the Politics of Race: The South and Universal Suffrage, 1952–1984* (1987). With Richard Niemi he edits *Vital Statistics on American Politics* (6th ed., forthcoming).

1

1997 and Beyond:
The Perils of Second-Term Presidents

Michael Nelson

The American people gave every sign of being disengaged from the elections of 1996. Less than 10 percent of them tuned in to Bill Clinton and Bob Dole's acceptance speeches at the Republican and Democratic National Conventions, down nearly one-third from 1992. Interest in the presidential and vice presidential debates was meager: the second debate between Clinton and Dole was seen by only 36 million viewers, the smallest audience for a presidential debate in history, and barely half as many people watched the debate between Al Gore and Jack Kemp as had watched the 1992 debate between the vice presidential candidates. Third-party candidate Ross Perot's half-hour "infomercials," one of which had drawn more viewers than a major league baseball playoff game in 1992, barely registered in the 1996 Nielsen ratings. In a late October poll, 39 percent of a sample of eligible voters said they were interested in the presidential campaign, compared with 78 percent at a comparable time in 1992. On election day, many of them stayed home: the voter turnout rate in 1996 was 49.0 percent, the lowest since 1924.[1]

Perhaps because the elections seemed so boring to so many people, post-election commentators reached back in history for ways to make the results appear interesting. As noted by several pundits, Clinton's victory in 1996 made him the first Democratic president since Franklin D. Roosevelt in 1936 (and only the fourth Democrat in history) to be elected to a second term, as well as the first Democrat ever to be elected along with a Republican Congress. Clinton's low vote totals also came in for comment: he was the first two-term president of either party since Woodrow Wilson, in the 1910s, not to win a majority of the popular vote in either of his victories and the only one never to receive at least four hundred electoral votes. Clinton's 49.2 percent share of the 49.0 percent voter turnout allowed him to claim the endorsement of just 24.1 percent of the voting-age population, slightly more than the 23.8 percent who voted for him in 1992 but the third lowest share for a winning presidential candidate since the 1820s. As for the Republican Congress, it was the first to be reelected since 1928. (Previous Republican victories in the 1946 and 1952 congressional elections had been undone by the voters two years later.) For the first time ever, the voters in 1996 maintained the combination of a Republican Congress and a Democratic president beyond two years.[2]

All of these historical landmarks were concerned with the results of the elections. So are most of the chapters in this book. Understanding why the elections turned out as they did is an important enterprise. Thus, in Chapter 2 Harold W. Stanley chronicles the presidential nominating process that in 1996 generated the candidacies of the Democrat Clinton, the Republican Dole, and the Reform Party nominee Perot. In Chapter 3 I carry forward the narrative and the analysis through the general election campaign that ended on election day in November. Matthew Robert Kerbel examines the media's role in the election in Chapter 4, and in Chapter 5 Jean Bethke Elshtain and Christopher Beem assess the campaign's issues and themes.

Understanding the consequences of the elections for politics and government is also an important task. Paul J. Quirk and Sean Matheson in Chapter 6 and Gary C. Jacobson in Chapter 7 write revealingly about the election campaign and results. But their main concerns are for how the elections will affect the presidency and Congress, respectively. John J. DiIulio Jr. offers additional insights into the elections and their consequences in Chapter 8.

Certainly no historical observation pervaded postelection commentary more thoroughly than that a president's second term almost invariably turns out to be less successful than the first term. Historians may argue about whether the second terms of eighteenth- and nineteenth-century presidents George Washington, Thomas Jefferson, James Madison, James Monroe, Andrew Jackson, Ulysses S. Grant, and Grover Cleveland fit this pattern.[3] But in the era of the modern presidency, second terms have been disappointing experiences for all of the presidents who have earned them. Although only Richard Nixon left office in disgrace, each of his two-term colleagues—Wilson, Franklin Roosevelt, Dwight D. Eisenhower, and Ronald Reagan—found their second terms to be less productive than their first terms.[4]

The Anomaly of Second-Term Disappointment

Why do second terms tend to be disappointing? After all, one might easily expect the opposite to be true. The second-term president, who under the two-term limit imposed by the Twenty-second Amendment cannot run again, is free from the cares of reelection politics that many presidents regard as an impediment to doing the best job possible. At least that is what they say when they endorse the proposal for a single, six-year presidential term, as several recent former presidents have done, including Eisenhower, Nixon, Gerald Ford, and Jimmy Carter.[5]

More important, presidents begin their second terms with four years of on-the-job training—they are in the ascending phase of the "cycle of increasing effectiveness" that comes with experience in office. As Paul Light, the inventor of the concept, writes:

> Presidents can be expected to learn over time. The presidential information base should expand; the president's personal expertise should increase. As the president and the staff become more familiar with the

working of the office, there will be a learning effect. They will identify useful sources of information; they will produce effective strategies for domestic choice. Clearly, prolonged contact with specific policy issues will produce specialization and knowledge.[6]

Clinton certainly has grown in the presidency, following the pattern of his long tenure as governor of Arkansas. His White House staff, hastily thrown together late in the transition period that followed the 1992 elections and correspondingly chaotic during his first two years in office, gradually became more surefooted after he appointed Leon Panetta as chief of staff. The president himself gained confidence as commander in chief when he discovered that the American people respected him for having the courage of his convictions to make the unpopular decisions that extended U.S. assistance to Bosnia, Haiti, and Mexico. He learned how to deal with a professional, independent-minded Congress after many years in which his only legislative experience was with the amateur legislature of Arkansas. Clinton's deportment mirrored his growth: out went the much photographed jogging shorts, self-revelations about his preferences in underpants, and limp salutes; in (after hours spent studying videotapes of Reagan) came a straight, shoulders-back posture and, with some coaching, crisp salutes.

Offsetting these advantages of the second term, however, are more numerous and significant disadvantages for the president. In the remainder of the chapter I describe these disadvantages, with special attention to Clinton, roughly in the order that they develop during a president's tenure in office.

Postponed Problems

During the second term, problems that were postponed from the first term because they were so controversial or intractable as to jeopardize the president's reelection come back to haunt the administration.[7] During his first term, for example, Franklin Roosevelt downplayed his important constitutional differences with the Supreme Court for fear that he would lose support among voters who approved of his policies but would resent any attack on the independence of the Court. Nixon engaged in a massive coverup of the Watergate affair hoping to prevent it from sullying his reelection campaign. Reagan blithely allowed his tax cuts and defense spending increases to drive the budget deficit skyward rather than engage in preelection belt tightening that might slow the politically popular economic recovery. In every case, the president's strategy of postponement was politically successful—Roosevelt in 1936, Nixon in 1972, and Reagan in 1984 were reelected handily. But after each election, the postponed problems loomed larger than ever over the second term.

The problems that Clinton postponed from his first term are legion. No one can predict the outcome of the several real and potential administration scandals: the skein of land deals and alleged coverups known as Whitewater, the gathering of FBI files on prominent Republicans by White House aides, the Paula Jones sexual harassment lawsuit, and the Democratic Party's unseemly relationship with foreign campaign contributors. Bosnia hovers darkly above the international horizon: having promised in December 1995 that American troops would be stationed there for only a year, Clinton said nothing during the 1996 campaign about the obvious need to leave them in place quite a bit longer. (That announcement came a few days after the election.) Welfare remains a vexing issue: before the election, even as Clinton signed a popular Republican bill that ended welfare's six-decade status as a federal entitlement program, he promised angry Democrats that he would "fix" the new law after the election. (One liberal critic suggested the following campaign slogan: "Vote for Clinton—Only He Can Undo What He Has Done.") As for Medicare, President Clinton may prove to be the victim of Candidate Clinton's success at reassuring elderly voters and their adult children that he would protect the program from the Republicans. On election day, "Medicare/Social Security" ranked second among the issues that concerned the electorate, according to the national exit poll, and Clinton won the votes of 69 percent of those who cared most about it.[8] During the second term, he must make the painful choices necessary to avert the Medicare trust fund's looming bankruptcy.

Empty Reelection Campaigns

Short-term political strategy also plants the seeds of second-term difficulties when presidents wage their reelection campaigns. Understandably, such campaigns tend to be "above party" affairs. The presidency, after all, is the nation's chieftainship of state as well as its more partisan chieftainship of government. As chief of state, the president embodies in a symbolic way all that unites Americans as a people, much as the monarch does in Great Britain.[9] Presidents seeking reelection naturally try to drape themselves in the broadly unifying garb of chief of state, which means avoiding controversial or even specific issues as much as possible and distancing themselves to some extent from the rest of their party's ticket. They are best able to do so when, as Stanley indicates in Chapter 2, they avoid a bruising intraparty battle for renomination. But the result, even when presidents win reelection landslides, is that they are in no position to claim a mandate to accomplish anything in particular during the second term. Nor do the president's fellow party members in Congress feel much obligation to help.

In addition to being weak on substance, presidential reelection campaigns tend to be long on announcements in the White House Rose Garden, elaborately staged appearances, and other media events and short on face-to-face campaigning among the voters and direct encounters with the press. Consequently, the president does not learn much from the campaign (as he did when first elected) about what the voters are thinking. This lack of immersion in the bath of public opinion can lead to serious miscalculations after the election. Ironically, all three of the presidents who have won the largest reelection majorities (thus demonstrating the unmatched sensitivity of their political antennae) blundered severely at the beginning of the second term: Roosevelt and his Court-packing scheme in 1937, Nixon and Watergate in 1973, and Reagan and the illicit sale of arms to Iran to fund the contra rebels in Nicaragua in 1985.[10] These self-inflicted political wounds ended any hopes for a successful second term.

A final characteristic of presidential campaigns for reelection creates problems for the second term. Almost by definition, such campaigns affirm the status quo. But as Jacobson argues in Chapter 7, it is hard to translate an "aren't things great?" theme into gains for the president's party in Congress. After all, if the country is doing so well, why should the voters want to turn out any incumbents, whether they are copartisans of the president or members of the opposition?

Roosevelt, Eisenhower, Nixon, and Reagan fell prey to most of these syndromes. In every case, the president asked the voters, in effect, to express their approval of the first term. Little was said about what the second term would bring. Even less was done to help the party's candidates for Congress. The predictable result: a landslide reelection for the president, but one whose significance was undermined by its themelessness and by disappointing results for the president's party in the congressional elections. Indeed, Republicans Eisenhower, Nixon, and Reagan each came out of his reelection with the same wholly or partially Democratic Congress with which he had entered it. The electorate that gave Eisenhower 57 percent of its votes also reelected 95 percent of the incumbent House members and 86 percent of the incumbent senators who were running for an additional term. Nixon's 61 percent victory was undermined by reelection rates of 94 percent in the Democratic House and 85 percent in the Democratic Senate. Similarly, in the same election in which Reagan earned 59 percent of the popular vote, 95 percent of House members and 90 percent of senators also were successful.[11]

Clinton's reelection campaign in 1996 fit the historical pattern. As noted in Chapter 3, after cruising to an easy renomination at the Democratic convention, he seldom called on the voters to elect a Democratic Congress—to do so would have jeopardized his efforts to rise above the partisan fray. Instead of pushing a change-oriented agenda, Clinton pointed with pride to the status quo, taking credit for the success of his first-term policies. Discussions of the future were shrouded in the empty, gauzy rhetoric of "building a bridge to the twenty-first century." In Chapter 5, borrowing a phrase from Alexis de Tocqueville, Elshtain and Beem aptly label Clinton's approach "small-party politics."

Not surprisingly, as in previous elections that returned a president to power, incumbents did well across the board in 1996: 95 percent of senators and 95 percent of representatives who sought reelection were successful. Democratic leaders in Congress, who had long resented Clinton's "triangulation" strategy for winning a second term (it placed the president as far above and apart from congressional Democrats as from congressional Republicans), understandably felt that they owed little to the president. As in 1992, almost every member of Congress outran the president at the polls.

Clinton did avoid one common failing of presidents seeking reelection: he did not seal himself off from the voters. With great zest born of a genuine love for electioneering, Clinton campaigned intensely, speaking before numerous crowds and handshaking his way through long lines of voters. At times he paused, once for half an hour, to debate and discuss the issues with an individual voter. He clearly was comfortable in the town-hall setting of the second presidential debate. Clinton's reelection campaign may have denied him a mandate and the promise of a good relationship with Congress, but it did not create the conditions for the sort of serious postelection political damage that several previous second-term presidents have inflicted on themselves.

No Honeymoon

A third element in the explanation of why presidents experience disappointment during their second terms is that they are not granted the honeymoon period that most first-term presidents enjoy.[12] Newly elected presidents usually receive the early approval of millions of voters who opposed them in the election.[13] Yet some crucial ingredients that make up the first-term honeymoon simply are not present the second time around, notably the general willingness of the public and the Washington community to give the new president a chance and the widespread (and, of course, impossible) hopes of all sectors of the nation that he will govern in their many and often contradictory interests.

The importance of the honeymoon period extends beyond good will and starry-eyed sentimentality. The honeymoon glow, its temporary nature noted ruefully by Lyndon B. Johnson in his remark that "[y]ou've got just one year when they treat you right," helps to explain, for example, why presidents make more new legislative requests to Congress in the first year of their administrations than in any other year, most of them during the first five months.[14] It also helps to explain why so many of the landmark legislative achievements for which presidents such as Wilson, Roosevelt, Johnson, and Reagan are remembered took place during the first year of their first terms.[15]

Clinton forfeited his first-term honeymoon in 1993 through a series of ill-conceived nominations (Zoë Baird, Lani Guinier), public relations blunders (the much-maligned $200 haircut on a Los Angeles airport runway), minor scandals (the improper firing of several White House travel office employees), and unpopular policy initiatives (allowing gays and lesbians to serve in the military). Indeed, Clinton's public approval rating at the one hundred day mark was the lowest in the history of presidential polling.[16] As for the second term, on election day 1996 the voters signaled their continuing doubts about Clinton even as they reelected him: the national exit poll found that 56 percent regarded the president as "not honest and trustworthy" and

55 percent said they were either "concerned" or "scared" about "what he will do in his second term." Clinton's relations with the media were so bad, according to presidential press secretary Michael McCurry, that "the only reason I would want to stay around here much longer . . . [would be] to try and see if you could get his head in a different place about that."[17] In the short term, the broadly centrist political strategies pursued by both political parties in 1996 may foster a measure of cooperation between Clinton and the Republican 105th Congress, as Quirk and Matheson suggest in Chapter 6. But Republican congressional leaders made clear after the election that they would cut the president no slack on controversial matters such as Medicare and campaign finance reform. When Clinton called for the creation of a bipartisan commission on Medicare, for example, Senate majority leader Trent Lott rejected the idea, saying, "he has been irresponsible. He has misled the people, he has misinformed them, he has been disingenuous."[18]

Midterm Election

Almost halfway into the second term comes the midterm congressional election and the fabled "six-year itch," the fourth ingredient of second-term frustration. Midterm elections of any kind seldom provide good news for presidents—the only midterm in history in which the president's party gained ground in both the House and the Senate was in 1934, during Franklin Roosevelt's first term. But a president's first midterm election, which occurs two years into the first term, generally is less punishing than the one that takes place during the second term, at the six-year mark. Roosevelt's Democrats lost seventy-one House members and six senators in 1938, midway through his second term; congressional Republicans lost forty-eight seats in the House and thirteen in the Senate in 1958, the sixth year of Eisenhower's tenure as president; Republicans lost forty-eight House members and five senators in 1974, six years after Nixon was first elected; and Reagan's Republicans lost five seats in the House and eight in the Senate (along with control of the Senate) in 1986, halfway through his second term. In all, since 1934 the average sixth-year loss for the president's party in Congress has been forty-three House members and eight senators, considerably greater than the average loss of twelve seats in the House and gain of two in the Senate during the midterm election of the president's second year.

These losses take their toll on the president's relationship with Congress as the second term wears on. As Michael Grossman, Martha Kumar, and Francis Rourke have shown, the final two years of second-term presidencies "have been accompanied by declines in presidential support in Congress on issues where the president took a clear stand." Their conclusion is borne out by data from the Eisenhower, Nixon, and Reagan administrations.[19]

Clinton is unlikely to experience midterm losses among congressional Democrats in 1998 of the magnitude faced by his two-term predecessors. The reason this is so, however, is of small comfort to him—namely, the abnormally large losses that the Democrats suffered during his first midterm in 1994. In that election, the Republicans gained fifty-two seats in the House, eight seats in the Senate, and control of both legislative bodies for the first time since 1952. In 1996 they maintained control of the House despite a modest loss of nine seats and extended their control of the Senate by gaining two seats. Thus, the "exposure" of congressional Democrats—that is, "the excess or deficit number of seats a party holds measured against its long-term norm"[20]—will be favorable to Clinton's party in 1998, especially in the House elections. (In the Senate, the Democrats are slightly more vulnerable: they will be defending eighteen seats and the Republicans sixteen.) Still, as Jacobson argues in Chapter 7, the likelihood is very low that the Democrats will gain ground in 1998. Clinton can expect to face a Republican Congress for his entire second term, the first Democratic president ever to govern under such circumstances.

Lame-Duck President

During Clinton's final campaign appearances in 1996, he noted wistfully to crowds that this was the last political campaign he ever would wage (unless he decided to run for a local school board someday). Political observers marked the underlying significance of this statement: at the moment of his reelection, Clinton, like all second-term presidents since Eisenhower, became a political lame duck, unable to run for another term as president.

One reason for the weakened political condition of the second-term president is the two-term limit imposed by the Twenty-second Amendment, which was passed by Congress in 1947 and ratified by the states in 1951. (The amendment exempted President Harry S. Truman, who was serving at the time, but he chose not to run in 1952.) To be sure, a two-term tradition had existed ever since Jefferson, willfully misinterpreting Washington's mainly personal decision not to serve a third term as president, proclaimed in 1807 that no one should violate Washington's "sound precedent."[21] In the years that followed, only Franklin Roosevelt lasted more than two terms, winning a third election in 1940 and a fourth in 1944. But several other presidents kept open the possibility of running again, which meant that second-term presidents could not be counted out as lame ducks until late in their tenure. By codifying the two-term tradition, the Twenty-second Amendment removed all doubt that, in beginning the second term, the president also was beginning the last term.

The disempowering effects of lame-duck status are at first subtle, manifested, for example, in the slow disappearance of the president from the evening news and the front pages as the media spotlight gradually shifts to the contest to select a successor. To the extent that the spotlight continues to shine on the president, its light becomes harsher: typically, the proportion of presidential news stories that are favorable declines and the proportion of unfavorable stories increases from the first to the last years of an administration.[22] Perhaps in response, the popularity of most second-term presidents undergoes a steeper descent than during the first term. A certain lassitude may ensue: Paul Brace and Barbara Hinckley find that "a significant drop in energy in second terms occurs," with the president less likely to take to the hustings or even the airwaves to defend the party or administration.[23]

As the end of the second term approaches, the lame-duck effects become more tangible and visible. Members of the president's team, both within the White House and in the departments and agencies of the bureaucracy, begin their exodus to greener pastures in the private sector, fully aware both that their employment with the president is drawing to an inevitable close and that their value in the job market will decline dramatically as soon as the president leaves office. Finding competent and loyal replacements to join the administration, at this late hour and for such a short time, is correspondingly difficult. Richard Schott and Dagmar Hamilton observe that "Candidates are less willing to make financial and other sacrifices for an appointment of merely a year or two, and much of the excitement and challenge of being part of a new administration have dissipated."[24] As for the members of the career civil service, their sense of commitment to the policies and programs of the administration dwindles steadily as the arrival of a new chief executive draws near.

During the final year of the second term, the Senate takes a jaundiced view of the president's Supreme Court nominations. Historically, the rejection rate for final-year nominations to the Court has been 48 percent, compared with 14 percent for nominations made earlier in the term. When the Senate is controlled by the opposition party, the final-year rejection rate rises to 75 percent.[25] Clinton's ability to fill the two or three seats on the Court that observers regard as likely to become vacant in the next few years (those held by John Paul Stevens, Chief Justice William Rehnquist, and possibly Sandra Day O'Connor) with nominees he wants will depend greatly on when the vacancies occur. Republicans in the Senate will naturally prefer to keep any seats that come open in 2000 unfilled pending the election of a new, possibly Republican president.

Clinton's lame-duck status will also cast long shadows over his second term in arenas other than media coverage, executive appointments, and Supreme Court nominations. He is the first Democratic president to bump up against the Twenty-second Amendment. Chastened by defeat in the 1994 midterm election, the Democrats papered over their intraparty differences in 1996. But they remain a divided party, and Clinton's looming departure probably will bring their differences to the fore. Most northern-based labor unions, racial and ethnic leaders, feminists, old-line liberals, and other "traditional Democrats" fear the global economy and want entitlement programs left alone. So-called New Democrats, many of them southerners, typically embrace global competition and are willing to address the entitlements question.[26]

Even as Clinton's reelection campaign was being waged in 1996, his party's attention had begun to turn to the choice of a successor in 2000. Vice

President Gore, freed by the two-term limit on Clinton to begin planting the seeds of his own candidacy for the Democratic presidential nomination,[27] emerged as the leader of the New Democrats. His campaign appearances on behalf of the Clinton-Gore ticket often were greeted by chants of "Gore in 2000" or "Twelve more years." As vice president, Gore is the heir apparent to Clinton as the Democratic standard bearer: six of the past nine vice presidents have subsequently been nominated for president by their parties.[28]

Yet the Democrats' continuing loss of congressional seats and governorships in the South to the Republicans has weakened the influence in the party of the New Democrats and the other moderates and conservatives who are most pervasive in that region. As recently as a generation ago, nearly every major elective office in the South was occupied by a Democrat. By 1997, with the loss of open, previously Democratic Senate seats in Arkansas and Alabama, the Democrats held only 7 of 22 southern seats in the Senate, 53 of 125 southern seats in the House (several of them representing liberal "majority-minority" districts, which had been established to encourage the election of minority members), and 3 of 11 southern governorships. Meanwhile, the traditional Democrat-dominated Northeast has become the party's strongest region. Leadership of the traditional Democrats in the presidential election of 2000 seems likely to pass to Rep. Richard Gephardt of Missouri, the House Democratic leader and a longtime rival of Gore. The news media's tendency to trivialize and personalize political conflict, which Kerbel describes in Chapter 4, can be expected to aggravate this rivalry.

To be sure, lame-duck presidents are not without resources. Hoping "to establish a final diplomatic victory as their legacy," they are "much more likely to schedule foreign trips in the final year of their administrations."[29] In addition, the constitutional powers of the presidency remain intact throughout the term, as Clinton's predecessor, George Bush, showed after losing the election of 1992. During his final two months as president, Bush dispatched 25,000 American troops to Somalia, signed the North American Free Trade Agreement (NAFTA), bombed Iraq, reached an arms control agreement with Russia, and pardoned six high-ranking former Reagan administration officials of any crimes they may have committed in connection with the Iran-contra affair. Clinton should find the lessons of Bush's lame-duck period easy to learn: in 1995 and 1996 he relied heavily on his executive power to act unilaterally as a way of thwarting the hostile Republican Congress. In addition, under a law passed by Congress in 1996 that took effect in January 1997, Clinton has a power that previous presidents have lacked: the line-item veto of particular provisions of tax and spending legislation.[30]

Conclusion

Pattern is not predestination, at least not in politics. To observe that modern presidents have been less successful in their second terms than in their first terms, even when that observation is adduced by explanations that are deeply grounded in the workings of the political system, is not to say that no second term ever will surpass a first term, or even that Clinton's second term will not turn out more successfully than his first term. Historical "what ifs" are of limited value, but who is to say, for example, that John F. Kennedy, a narrowly elected president in 1960 who used his first term mainly to set the agenda for a massive, mandate-giving reelection in 1964, would not have reaped the harvest of his earlier efforts in the form of historic legislative achievements in a second term?[31] Clinton was denied an overwhelming reelection in 1996, but he certainly has displayed impressive growth in his conduct of the presidency, along with shrewd experience at dealing with a Republican-controlled Congress. He also governs, as DiIulio argues in Chapter 8, during unusually volatile times, in which the past is no sure predictor of the future.

Still, the historical pattern and the explanations that underlie it do not augur well for Clinton's second term: the postponement of thorny problems until after the election, the mostly nonpartisan vacuousness of the reelection campaign, the absence of a postelection honeymoon period, the midterm election in 1998, the coming exodus of talented and experienced presidential lieutenants and the difficulty of replacing them, and the growing problems attendant with advanced lame-duck status during the waning years of the term.

Underlying most of these problems is the Twenty-second Amendment. No constitutional amendment has undone the Framers' intentions more completely than the two-term limit: the delegates to the Constitutional Convention of 1787 designed all of their provisions for the term and election of the executive around the central goal of allowing the president to be ever eligible for reelection. They believed strongly that presidential reeligibility was good for the president, who would have every incentive to do the best possible job, and good for the country, which would have the option of keeping a president it liked in office. Nor has any amendment been rushed to enactment by Congress in such haste and with such disregard for the original constitutional design. Briefly restored to power in the 1946 congressional election after a long absence, Republicans passed the amendment in posthumous resentment of Franklin Roosevelt's four victories. An argument could have been made, after careful consideration of the debates at the Constitutional Convention, that the Framers had been wrong not to impose a presidential term limit in the first place or that the times had changed since 1787 in ways that made such a limit necessary. But the enactors of the Twenty-second Amendment were uninterested in serious constitutional argument and unwilling to take the time to construct one.[32]

Most Americans support the two-term limit on presidents. If anything, they want to extend the constitutional term-limit principle to members of Congress. One can only hope that at some point, putting fervor aside, they will pause to consider what they have done to the second-term presidents whom they have elected.

Notes

1. The data in this paragraph were drawn from "Debate Garners Lower TV Numbers," *Memphis Commercial Appeal*, October 18, 1996; "Hey! Is Anyone Listening?" *Washington Post National Weekly Edition*, October 21–27, 1996; and various documents at the *New York Times* Web site *(www.nytimes.com/web/docsroot/politics)*.

2. In the midterm elections of 1894, 1918, and 1946, the Republicans won control of Congress during a Democratic administration. In each case, however, the voters elected a president and Congress of the same party two years later.

3. Although not comparing second-term to first-term success, one recent work rates Washington, Madison, and Jackson as having had "successful second terms," Jefferson and Monroe as having had "troubled second terms," and Grant and Cleveland as having had "failed second terms." Alfred J. Zacher, *Trial and Triumph: Presidential Power in the Second Term* (Fort Wayne, Ind.: Presidential Press, 1996), 333.

4. Only presidents who (a) were elected to at least two terms and (b) served at least a year of the second term are included in this analysis. The first criterion excludes successor presidents, even those who were later elected to one full term, such as Theodore Roosevelt, Calvin Coolidge, Harry S. Truman, and Lyndon B. Johnson; the second excludes presidents who died in office early in their second terms, such as Abraham Lincoln and William McKinley.

5. Jackson proposed the single, six-year term during his first term as president. In 1913, Republican senator Miles Poindexter of Washington stated the case against such proposals with unsurpassed succinctness: "Six years is entirely too long for a bad man, and it is too short for a good man." James L. Sundquist, *Constitutional Reform and Effective Government*, rev. ed. (Washington, D.C.: Brookings Institution, 1992), 46–54.

6. Paul C. Light, *The President's Agenda: Domestic Policy Choice from Kennedy to Reagan* (Baltimore: Johns Hopkins University Press, 1991), 37.

7. In their study of the Eisenhower, Nixon, and Reagan presidencies, Brace and Hinckley found that "the ratio of negative to positive events was much larger during the second terms," mostly because of "things set in motion [by these presidents] during their first terms." Paul Brace and Barbara Hinckley, *Follow the Leader: Opinion Polls and the Modern Presidency* (New York: Basic Books, 1992), 40, 41.

8. National exit poll data were obtained from the PoliticsNow Web site *(http://www.politicsnow.com)*.

9. Erwin C. Hargrove and Michael Nelson, *Presidents, Politics, and Policy* (Baltimore: Johns Hopkins University Press, 1982), 20–24.

10. One could add Johnson and the massive escalation of the Vietnam War in 1965 to this list.

11. Charles O. Jones, *The Presidency in a Separated System* (Washington, D.C.: Brookings Institution, 1994), 34–35.

12. Light, *The President's Agenda*, 39.

13. Hargrove and Nelson, *Presidents, Politics, and Policy*, 21–22.

14. Light, *The President's Agenda*, 41–45, 241. Johnson is quoted in Harry McPherson, *A Political Education* (Boston: Little, Brown, 1972), 268.

15. William Lammers, "Domestic Policy Leadership in the First Year," in *Understanding the Presidency*, ed. James P. Pfiffner and Roger H. Davidson (New York: Longman, 1997), 215–232.

16. Sidney M. Milkis and Michael Nelson, *The American Presidency: Origins and Development, 1776–1993* (Washington, D.C.: CQ Press, 1994), 398.

17. Ken Auletta, "Inside Story," *New Yorker*, November 18, 1996, 59.

18. "Bipartisan Mood Starting to Fade on Potent Issues," *New York Times*, November 11, 1996.
19. Michael B. Grossman, Martha Joynt Kumar, and Francis E. Rourke, "Second-term Presidencies: The Aging of Administrations," in *The Presidency and the Political System*, 2d ed., ed. Michael Nelson (Washington, D.C.: CQ Press, 1988), 217–219.
20. Bruce I. Oppenheimer, James A. Stimson, and Richard W. Waterman, "The President's Party in Midterm Elections: Going from Bad to Worse," *Legislative Studies Quarterly* 11 (May 1986): 228.
21. Michael Nelson, "Constitutional Beginnings," in *Guide to the Presidency*, 2d ed., Vol. 1, ed. Nelson (Washington, D.C.: Congressional Quarterly, 1996), 49–50. Jefferson is quoted in "Thomas Jefferson's 'No Third Term' Letter" in *Historic Documents on Presidential Elections, 1787–1988*, ed. Michael Nelson (Washington, D.C.: Congressional Quarterly, 1991), 102.
22. Michael Baruch Grossman and Martha Joynt Kumar, *Portraying the President* (Baltimore: Johns Hopkins University Press, 1981), 262.
23. Brace and Hinckley, *Follow the Leader*, 41–43, 60–61, 194–197.
24. Richard L. Schott and Dagmar S. Hamilton, *People, Positions, and Power* (Chicago: University of Chicago Press, 1983), 27.
25. Calculated from data presented in John Anthony Maltese, *The Selling of Supreme Court Nominees* (Baltimore: Johns Hopkins University Press, 1995), 2–8.
26. John L. Judis, "Beyond the Clinton Presidency," *New Republic*, September 16 and 23, 1996, 24–26.
27. The freeing of second-term vice presidents to begin their own presidential campaigns well in advance of the election was a wholly unanticipated consequence of the Twenty-second Amendment.
28. For a discussion of this phenomenon, see Milkis and Nelson, *The American Presidency*, chap. 15.
29. Brace and Hinckley, *Follow the Leader*, 61, 196–197.
30. The Republican 104th Congress, in passing the line-item veto act, delayed its implementation until after the elections in the hope that a Republican president would be the first to benefit from it. The act's constitutionality is being challenged in federal court.
31. Michael Nelson, "The Presidency: Clinton and the Cycle of Politics and Policy," in *The Elections of 1992*, ed. Nelson (Washington, D.C.: CQ Press, 1993), 149–150.
32. Milkis and Nelson, *The American Presidency*, 303–305.

2

The Nominations: Republican Doldrums, Democratic Revival

Harold W. Stanley

Viewed from the fall of 1995, the coming 1996 presidential race looked highly uncertain. President Bill Clinton's political standing was shaky. The judgment rendered on his presidency and the Democrats by the voters in the 1994 midterm elections had been harsh: Democrats lost control of both the House and the Senate. Not a single Republican incumbent was defeated for reelection to the Senate, the House, or to a governorship. Clinton was not on the midterm ballot, but his presidency had provided more problems than promise for Democratic allies.[1] In 1995 Republicans, controlling both branches of Congress for the first time in forty years, went to work on their Contract with America. Talk of a Republican revolution signaled Republicans' desire to put their partisan stamp on government. They had high hopes of recapturing the White House in 1996.

Although Republicans had yet to rally fully behind him, Senate majority leader Robert Dole, R-Kan., appeared likely to be the candidate to challenge Clinton. Yet the Dole and Clinton candidacies were not generating the widespread enthusiasm attached to a possible presidential bid by Gen. Colin L. Powell Jr., former chairman of the Joint Chiefs of Staff. Powell was leading in many presidential preference polls. Whether he would run as an independent or a partisan, or whether he would run at all, was unknown in early November 1995. Meanwhile, Ross Perot, a surprisingly strong independent presidential candidate in 1992, seemed likely to run again. Other independent candidacies were possible. The public's yearning to turn away from politics as usual was evident.

Political Context
The Shadow of a Powell Candidacy

The possibility of Powell entering the race shaped the start of the 1996 presidential campaign. To promote his autobiography, *My American Journey*, in September 1995 he began a publicity tour that had many of the trappings of a presidential campaign. The media launch was extraordinary. Powell appeared again on the cover of *Time* magazine—his sixth cover of *Time*, *Newsweek*, or *U.S. News and World Report* in two years. As public attention focused on Powell, his political standing rose. In one poll's head-to-head matchup against President Clinton, Powell had a fifteen percentage point advantage; in a three-way matchup, Powell and Clinton each polled 33 percent, Dole 30 percent.[2] Although Powell had not stated he would run, he had not discouraged speculation that he might. He promised to announce his decision after his book tour ended in mid-October.

On November 8, to the disappointment of many, Powell declared that he was a Republican but would not be a candidate for president in 1996. His withdrawal cleared the way for the already declared presidential candidates to seek greater attention from reporters, financial contributors, and voters. These Republicans included Senator Dole, former Tennessee governor Lamar Alexander, commentator Pat Buchanan, millionaire publisher Steve Forbes, and Sen. Phil Gramm of Texas.[3]

But the declared Republican candidates faced a difficult audience. The day after Powell's announcement, one CNN/USA Today/Gallup poll found that more than half the Republicans surveyed were not satisfied with the GOP's field of candidates.[4] Several prominent Republicans had previously said that they would not run for president: former vice president Dan Quayle, former secretary of state James A. Baker III, former defense secretary Dick Cheney, former housing secretary Jack Kemp, former education secretary Bill Bennett, Wisconsin governor Tommy Thompson, and Massachusetts governor William Weld.

A number of potential independent and third-party candidacies also were discussed in late 1995, suggesting that the 1996 election could be one in which the two-party system would again be sorely tested. A Perot candidacy seemed likely, but on September 25 Perot surprised the political world by announcing on "Larry King Live" that he would form a new, nationwide third party. Previously, he had opposed calls to form a third party. The purpose of the new party was to field a "world class" presidential candidate—"George Washington II"—Perot insisted. Nevertheless, suspicions were strong that the candidate might ultimately be Perot himself.

Sensing that Perot backers were more likely to be Republicans than Democrats, the Democrats were delighted, Republicans riled. House Speaker Newt Gingrich branded Perot's idea "as a fantasy of delusion." Dole was miffed: "It seems to me he has a checklist, and if we don't do it in a week, he's going to run for president."[5] In addition, a group of seven or eight political moderates, principally former elected officials such as Bill Bradley and Lowell Weicker, explored prospects for fielding a centrist presidential candidate; Ralph Nader signaled his intention to run as the Green Party candidate; and Rev. Jesse Jackson, twice a candidate for the Democratic nomination, contemplated running as an independent.[6] Given the volatility of public opinion and the previous public fascination with Powell, the possible political repercussions of such candidacies offered little reason for activists in either major party to think that 1996 could be counted on to turn out well.

Federal Government Shutdowns

When an incumbent president seeks reelection, the election often constitutes a referendum on the first term.[7] Following the 1994 elections, which left the president and congressional Democrats in disarray, the aggressively conservative Republican Congress believed it had been given a mandate to reverse decades of Democratic policies. However, just a year into the session, the Republicans miscalculated, giving Clinton an opportunity to exert political leadership and regain the political advantage.

A few days after Powell announced that he would not be a candidate, wrangling over the 1996 budget led to a federal government shutdown. Republicans in the House and Senate were intent on using the budget to establish legislative priorities and were not reluctant to challenge the president over those priorities. But Clinton stood firm. "Instead of a waffling, eager-to-please president they might have thought they could bully into making quick concessions, Republicans encountered a determined chief executive who had been badly wounded by accusations that he was a spineless flip-flopper."[8] On November 14, budget battles resulted in a government shutdown, which meant that most federal workers were told to stay home and all but essential federal services were suspended. The government had been shut down nine times before but never for more than three days. The most recent was the three-day stoppage in the fall of 1990 when President George Bush broke his "Read my lips, no new taxes" pledge. The November shutdown lasted for six days; a second one in December and January lasted three weeks.

The political brinkmanship that brought about the shutdowns proved costly to Republicans and their congressional leadership, Dole and especially Gingrich. To make matters worse, Gingrich explained that he had forced the shutdown in part because of personal pique over how the president had treated him on *Air Force One* during a trip to attend the funeral of Israeli prime minister Yitzhak Rabin. Gingrich complained that he and Dole had been made to exit by the rear of the plane rather than at the front as the president does. Gingrich also contended that the president had not taken advantage of the trip to confer with the Republican leaders about the budget impasse. (The White House released a photo from the trip showing Dole, Gingrich, and the president in conversation.) This display of personal peevishness helped turn the public against Gingrich and the Republicans.[9]

Neither Clinton, nor congressional Democrats, nor congressional Republicans were blameless in the shutdown. Yet the public, by a two-to-one margin, saw the Republicans as more at fault.[10] As public support for the Republican Congress waned, a suddenly more presidential Clinton, standing firm for his beliefs, began rising, shedding the flip-flop image that had long marred his presidency. Republicans ended the shutdown standoff early in 1996, with Dole explaining, "Our message is a balanced budget over seven years. Our message is not some government shutdown. . . . Somewhere along the way, we've gotten off message."[11]

The Clinton Candidacy

Clinton's responses to the federal government shutdowns, as well as to the earlier bombing of the Oklahoma City federal building and the crisis in Bosnia, allowed him to regain his political footing in 1995 and grow in presidential stature.

Republican rhetorical questioning of, among other things, the value of government regulation and bloated federal bureaucracies met with an altered political context after the bombing of the Alfred P. Murrah Building in Oklahoma City on April 19, 1995. Apparently attributable to domestic terrorism, the deaths of so many federal workers shocked the public. In times of national tragedy, presidents can symbolize national concerns and feelings. Clinton proved to be no exception.

With the end of the cold war, foreign affairs exerted less influence on national politics than in the past. But in the fall of 1995 Clinton, against political advice, committed U.S. troops to Bosnia. The extended commitment of troops was widely perceived as politically risky—if heavy casualties ensued, Clinton's reelection prospects could be a casualty as well.[12] Yet the public admired the president's steadfastness. Clinton had been accused in the 1992 campaign of draft-dodging in the 1960s, and as president he had worn the commander in chief mantle uncomfortably. With Bosnia, as with the Oklahoma City bombing and the federal government shutdowns, Clinton was seen as moving more assuredly into being president.

A major political accomplishment for Clinton in the run-up to the presidential election year was avoiding a challenge for the 1996 Democratic nomination. In the immediate aftermath of the 1994 elections, such a challenge looked virtually certain. One means of warding off opposition was to raise a considerable financial war chest, which Clinton did in 1995. Because no challenger for the nomination emerged within the Democratic Party, the funds were spent on preconvention advertising to bolster Clinton's standing and undermine Dole's.

By the end of 1995, Clinton's political stock was rising, and he was leading Dole in the presidential trial heat polls. But would his lead hold? Historically, a presidential lead going into the election year is commonplace: the incumbent led the other party's front-runner in the Gallup poll on nine of ten occasions between 1948 and 1992. Only Harry S. Truman trailed going into the 1952 election year. Three of those nine incumbents ultimately lost—Ford in 1976, Carter in 1980, and Bush in 1992. Another, Johnson in 1968, dropped out after a weak showing in the New Hampshire primary. Truman in 1948 fell behind before dramatically battling back to secure reelection.

Talk of scandals and investigations hung over the Clinton White House, complicating the president's new hold on public opinion. The Clintons' Whitewater real estate transactions, White House acquisition of FBI files on major Republicans, and the 1993 firing of most of the White House travel office all represented potential time bombs for a Clinton reelection bid.[13]

Clinton's lead in the polls in late 1995 could prove as fleeting as those for some previous presidents had been.

The Dole Candidacy

Dole's candidacy for the Republican nomination enjoyed considerable advantages compared with the rest of the Republican field. As Senate majority leader he had proven his political abilities and accumulated extensive credits in the party's favor bank. As a would-be presidential candidate in 1980 and 1988 and a vice presidential candidate in 1976, he had acquired substantial experience in national campaigning. Having lost before was not a stigma: the three most recently elected Republican presidents—George Bush, Ronald Reagan, and Richard Nixon—each had sought the presidency unsuccessfully before winning it. As Dole frequently told primary and caucus audiences, "I have the experience. I have been tested, and tested and tested in many, many ways. I am not afraid to lead and I know the way." [14] One testament to Dole's candidacy was that in the early going, the other candidates for the Republican nomination all sought to position themselves as his prime competition.[15]

Dole's campaign, by lining up big-name endorsements from party leaders, followed the strategy of Bush, to whom he had lost the Republican nomination in 1988. For example, the day Powell announced that he would not be a candidate, helpfully clearing the way for Dole, Dole secured the "long-awaited, much-coveted endorsement of GOP Governor Stephen Merrill of New Hampshire"—a combination of events that Jack Kemp labeled "a spectacular breakthrough for Bob Dole." [16]

Dole's military service to the nation in World War II contrasted pointedly with Clinton's record of avoiding service during the Vietnam War. Dole's war wounds—his right arm was disabled—were vivid reminders of his military record.

Dole's fund-raising ability was much in evidence in 1995, giving him a formidable war chest from the start. But, unlike Clinton, Dole had challengers with whom to contend. Gramm was an effective fund-raiser, too, gathering $4.1 million at one dinner in Dallas. "Thanks to you," Gramm told the audience, "I have the most reliable friend you can have in American politics, and that's ready money." [17] Money was not everything in 1996, but few anticipated the small return Gramm would get on his spending or foresaw how the large sums Forbes spent would change the dynamics of the nominating contest.

Dole had vulnerabilities as well as assets. The principal characteristic the public associated with him was his age. Seventy-two years old during the nomination season, Dole would be the oldest person ever elected president if he succeeded in 1996. Dole's legislative skills did not translate readily into public campaign settings. He was not as effective a speaker as audiences expected presidential candidates to be.

Dole's road to the Republican nomination was rocky. The odds-on favorite before the voting began, Dole secured the nomination, but in doing so he encountered obstacles that called into question his command of Republican loyalties and, to the extent the wider public was watching, raised questions about his ability to broaden his base of support for the general election. Ultimately, his organizational advantages prevailed to win him the nomination. But the quest was costly, both financially and politically.

The 1996 Nominating Process

The presidential nominating process has undergone substantial reforms since the 1960s. Campaigns have become more public, with greater numbers of convention delegates being selected in primaries. Campaign finance reforms in the 1970s provided for public funding, limited the amount of money that can be raised from individuals or groups, and restricted how much candidates taking public funds can spend. These reforms have tended to make presidential campaigns longer, to make media coverage more central to success, to place a premium on organizing the early-voting states well, and to make it crucial for candidates to do better than expected to keep the momentum for subsequent primaries.[18]

After 1992 the nominating process underwent further changes. Concerns had been expressed in recent years about a "front loaded" calendar in which the states clustered their primaries and caucuses early in the election year. The 1996 calendar gave new meaning to the term. The accelerated schedule of primaries and caucuses seemed to favor Dole's candidacy. Only severe early setbacks for Dole could imperil his dominance, preventing him from scoring a quick knockout and throwing open the quest for the nomination.

States jockeyed for position in preparation for the 1996 nominating contest, causing dramatic changes in the pace and timing of the primaries and caucuses. Although the primary and caucus schedule extended from February to June, states sought greater influence in the process by moving their contests up. Almost two-thirds of the convention delegates would be selected before the end of March. California, the largest state, had long felt slighted during the nominating process. Nominations had generally been decided well before its primary in early June. For 1996 California moved its race to March 26. New York also moved its primary from early April to March 7. These changes increased the organizational and financial resources that candidates needed right from the start.

Previously, southern states had led the way in scheduling primaries for the same day (called "Super Tuesday" since 1988) in an attempt to maximize regional clout.[19] For 1996 more states made a concerted effort to group primaries in regional clusters: North Dakota and South Dakota led off with a small regional primary on February 27; all the New England states except New Hampshire voted March 5 in "Junior Tuesday"; six southern states including Florida and Texas held primaries on March 12 ("Super Tuesday"); and the industrial heartland of Illinois, Michigan, Ohio, and Wisconsin voted on March 19.

Some states even tried to take Iowa and New Hampshire's place as the opening rounds of the nominating process. For years states had envied the first-in-the-nation position of the Iowa caucuses and the New Hampshire primary. In 1996 Alaska and Louisiana each tried to leapfrog Iowa and New Hampshire and become the first state in the nation to pick convention delegates. Iowa and New Hampshire persuaded most of the Republican candidates to skip the new early events. In Louisiana all but Buchanan and Gramm obliged. Candidates and the media continued to focus principally on Iowa and New Hampshire as the accepted starting points of the campaign, but the earlier events did boost Buchanan's candidacy and forced Gramm to an early exit from the field.[20]

The march of the states toward the front of the nominating calendar did not overshadow the importance of the earliest events. Indeed, given the number of delegates at stake in the weeks immediately following the first primaries and caucuses, the importance of the early events was magnified. Doing well early could bring huge rewards in terms of media attention and momentum in time for the delegate-rich primaries. A slow start could be fatal because fewer delegates were up for grabs later in the process.

Although Democratic nomination rules require states to award delegates in rough proportion to the candidates' share of the primary or caucus vote, Republican rules allow state parties, if they so choose, to allot all their delegates to the candidate polling the most votes. The Republicans' winner-take-all process rewards candidates who break out of the pack early, piling up delegates far beyond what a proportional allocation would permit.[21]

Political outcomes are not self-interpreting. In the quest for a presidential nomination, results take on meaning in relation to expectations. Winning seldom suffices, especially if a candidate's first-place finish was expected. How candidates fare relative to expectations goes a long way toward determining who is seen as gaining strength and who is thought to be faltering. Greater and more positive press coverage accrues to candidates who meet or exceed expectations; negative press coverage snowballs for those who fall below expectations. The resulting momentum for candidates meeting or surpassing expectations proves a real asset in the relentless schedule of primaries and caucuses. The struggle between candidates and journalists to define the expectations by which the results are judged is a crucial aspect of the nominating process.

Before delegate selection began in earnest in 1996, events indicated that Dole's path to the nomination was not going to be an easy one. A presidential straw poll at the Iowa Republican Convention on August 19, 1995, attracted attention despite its rules: anyone who paid the $25 entry fee could vote in the straw poll. Some campaigns flexed their organizational muscles and financial coffers in an attempt to get the straw poll to come out right.

Dole, the presumed front-runner, tied Gramm with 24 percent of the 10,598 voters; Buchanan pulled in 18 percent. Although no convention delegates were at stake, the results raised questions about Dole's grasp on the nomination and the party.

A nonbinding straw poll at the Florida Republican Convention November 17–18, 1995, offered another test of the candidates' organizations and abilities to spend. Again, the event attracted considerable media coverage even though no delegates were at stake. Dole had the required organization and resources to place first with 33 percent, but Gramm made a surprisingly strong second-place showing with 26 percent, suggesting Dole's vulnerability. Alexander was a close third with 23 percent.

A nationally televised address by Dole on January 23, 1996, suggested further vulnerability. Giving the Republican response to Clinton's State of the Union address, Dole came across as wooden, almost funereal. Republican presidential rivals, media analysts, and party activists panned Dole's speech, suggesting that he had fallen far short of what would be required to compete against Clinton in a presidential campaign. Dole's appearance raised concerns about whether he might be too old to run for the presidency, a problem that lingered throughout the campaign. In contrast, Clinton's speech that night set the stage for the presidential campaign to follow. Clinton declared, "The era of big government is over. But we cannot go back to the time when our citizens were left to fend for themselves." Clinton borrowed heavily from previously successful Republican themes.[22]

Early Delegate Selection

The first Republican balloting occurred in Alaska. Caucuses were held January 27–29, 1996 (see Table 2-1). Fewer than ten thousand voters participated in a straw poll held in conjunction with the precinct caucuses. Delegates were not at stake; they would be chosen at the party's state convention in April. For Dole, the results proved to be "another jolt in a period of turbulence," replacing "his aura of inevitability with an air of vulnerability." Buchanan placed first with 32.6 percent, Forbes second with 30.7, and Dole a distant third with 17.1. Dole attempted to dismiss the results, telling reporters in Iowa, "That's all right. Forbes spent a lot of money up in Alaska on TV, and I didn't get to Alaska because of the budget talks." To Gramm's embarrassment, conservative radio talk show host Alan Keyes polled 10 percent to his 9 percent.[23]

The first vote to select convention delegates did not involve Dole directly—Gramm and Buchanan were the principal competitors for twenty-one delegates in Louisiana on February 6. Gramm's supporters had engineered the establishment of the early delegate contest in Louisiana, which borders on Gramm's home state of Texas. They hoped to demonstrate Gramm's strength to bolster his favorite-son status in the South and to provide momentum going into Iowa. Gramm boasted that he would take all twen-

Table 2-1 Republican Presidential Caucus Results, 1996

State (date)	Turnout	Alexander	Buchanan	Dole	Forbes	Keyes	Uncommitted
Alaska (Jan. 27–29)	9,172	0.6%	32.6%	17.1%	30.7%	9.8%	9.2%
Louisiana (Feb. 6)	22,846	—	44.4	—	—	4.0	51.6
Iowa (Feb. 12)	96,451	17.6	23.3	26.3	10.2	7.4	15.1
Wyoming (March 2)	915	7.2	19.8	40.4	17.6	6.7	8.3
Minnesota (March 5)	28,256	4.6	33.1	41.2	10.3	9.5	1.4
Washington (March 5)	26,158	2.1	28.1	36.4	21.8	7.9	3.8
Missouri (March 9)	10,000	—	36.5	28.5	0.9	9.2	25.0

Source: Congressional Quarterly, *Guide to the Republican National Convention* (Washington, D.C.: Congressional Quarterly, 1996), supplement to vol. 54, no. 31, 62.

Note: Empty cells indicate the candidate was not listed on the caucus ballot or his votes were not tabulated separately. In most cases, results are based on straw votes of caucus participants at first-round caucus events. In Louisiana, however, voters balloted directly for national convention delegates, and in Missouri the results reflected the preferences of delegates elected to the next stage of the caucus process. Turnout is estimated for Missouri. Percentages do not always add to 100 percent due to rounding.

ty-one of the delegates, then reduced that prediction to a strong win. "To become president of the United States," he said, "I have to win here in Louisiana. . . . Eleven to ten would still be victory, but it would be an awful lot like kissing your sister." When the results came in Buchanan beat Gramm, thirteen delegates to eight. Less than 5 percent of registered Republicans participated, with conservatives and the religious right making up a majority of the voters. Gramm's loss fueled Buchanan's drive for the nomination and knocked the Texan's campaign into a tailspin. The Alaska and Louisiana results suggested that although Buchanan might not dominate the quest for the nomination, he could dominate Gramm (and perhaps others) as the favorite of the Republican right. Meanwhile, the decision of these two candidates to compete seriously in the earliest 1996 events had rankled Republican leaders in Iowa and New Hampshire, jealous of their first-in-the-nation status.[24]

The Iowa Caucuses

The Iowa caucuses on February 12 were presumably neighboring Kansan Dole's to lose, even though neighborliness had proven more promising than productive for Gramm in Louisiana. Interest centered not on whether Dole would win but by how much and on which of the remaining candidates would do better than expected. Opponents sought to raise the bar for Dole, suggesting that he needed to match his winning showing of 37 percent against Bush in 1988. Dole forces resisted that high hurdle.[25]

Iowa Republican voters came through for Dole but not resoundingly—Dole edged Buchanan by only 26.3 percent to 23.3 percent (Table 2-1). Alexander, having spent eighty days campaigning in Iowa, finished a respectable third with 18 percent of the vote. Dole's narrow victory did not put enough distance between himself and the other Republican candidates to suggest that the nominating contest would be over soon. Yet Dole's campaign benefited from Forbes's weak showing (fourth with 10.2 percent) and the even weaker showing of Gramm (fifth with 9.3 percent). Gramm, the candidate most pundits had thought would be Dole's chief rival, ended his campaign two days later, on Valentine's Day.

Gramm's strategy was to target conservative party activists and to show organizational strength and an air of inevitability through several straw vote victories in the South and West during 1995. Neither telegenic nor personally attractive to voters, Gramm proved to have limited appeal once the balloting began. He set high expectations and then failed to live up to them: a top-two finish in Alaska (he placed fifth), a strong majority of Louisiana delegates (he got less than 40 percent), and a top-three showing in Iowa (he fell to fifth). "Rather than casting himself as an underdog and rising up, he declared himself the big dog early on and went downhill from there."[26] Gramm endorsed Dole on February 16 in an attempt to deflate Buchanan among conservatives.[27]

Gramm's candidacy had constituted a potential problem for Dole that did not materialize; Forbes proved to be a much more formidable challenge for Dole. Forbes had one big idea—an overhaul of the tax system featuring a 17 percent flat tax—and a vast personal fortune that he was willing to spend to promote that idea and his presidential candidacy. Forbes stressed "hope, growth, and opportunity," giving his campaign an upbeat and optimistic tone.

In late January Forbes emerged as a principal challenger to Dole. He appeared on the cover of *Time* and *Newsweek* just prior to the start of the actual delegate selection process. The political ads Forbes ran, critical of Dole, reworked the political landscape to Dole's disadvantage. Forbes spent heavily on targeted media buys in Iowa, New Hampshire, and other pivotal states. Because he used his own money ("loaned" to his campaign) instead of taking federal matching funds, he was not subject to federal spending limits in the primary and caucus states, as were Dole and the other candidates who took federal matching funds. For them, the expenditure ceiling for New Hampshire was $618,200, and for Iowa a little more than $1 million.[28] Forbes reportedly spent $500,000 on advertising in New Hampshire alone in September and October 1995, the first weeks of his presidential bid. Between September and the end of December, Forbes spent about $18 million overall, much of it in the early balloting states, a sum similar to what Dole and Gramm together had spent nationally in all of 1995. Two-thirds of Forbes's spending—$12.5 million—went to media advertising in late 1995, an overwhelming sum compared with what the other candidates spent.[29]

The presidential nominating process had seen nothing to match Forbes's finances.[30] (For an overview of the preconvention spending and fund-raising in 1996, see Table 2-2.) Door-to-door "retail" politics had always characterized the small-scale Iowa and New Hampshire contests. Retail politics was, if not replaced, overwhelmed by massive, unprecedented media buys in 1996.

Forbes's media buys had a particular political kick because the ads "fastened on Dole, ripping his record of legislative compromise on taxes and other issues."[31] Of Dole, Forbes asked, "Where is his compass?" Forbes's ads criticized Dole for canceling a Senate vote on term limits in fall 1995 and for supporting sixteen tax hikes during the past fourteen years—as Forbes put it, "a mind-numbing and wallet-emptying $962 billion in additional taxes."[32] Late January polls had Forbes running even with Dole in New Hampshire and Arizona. Forbes's support ebbed in the days before the Iowa caucuses and New Hampshire primary, a reaction in part to the perceived negativity and extravagance of his campaign. Forbes, who reputedly spent $4 million on media alone in Iowa, blamed the caucus mechanism for his fourth-place finish there. His late-starting, media-intensive campaign had slighted the grassroots organization that caucus politics demands. But Forbes's attacks took their toll on Dole's political standing.

Table 2-2 Presidential Nomination Campaign Finance, 1996

Candidates	Federal matching funds	Individual contributions minus refunds	Candidate contributions	Candidate loans minus repayments	Transfers from prior races	Other receipts[a]	Adjusted total receipts	Adjusted total disbursements
Democrats								
Bill Clinton	$13,412,197	$28,285,108	$0	$0	$250,000	$542,243	$42,489,548	$38,105,490
Lyndon Larouche[b]	624,691	3,058,562	0	0	0	1,000	3,684,253	3,706,949
Total	14,036,888	31,343,670	0	0	250,000	543,243	46,173,801	41,812,439
Republicans								
Lamar Alexander	4,573,442	12,635,615	9,583	0	0	396,338	17,614,978	16,353,539
Pat Buchanan	9,812,517	14,659,228	0	0	0	29,431	24,501,176	24,489,005
Bob Dole	13,545,770	29,555,502	0	0	242,169	1,260,651	44,604,092	42,173,706
Bob Dornan	0	297,511	0	44,000	0	5,374	346,885	341,718
Steve Forbes	0	4,203,792	1,000	37,456,000	0	32,689	41,693,481	41,657,444
Phil Gramm	7,356,218	15,880,676	0	0	4,782,085	772,523	28,791,502	28,038,313
Alan Keyes	892,436	3,442,056	2,500	5,000	0	6,173	4,348,165	4,252,471
Richard Lugar[b]	2,643,477	4,803,612	0	0	85,000	237,294	7,769,383	7,631,213
Arlen Specter[b]	1,010,455	2,284,901	0	0	17,000	177,939	3,490,295	3,391,843
Morry Taylor	0	37,854	3,342	6,471,754	0	3,900	6,516,850	6,504,966
Pete Wilson	1,724,254	5,285,889	0	0	2,000	351,072	7,363,215	7,219,912
Total	41,558,569	93,086,636	16,425	43,976,754	5,128,254	3,273,384	187,040,022	182,054,130

(Continued)

Table 2-2 (Continued)

Candidates	Federal matching funds	Individual contributions minus refunds	Candidate contributions	Candidate loans minus repayments	Transfers from prior races	Other receipts[a]	Adjusted total receipts	Adjusted total disbursements
Others								
Harry Browne (Libertarian)	$0	$1,112,482	$34,271	$0	$0	$1,244	$1,147,997	$1,073,600
John Hagelin (Natural Law)	358,883	700,085	15,250	50,000	0	100	1,124,318	1,117,266
Ross Perot (Reform)	0	82,781	8,215,746	0	0	0	8,298,527	8,031,229
Dick Lamm[b] (Reform)	0	140,281	5,000	25,000	0	0	170,281	39,364
Total	358,883	2,035,629	8,270,267	75,000	0	1,344	10,741,123	10,261,459
Grand total	55,954,340	126,465,935	8,286,692	44,051,754	5,378,254	3,817,971	243,954,946	234,128,028

Source: Federal Election Commission, "Financing the 1996 Presidential Campaign," *http://www.fec.gov/pres96/presmstr.htm.*

Note: Figures are from inception through August 31, 1996.

[a] Other receipts include party contributions minus refunds, other committee contributions minus refunds, and other loans minus repayment.

[b] Reports covering August 1996 not yet received.

The New Hampshire Primary

The New Hampshire results on February 20 ensured that the nominating contest would be longer than Dole would have liked. Buchanan won, upsetting Dole by 27.2 percent to 26.2 percent (Table 2-3). The results also upended the conventional wisdom. Caucuses, which are low-turnout affairs, are generally thought to test a campaign's organizational abilities, thereby rewarding ideological candidates who have fervent supporters. Primaries are much more participatory and require candidates to appeal to a broader range of voters. Buchanan was thought to be favored by caucuses and disadvantaged by primaries. New Hampshire was an exception to the rule, but it was Buchanan's only primary victory. (He won three of seven caucuses.)

New Hampshire polls had suggested as recently as two days before the vote that Dole would win, which made his defeat seem more serious.[33] Buchanan and Dole were followed closely by Alexander (22.6 percent) and Forbes with—as in Iowa—a weak fourth-place finish (12.2 percent). During the next four weeks, Republican voters would sort out this field in twenty-nine primaries. Although Dole had more money, more prominent endorsements, and a stronger organization, his momentum had been halted, and his campaign appearances lacked spark. It was far from certain that Dole would parlay his considerable advantages into primary wins.[34]

Buchanan won New Hampshire by consolidating conservative support in the absence of Gramm, while Dole split the moderate vote with Alexander. Buchanan boasted, "We are taking our party back [from] the forces of the old order." According to Buchanan, the establishment was "in a terminal panic. They hear the shouts of the peasants coming up the hill. You watch the establishment, all the knights and barons when we ride in at the castle, pulling up the drawbridge. All the peasants are coming with pitchforks at them. We are going to take this over the top."[35] Buchanan portrayed his campaign as giving voice to the voiceless, everyone from the unborn threatened by abortion to economically anxious working-class families threatened by corporate downsizing. Buchanan's opposition to abortion fit within the party mainstream, but his tirades against foreign trade agreements and his desire to restrict immigration alarmed many Republicans.[36]

Buchanan, a conservative commentator, was experienced in presidential politics, having challenged Bush's renomination in 1992 in protest of the president's breaking his pledge of no new taxes. Buchanan's prime-time speech at the 1992 Republican convention had raised the hackles of many politically centrist viewers, complicating Bush's general election strategy of reaching toward the middle.

Bruised by Buchanan's victory in New Hampshire, Dole portrayed the upcoming contests as a "fight for the heart and soul of the Republican Party. . . . In the month ahead we will decide if we are the party of fear or of hope, if we are a party that keeps people out or brings people in." Alexander insisted that Dole, who "doesn't seem to have any ideas," should step aside

Table 2-3 Republican Presidential Primary Returns, 1996

State (date)	Turnout	Alexander	Buchanan	Dole	Forbes	Keyes	Uncommitted
New Hampshire (Feb. 20)	208,993	22.6%	27.2%	26.2%	12.2%	2.7%	9.1%
Delaware (Feb. 24)	32,773	13.3	18.7	27.2	32.7	5.3	2.8
Arizona (Feb. 27)	347,482	7.1	27.6	29.6	33.4	0.8	1.5
North Dakota (Feb. 27)	63,734	6.3	18.3	42.1	19.5	3.2	10.6
South Dakota (Feb. 27)	69,170	8.7	28.6	44.7	12.8	3.4	1.8
South Carolina (March 2)	276,741	10.4	29.2	45.1	12.7	2.1	0.6
Puerto Rico (March 3)	238,748	0.5	0.4	97.9	0.5	0.0	0.7
Colorado (March 5)	247,752	9.8	21.5	43.6	20.8	3.7	0.6
Connecticut (March 5)	130,418	5.4	15.1	54.4	20.1	1.7	3.3
Georgia (March 5)	559,067	13.6	29.1	40.6	12.7	3.1	0.9
Maine (March 5)	67,280	6.6	24.5	46.3	14.8	1.8	5.9
Maryland (March 5)	254,246	5.5	21.1	53.3	12.7	5.4	2.0
Massachusetts (March 5)	284,833	7.5	25.2	47.7	13.9	1.8	3.8
Rhode Island (March 5)	15,009	19.0	2.6[a]	64.4	0.9[a]	0.2[a]	12.9
Vermont (March 5)	58,113	10.6[b]	16.7	40.3	15.6	—	16.8
Florida (March 12)	898,070	1.6	18.1	56.9	20.2	1.9	1.3
Louisiana (March 12)	77,789	2.1	33.1	47.8	13.2	3.2	0.6
Mississippi (March 12)	151,925	1.8	25.9	60.3	8.0	1.9	2.1
Oklahoma (March 12)	264,542	1.3	21.5	59.3	14.1	2.4	1.4
Oregon (March 12)	407,514	7.0	21.3	50.8	13.3	3.5	4.1
Tennessee (March 12)	289,043	11.3	25.2	51.2	7.7	2.7	1.9
Texas (March 12)	1,019,803	1.8	21.4	55.6	12.8[b]	4.1	4.2
Illinois (March 19)	818,364	1.5	22.7	65.1	4.9	3.7	2.1
Michigan (March 19)	524,161	1.5	33.9	50.6	5.1	3.1	5.9

	Votes					
Ohio (March 19)	955,017	2.0	21.5	66.4	6.0	2.9	1.1
Wisconsin (March 19)	576,575	1.9	33.8	52.3	5.6	3.1	3.3
California (March 26)	2,452,312	1.8	18.4	66.1	7.5	3.8	2.5
Nevada (March 26)	140,637	2.3	15.2	51.9	19.2	1.4	10.0
Washington (March 26)	120,684	1.3	20.9	63.1	8.6	4.6	1.4
Pennsylvania (April 23)	684,204	—	18.0	63.6	8.0	5.8	4.5
District of Columbia (May 7)	2,941	—	9.5	75.5	—	—	15.0
Indiana (May 7)	498,444	—	19.4	70.6	9.9	—	—
North Carolina (May 7)	283,213	2.7	13.0	71.5	4.1	4.1	4.5
Nebraska (May 14)	170,591	2.6	10.4	75.7	6.2	3.0	2.1
West Virginia (May 14)	125,413	2.9	16.3	68.8	4.9	3.8	3.3
Arkansas (May 21)	42,648	—	23.5	76.5	—	—	—
Idaho (May 28)	118,715	—	22.3	62.3	—	5.0	10.4
Kentucky (May 28)	103,206	3.2	8.1	73.8	3.3	3.7	7.8
Alabama (June 4)	143,295	—	15.7	74.9	—	3.6	5.8
Montana (June 4)	114,463	—	24.4	61.3	7.2	—	7.1
New Jersey (June 4)	209,998	—	11.0	82.3	—	6.7	—
New Mexico (June 4)	67,122	3.9	8.2	75.4	5.7	3.2	3.7
Total	14,115,048	3.5	21.3	59.1	10.1	3.2	2.8

Source: Congressional Quarterly Weekly Report, March 9, 1996, 646; Congressional Quarterly, Guide to the Republican National Convention (Washington, D.C.: Congressional Quarterly, 1996), supplement to vol. 54, no. 31, 63–64.

Note: Empty cells indicate that the candidate or the uncommitted line was not listed on the ballot. Results are based on official returns for the primaries held through April (except for Ohio) and on nearly complete but unofficial returns for the primaries held in May and June (except for Idaho and Nebraska, where official returns were available). The New York primary, March 7, not listed above, was for election of delegates only; Dole won all ninety-three at stake.

[a] Votes won by Buchanan, Forbes, and Keyes in Rhode Island were write-ins.

[b] Alexander withdrew from the race March 6. Forbes withdrew from the race March 14.

in favor of the more youthful Alexander and his "fresh conservative ideas" as a way to check Buchanan's "wrong ideas." Dole's deputy campaign chairman, William B. Lacy, blamed Dole's loss on Forbes's saturation of the airwaves with anti-Dole advertising.[37]

An energized Buchanan immediately became a cautionary example of the importance of image in presidential campaigns. New Hampshire gave Buchanan a moment in the public limelight, but he squandered it. The week after the New Hampshire primary, Buchanan made a campaign stop at Mount Rushmore. Framed against the sculptured faces of Washington, Jefferson, Lincoln, and Roosevelt, Buchanan inevitably invited negative comparisons with these legendary figures. In Tombstone, Arizona, he dressed up with six shooters and a black cowboy hat, forgetting that in the movies the bad guys wear black hats, the good guys white ones. In the days to follow, Buchanan appeared raising a rifle over his head, fueling concerns about his extreme views, and in an Uncle Sam hat more suitable for a carnival huckster than a presidential candidate. These images made for memorable campaign vignettes but did not help Buchanan broaden his base of support.

Finishing third in the New Hampshire primary constituted a significant downturn in Alexander's nomination prospects. Being edged out by Dole made his campaign themes ring hollow. In the last days before the New Hampshire vote, Alexander was short of money to answer Dole's media blitz of critical ads. Alexander had counted on bettering Dole in New Hampshire, gaining validity for the claim that he, not Dole, would be the stronger challenger to Clinton. Alexander's "ABC" slogan, frequently repeated, meant "Alexander Beats Clinton." Unfortunately for Alexander, he could point to no primary or caucus returns in which he beat Dole, much less public opinion polls suggesting that he could beat Clinton.[38]

The early primaries and caucuses usually winnow the field of candidates to a small number. In 1996, because these contests furnished alternative arenas in which different candidates campaigned to their own advantage, only Gramm dropped out. After a fourth-place finish in both Iowa and New Hampshire, Forbes concentrated on Delaware (February 24) and Arizona (February 27), winning both. Voters had recoiled from his negative ad campaigns in Iowa and New Hampshire. A more positive message in Arizona highlighted his flat tax proposal and outsider status. Forbes told supporters celebrating his victory in Arizona: "A week ago they wrote our obituary. Tonight we can perhaps write the obituary for conventional political punditry in America." Dole pointed out that Forbes had spent $4 million on media in Arizona, remarking to reporters: "This guy is trying to buy the election." Forbes dismissed Dole's charge as sour grapes and asserted that the contest was now between himself and Buchanan.[39]

Although Dole had stumbled in New Hampshire, he picked up primary victories on February 27 in North Dakota and South Dakota. By early March the Republican nominating contest appeared muddled, with no clear end in sight. But appearances proved to be deceiving; the uncertainty ended quickly.

The March Primaries

The South Carolina primary on March 2 loomed large as the month began. In the ten days following this vote, sixteen states would hold primaries. Both Buchanan and Alexander hoped to capitalize on the promise of their New Hampshire primary showings. If Buchanan was ever to amass a considerable number of delegates, the conservative, Christian primary voters in the South constituted a prime target audience. Alexander hoped to connect with southern voters by emphasizing his regional ties. South Carolina would prove to be a turning point in the 1996 Republican nomination, as it had in 1980 and 1988.[40]

Dole won South Carolina handily, 45.1 percent to Buchanan's 29.2 percent, sweeping the state's thirty-seven convention delegates. Critical to Dole's victory in South Carolina was his endorsement by former governor Carroll A. Campbell Jr., Sen. Strom Thurmond, and Gov. David Beasley. Beasley in particular had strong support in the religious right movement, and Christian conservatives made up one-third of the primary voters according to exit polls. Within this group, Dole garnered 40 percent support, virtually matching Buchanan. Buchanan's protectionist stance on trade did not help him in a state that had developed economically in part through foreign investment. Nor did Buchanan's embrace of Old South causes such as flying the Confederate flag and an all-male Citadel prove to be the winning ticket in the New South. Forbes nosed out Alexander for third place, 12.7 percent to 10.4 percent, although neither's showing was good news.

On March 5, three days after his victory in South Carolina, Dole won eight mostly winner-take-all state primaries (for "Junior Tuesday" races, see Table 2-3), all by double-digit margins, and secured 176 of the 195 delegates at stake. Two days later, in New York, Dole added another 93 delegates, bringing his total to 361 of the 996 needed for nomination (see Table 2-4). Buchanan lagged far behind with a total of only forty-five delegates. His New Hampshire victory inadvertently had framed the presidential nomination contest as a battle to prevent him from winning. Party leaders and primary voters were quickly, albeit unenthusiastically, settling on Dole as the best choice to stop Buchanan.[41]

On March 5 Kemp endorsed Forbes. The widespread response in the political community was that Kemp was jumping onto a sinking ship. On March 6 Alexander and Sen. Richard Lugar, whose campaign had never caught on, dropped out of the race. Buchanan and Forbes declared their intention to continue—Buchanan to give voice to his supporters and their conservative agenda at the convention (and perhaps beyond if he mounted an independent campaign), and Forbes to ensure a "vigorous debate" that would help shape a stronger party and a stronger candidate.[42]

With 362 delegates up for grabs on "Super Tuesday" (March 12)—virtually all of them in winner-take-all primaries—Dole's new-found momentum, along with the strength of his organization, meant that he might clinch

Table 2-4   Accumulation of Republican Delegates, 1996

Through	Dole	Buchanan	Forbes	Alexander	Uncommitted
February 23	8	21	2	4	6
February 28	27	31	57	5	8
March 7	361	45	67	5	14
March 14	710	55	70	—	19
March 19	933	80	—	—	64
March 26	1,126	84	—	—	64

Source: Tallies are Associated Press counts as reported in *Congressional Quarterly Weekly Report* (1996), 442, 576, 650, 715, 826, 907.

Note: A majority of the convention delegates was required for nomination: 996. Empty cells mean the candidate had dropped out of the presidential race.

the nomination by the end of March. Sen. Arlen Specter said it best: "It's like Nebraska playing [Kansas] State. In the second half, Nebraska just wears them out."[43]

Super Tuesday proved to be a dramatic Dole sweep as he gained 349 of the 362 delegates at stake in seven primaries. Dole's triumph led Forbes to bring his big-spending campaign to an end; he quit the race on March 14 and endorsed Dole. Super Tuesday put Dole within fewer than 300 delegates of the 996 needed for nomination. (Clinton, uncontested, accumulated the number needed for the Democratic nomination on Super Tuesday.) Although Buchanan remained in the race, exit polls showed that Dole was increasingly the choice, if not the voice, of the religious right, which made up 40 percent of the Super Tuesday vote: conservative Christian voters favored Dole over Buchanan by more than ten percentage points.

The next week the primary schedule turned to the industrial heartland of Illinois, Michigan, Ohio, and Wisconsin. Dole swept all four March 19 contests with clear majorities of the primary vote, gaining 196 of the 219 delegates at stake. Buchanan picked up the remainder in Michigan. Dole's impressive showing nonetheless raised questions about his general election appeal. In particular, he had difficulty corralling the support of Republican primary voters who considered themselves independents or Democrats. A general election nominee would need not only to solidify the Republican base but also to reach out to voters in the middle.[44]

With a lopsided win in the California primary on March 26, Dole clinched the Republican nomination. As the primary season wound down through the spring, Dole had continued to increase his share of the vote. Republican primary voters were not showing "buyer's remorse": in Junior Tuesday primaries during the week of March 5, Dole won 52 percent of the primary vote; the next week on Super Tuesday, he gained 55 percent; the next week in the midwestern primaries, 60 percent; in the late March western primaries, 65 percent. In the remaining April, May, and June primaries, Dole won 70 percent. To be sure, the field of candidates had narrowed. But the voters were not backing Buchanan even as a protest against Dole's impending nomination.

Dole had lost New Hampshire, the first primary, February 20 to Buchanan, then lost to Forbes in Delaware four days later, and again to Forbes in Arizona February 27. After that, Dole's only primary or caucus defeat occurred March 9 when an estimated ten thousand Missouri caucusgoers preferred Buchanan to Dole, 36.5 percent to 28.5 percent. From then on, Dole won every primary for a total of forty wins out of forty-three primaries. The Dole vote amounted to 59.1 percent of the total primary vote. Of the seven caucuses Dole won four.

Although Dole's nomination was no longer in doubt, concerns about his candidacy gave Republicans pause. In late April Bill Kristol wrote in the conservative *Weekly Standard*: "Bob Dole is likely to lose the presidential race to Bill Clinton. He may lose badly." The relentless publication of polls provided more bad news for Dole. Clinton led Dole in virtually every national survey that was publicly released in 1996.[45]

Exit Polls: An Overview of Primary Voting

Exit polls from twenty-eight Republican primary states traced the characteristics of the voters who favored Dole (Table 2-5). Dole drew proportionately greater support from voters sixty years or older, one-third of the Republican primary voters. Dole also drew strong support from the 77 percent of the Republican voters who had graduated from high school or attended college, but he fell down sharply (as did Buchanan) among the 19 percent with at least some postgraduate education. Dole garnered strong support from the voters who considered themselves Republicans. But the 21 percent who considered themselves independents and the 4 percent who thought of themselves as Democrats were not so keen on him, suggesting that he had work ahead if he hoped to reach out to independents and defecting Democrats in the general election.

About 70 percent of the Republican primary voters considered themselves moderate or somewhat conservative. Among these groups Dole won almost 60 percent of the vote. Even among the 21 percent of the voters describing themselves as very conservative, Dole beat out Buchanan, 44 percent to 38 percent. The divisive, polarizing nature of Buchanan's candidacy was apparent in the exit polls: 56 percent of the Republican primary voters considered Buchanan too extreme, and two-thirds of the 56 percent backed Dole.

Opposition to abortion was a cornerstone of the Buchanan campaign. Exit polls revealed that most Republican primary voters opposed a plank advocating a constitutional ban on abortion in the party platform: 57 percent opposed such a plank, and 38 percent backed it. Even among those who sup-

Table 2-5   Vote in the 1996 Republican Primaries, by Groups (percent)

Group	Percentage of voters	Buchanan	Dole	Forbes	Other
Age					
Under 30	10%	25	52	12	11
30-44	30	25	50	12	11
45-59	28	24	52	13	11
60 or older	32	18	65	10	7
Education					
Not a high school graduate	3	24	49	8	19
High school graduate	20	27	57	9	7
Some college	30	24	54	11	11
College graduate	27	20	55	13	12
Postgraduate	19	12	39	10	39
In 1992 voted for					
Bill Clinton	12	24	40	16	20
George Bush	66	20	63	9	6
Ross Perot	13	29	38	20	13
Party affiliation					
Republican	75	21	61	10	8
Independent	21	28	41	15	16
Democrat	4	29	29	11	31
Ideology					
Very liberal	2	19	45	10	26
Somewhat liberal	7	19	53	14	14
Moderate	33	16	59	13	12
Somewhat conservative	37	20	59	11	10
Very conservative	21	38	44	9	9
Constitutional ban on abortion in Republican Party platform					
Favor	38	35	49	7	9
Do not favor	57	18	58	15	12
U.S. trade					
Creates more jobs in own state	43	14	61	11	14
Costs more jobs in own state	39	34	49	8	9
Pat Buchanan					
Too extreme	56	5	71	13	11
Not too extreme	41	47	35	10	8
Percentage of 11.9 million total vote		22.7	55.5	12.6	9.2

Source: New York Times, March 31, 1996.

Note: Based on combined vote totals and results from exit polls conducted in twenty-eight states by Voter News Service. Some questions were not asked in each state. There was no exit poll in Nevada.

ported a constitutional ban on abortions, Dole won 49 percent of their votes, beating Buchanan by fourteen percentage points.

Republican Reform of the Nominating Process

From the start, Republican activists had doubts about whether the party would be well served by the compressed, front-loaded nominating process that had evolved for 1996. A Republican Party task force to study the question and make recommendations was appointed in January 1996 and charged to report after the primaries and caucuses were over. As Haley Barbour, then chairman of the Republican National Committee, explained, "There is some concern that our nominating process may have become so compressed that it may not serve the party or the voters well. With the primaries and caucuses so close together, voters don't have much time to reflect as some candidates drop out and others emerge." [46] The task force found that the compressed schedule had two disadvantages: it did not provide enough time between primaries to allow the voters to assess the field of candidates that remained after the previous primary results, and it dampened turnout in later primaries once Dole's nomination became apparent in early March.[47]

To remedy the problems of a compressed calendar the Republican convention adopted three changes: all states must establish their delegate-selection plans for 2000 by July 1, 1999; all primaries and caucuses must be held between the first Monday in February and the third Tuesday of June; and extra delegates will be awarded to states that decide to hold their primary or caucuses later in the process. States voting between March 15 and April 14 will get a 5 percent delegate bonus; those voting between April 15 and May, 7.5 percent; and those that vote on or after May 15, 10 percent.[48]

Dole's Campaign

Although Dole had the nomination locked up by late March, his campaign's financial situation looked ominous—he was bumping up against the federal spending limit for the preconvention period. During the more than four months that remained until the August convention, when federal money would be released, the Dole campaign had to practice extreme frugality. Dole's financial predicament contrasted sharply with Clinton's overflowing coffers. Clinton, who faced no challenge for the Democratic nomination, had nonetheless raised a substantial war chest (Table 2-2). He mounted a massive ad campaign in the spring that Dole could not match.

Not only was Clinton's financial advantage imposing, his political health had continued to improve. Since the previous fall Clinton's public approval rating had risen to and remained within the politically robust zone of 50 percent or higher, putting him at the level of Eisenhower, Nixon, and Reagan during the fourth year of their first terms. Each of these presidents had won a landslide reelection. Bush in 1992 and Carter in 1980 had approval ratings of about 40 percent at a comparable point in their terms and were defeated. As Clinton grew more formidable, Dole faced the daunting task of whittling down the president's lead without spending much on his campaign.

Dole was the first presidential nominee in history who was also the Senate majority leader. Hoping to draw on his experience as an effective legislative leader, Dole chose to campaign against Clinton from Capitol Hill rather than travel across the country. It seemed the most effective avenue available to him: Dole's campaigning had been lackluster, and he could no longer afford to do much anyway. But the task of running for president while serving as majority leader proved daunting. For example, on the day he clinched his party's presidential nomination, Senate Democrats embarrassed Dole by outmaneuvering him on a vote to hike the minimum wage. Dole was publicly opposed to such an increase, and a new Senate vote on the popular measure could only remind voters of that. Moreover, Republican senators and especially Republican House members had priorities of their own. A House-passed bill to repeal the popular ban on certain assault weapons presented Dole with a Republican accomplishment that posed campaign problems for him.[49] Tying his political fortunes so tightly to Gingrich and the Republican Congress provided drag and no boost for Dole.

On May 15 Dole announced that he would resign from the Senate on June 11 and would devote himself full time to his quest for the presidency. "I will seek the presidency with nothing to fall back on but the judgment of the people," he said, "and nowhere to go but the White House or home."[50] Stepping down from the Senate offered the potential of liberating Dole from legislative gridlock and, for the benefit of Republican activists, signaled a total commitment to his presidential campaign. Former rival Alexander commended Dole: "This is the general saying to the troops, 'I'm willing to risk it all. Follow me.'"[51] Moreover, in the words of one senior Republican strategist: "The idea of trying to be president from the Senate floor reinforces all of Dole's deal-making imagery rather than laying out a clear case against Clinton."[52]

Dole's resignation from the Senate brought no end to the unfavorable polling numbers, however. Although a CNN/*Time* poll June 12–13 showed Dole closing the gap to just six percentage points, later polls had Clinton's lead back in double digits. Dole's supporters argued that such early polls were not to be taken seriously. In the months that followed, they claimed that the race would tighten as Dole did the following: solidified his Republican base, announced his economic program, picked his vice presidential candidate, gave his convention acceptance speech, began the real campaign after Labor Day, won the presidential debates. Such were the hopes, but the reality would prove harsh.

Dole's campaign sputtered along through the summer. Against the backdrop of plentiful polling evidence that he was not making headway against Clinton, critical press coverage was frequent. Campaigning in Kentucky in June, Dole questioned findings that tobacco is addictive. The outcry that followed put Dole in the news but at a disadvantage. For the most part, Dole's infamous temper was held in check, but he turned testy at times. When pressed by Katie Couric of the NBC *Today* show about campaign contributions received from the tobacco industry, Dole questioned whether "people like you [in the media violated FCC] regulations by always . . . sticking up for the Democrats." Turning down an invitation to speak to the NAACP annual convention in July, Dole suggested that NAACP president Kweisi Mfume, a former Democratic House member, "was trying to set me up" by inviting him to appear before the liberal organization.[53]

As always, the conventions that climax the nominating process provided a showcase for the nominees and their parties. If Dole was to turn things around for the general election, the Republican convention offered one of the few remaining opportunities to do so. Such hopes were not without foundation. Although Dole still trailed Clinton 50–34, sixteen percentage points, in early August, recent political history offered grounds for optimism. Both Clinton in 1992 and Bush in 1988 had trailed their opponents before the first convention, albeit by smaller margins—Clinton by five points, Bush by six points. The actual general election results represented eleven-point and fourteen-point swings, respectively, from the preconvention standings.[54] In the days before the conventions, Dole hoped to jump-start his campaign and begin closing the gap by announcing his economic plan and naming his vice presidential running mate.

On August 5, a week before the Republican convention, Dole unveiled his economic plan, promising a 15 percent tax cut for all taxpayers. In addition, the top tax rate on capital gains would be cut by 50 percent, a $500–per-child tax credit would be given to low- and middle-income parents, the federal budget would be balanced in six years, enforcement by the Internal Revenue Service would be tempered, and the damages recoverable in civil lawsuits would be limited.

The plan marked a sharp departure from Dole's career-long stance as "a flinty deficit hawk who repeatedly angered his party's right wing by pushing tax increases as well as spending cuts to try to shrink the burgeoning deficits."[55] Critics contended that Dole's proposal did not explain how he would pay for the resulting $551 billion decrease in taxes. Indeed, Dole promised not to cut Medicare, defense spending, and Social Security, leaving only 30 percent of the budget to absorb the cost of the tax cut.[56]

In the week before the Republican Convention, the polls showed that Dole's economic plan had not captured the public's attention. Clinton continued to lead Dole by a decisive margin.

The Nominating Conventions
The Republican Convention

Dole had promised to depart from custom and name his running mate before the Republican convention. On Saturday, August 10, two days before the convention opened, Dole picked Jack Kemp, an optimistic advocate of supply-side economics and tax cuts, who had served as a House member from Buffalo, New York, and as housing secretary in the Bush cabinet. The choice of Kemp, "a galvanizing and sometimes controversial politician with whom [Dole] had often been at odds,"[57] avoided a weekend of preconvention media coverage that might otherwise have recapitulated the difficulties the Dole campaign had encountered to date. By picking Kemp, an abortion rights opponent, Dole also avoided the conflict threatened by the religious right if he chose a pro–abortion rights running mate.

The Republican convention in San Diego, California, provided several days of favorable press coverage. "GOP leaders melded the twin themes of compassion and conservatism" was a standard headline. The platform contained strong and potentially unpopular planks on controversial social issues to please Republican conservatives, but its adoption took place in a morning session. (Dole dismissively noted before the convention that although he probably agreed with almost everything in it, he had yet to read the platform and he did not feel bound by it.[58] Prime-time convention speakers stressed inclusion and moderation. The unity of the delegates contrasted sharply with the divisions that had marked the 1992 convention. Buchanan's polarizing speech that year had hindered Bush's campaign. But Buchanan did not have enough delegates (142, or 7 percent) to parlay into a presence at the 1996 convention. The Dole forces were unwilling to provide him with a platform for a repeat performance.[59]

The Republican convention, coming on the heels of Dole's launch of his economic plan and his selection of Kemp, helped Dole to unify and excite his Republican base. The general election challenge was uphill—the nation was at peace, the economy prosperous, and Clinton enjoyed a large lead—but in Dole's acceptance speech, he told the delegates: "Tonight, I stand before you tested by adversity, made sensitive by hardship, a fighter by principle, and the most optimistic man in America."[60] Dole got a boost from the convention. ABC tracking polls taken six days before the meeting opened and six days after showed that Clinton dropped from 50 percent to 44 percent and Dole increased from 34 percent to 40 percent, netting a twelve percentage point swing. But these gains did not last. By the time the Democratic convention opened a week later, Clinton led Dole 51 percent to 36 percent, a fifteen-point gap.[61]

The Reform Party Conventions

In late 1995 Perot established the Reform Party as a third-party challenge to the two major parties. On July 9, 1996, former Democratic governor Richard D. Lamm of Colorado announced that he would seek the Reform Party nomination. Two days later Perot declared that he would run for the nomination himself. The nominating process involved ballots sent to 1.3 million individuals who were either registered party members or signers of ballot-access petitions for the Reform Party in their states. The candidates who received 10 percent of their votes—Lamm and Perot—were invited to speak to the Reform Party convention in Long Beach, California, on August 11. Subsequently, another vote—by phone, mail, and electronic means—was taken and the nominee was announced at another convention on August 18 in Valley Forge, Pennsylvania.

The Reform Party was Perot's creation, and he had little trouble sewing up its nomination, defeating Lamm by a two-to-one margin. The total number of votes cast was tiny in contrast to the more than one million ballots that were circulated, however, and some would-be Reform voters, Lamm included, complained about the difficulties of securing a ballot. After losing, Lamm congratulated Perot, but stopped short of endorsing him. News coverage of the fledgling Reform Party was eclipsed by the media's focus on the Republican convention. Perot postponed his announcement of a running mate until September 10, when he picked Pat Choate, a Washington, D.C., economist, consultant, and author. In 1992 Perot had achieved an impressive 19 percent of the popular vote, but in 1996 his appeal had shrunk. After the Reform Party convention, polls showed Perot's support hovering in the single digits.

The Democratic Convention

The Democratic convention reinforced the centrist political position that Clinton had attempted to occupy since his party's defeat in 1994. A well-planned convention contained little suspense, the only news jolt coming on the morning of Thursday, August 29, when Clinton's chief campaign strategist, Dick Morris, resigned in response to tabloid newspaper stories about his liaisons with a prostitute. Republicans reacted by reminding voters about the "sleaze factor" they contended characterized the Clinton White House. Dole suggested that the loss of Morris, a centrist, meant that Clinton would become more liberal.[62]

The Democratic convention, like its Republican counterpart, made a considerable effort to portray the party as sensitive to the plight of the less fortunate, particularly the disabled. Carefully selected political speeches filled prime time, but even more carefully selected vignettes were crafted to stir the viewers' emotions. On opening night, the Democrats featured actor Christopher Reeve, paralyzed from a riding accident, and gun control advocates Jim and Sarah Brady. Jim Brady, formerly Reagan's press secretary, had been disabled in the 1981 assassination attempt against Reagan. Polls taken in the aftermath of the Democratic convention showed that Clinton retained his comfortable double-digit lead over Dole.

The staging of the 1996 Republican and Democratic conventions raised questions about the role of quadrennial nominating conventions. With the reformed nominating process emphasizing the primaries and caucuses, conventions are devoid of suspense. Measuring newsworthiness in the standard media terms—that is, as surprising turns of events—meant the conventions were also limited as newsmakers. In a television age, the parties have a great incentive to script the conventions to produce a watchable television show. Each party did that in 1996, but the major networks demurred, cutting back on their coverage. On most nights the three major networks aired only one hour of convention programming.[63] The ratings for the networks' convention broadcasts fell well below the figures from 1992. Expectations were strong that conventions in 2000 would be very different events, although no alternative format commanded consensus support.

Conclusion

The nominating process marked a critical period in the 1996 presidential election. The political dynamics established during the nomination season persisted through the general election. Before the primary and caucus voting began, President Clinton had recovered politically to an extent thought improbable in the aftermath of the 1994 elections. The unfolding of the nominating process presented problems for Senator Dole, but not for Clinton. The absence of a challenger for the Democratic nomination gave Clinton an almost free hand in moving toward the center of the political spectrum. Dole, battered and bruised from fighting off Forbes, Alexander, and Buchanan, was lumbered with ties to an increasingly unpopular Republican Congress. Many voters had yearned for a fresh figure in politics, such as Powell, but no such alternative was on offer.

Despite the doubts and difficulties, Dole managed to secure the Republican nomination. But the task remaining before him was formidable. With his party's nomination in hand, Dole would attempt to triumph over a centrist incumbent presiding in a time of peace and prosperity.

Notes

1. Harold W. Stanley, "The Parties, the President, and the 1994 Mid-term Elections," in *The Clinton Presidency: First Appraisals,* ed. Colin Campbell and Bert Rockman (Chatham, N.J.: Chatham House, 1995), 188–211.
2. Gallup Poll, September 22–24, 1994, as reported in Lydia Saad, "Powell's Best Bet: Run as a Republican," *The Gallup Organization October 1995 Newsletter Archive,* vol. 60, no. 21, October 7, 1995.
3. Other declared Republican candidates were Rep. Bob Dornan of California; former chairman of the Civil Rights Commission, Arthur Fletcher; radio talk show host Alan Keyes; Sen. Dick Lugar of Indiana; Sen. Arlen Specter of Pennsylvania; businessman Maurice M. "Morry" Taylor; and Gov. Pete Wilson of California. Wilson suspended his presidential campaign September 29, 1995, and Specter suspended his campaign November 22, 1995.
4. CNN/*USA Today*/Gallup Poll, November 8, 1995.
5. Quotations in Rhodes Cook, "In Surprise Move, Perot to Launch Third Party: Focus Will Be on Choosing Candidate for 1996 Presidential Run," *Congressional Quarterly Weekly Report,* September 30, 1995, 3022–3024.
6. "White House '96—Independent Candidate: Introducing the Gang of Seven," *Hotline,* November 27, 1995; Ronald D. Elving, "Benefits from Powell Decision

Spread Among Candidates," *Congressional Quarterly Weekly Report,* November 11, 1995, 3470–3472.

7. Paul R. Abramson, John H. Aldrich, and David W. Rohde, *Change and Continuity in the 1992 Elections,* rev. ed. (Washington, D.C.: CQ Press, 1995), 195–220.

8. George Hager, "Budget Battle Came Sooner than Either Side Expected, *Congressional Quarterly Weekly Report,* November 18, 1995, 3503–3509.

9. Jackie Koszczuk, "'Train Wreck' Engineered by GOP Batters Party and House Speaker," *Congressional Quarterly Weekly Report,* November 1, 1995, 3506–3507.

10. Hager, "Budget Battle," 3503–3509; "A lesson of 1995 was that no matter how Republicans set up an impasse, they are likely to get the blame because the president controls the spin." Stephen Gettinger, "Game Has Changed for GOP Majority," *Congressional Quarterly Weekly Report,* February 17, 1996, 422.

11. But even the ending of the shutdown in early January 1996 created problems for Dole with some Republican conservatives. Some House Republicans, thinking Dole had been unduly conciliatory toward the president in ending the impasse, wanted to continue the strategy of using the government shutdown to pressure Clinton to approve a balanced budget agreement along Republican lines. David S. Cloud, "Dole Gambles on Budget Crisis," *Congressional Quarterly Weekly Report,* January 6, 1996, 54; Alissa J. Rubin, "'CR' Ends Shutdown," 3598; George Hager, "Day by Day: Talks Wax and Wane as Anger, Miscues Punctuate Week," *Congressional Quarterly Weekly Report,* December 23, 1995, 3876–3877; George Hager, "A Battered GOP Calls Workers Back to Job," *Congressional Quarterly Weekly Report,* January 6, 1996, 53–57.

12. Jack W. Germond and Jules Witcover, "Clinton's Can't-Win Policy on Bosnia," *National Journal,* December 2, 1995, 2995.

13. Rhodes Cook, "Convictions in Arkansas Revive Clinton's Whitewater Woes," *Congressional Quarterly Weekly Report,* June 1, 1996, 1547–1549; Rhodes Cook, "Third Parties Push to Present a Respectable Alternative," *Congressional Quarterly Weekly Report,* July 13, 1996, 1986–1988. For a listing of ethical questions surrounding Clinton and his cabinet during his first term, see Jonathan D. Salant, "Term Full of Questions," *Congressional Quarterly Weekly Report,* August 17, 1996, supplement to vol. 54, no. 33, 12.

14. Bob Dole, announcing his presidential candidacy, *Hotline,* April 10, 1995.

15. Rhodes Cook, "GOP Hopefuls Gather in New Hampshire for First Televised Debate," *Congressional Quarterly Weekly Report,* October 14, 1995, 3159.

16. Elving, "Benefits from Powell," 3470–3472.

17. Sam Howe Verhovek, "Strategic Mistakes Brought Down Gramm," *New York Times,* February 15, 1996.

18. For an insightful analysis of momentum in the presidential nominating process, see Larry M. Bartels, *Presidential Primaries and the Dynamics of Public Choice* (Princeton: Princeton University Press, 1988). For an analysis of the Democratic reforms of the presidential nominating process up to 1984, see David E. Price, *Bringing Back the Parties* (Washington, D.C.: CQ Press, 1984), 145–187.

19. Charles D. Hadley and Harold W. Stanley, "Super Tuesday 1988: Regional Results and National Implications," *Publius* 19 (summer 1989): 19–37.

20. Indeed, when presidential candidate, Gov. Pete Wilson of California, announced September 11, 1995, that he would not compete in the early February Iowa caucuses, preferring instead to concentrate on the New Hampshire primary and other early primary states, political observers placed his campaign under a "death watch"—"the Iowa pullout was widely viewed as an act of desperation by a potentially formidable candidate who had failed to gain altitude." Rhodes Cook, "Wilson Campaign Succumbs to Weak Fundraising," *Congressional Quarterly Weekly Report,* September 30, 1995, 3025.

21. In only a dozen states were Republican delegates awarded proportionately according to each candidate's share of the vote; in the remaining states winner-take-all rules prevailed. Rhodes Cook, "GOP's Rules Favor Dole, If He Doesn't Stumble," *Congressional Quarterly Weekly Report,* January 27, 1996, 228–231.
22. Jackie Koszczuk, "Clinton Embraces GOP Rhetoric," *Congressional Quarterly Weekly Report,* January 27, 1996, 211.
23. Percentages are based on vote tallies in thirty-eight of Alaska's forty election districts. Rhodes Cook, "Dole Suffers Bit of a Chill in Alaska Straw Vote," *Congressional Quarterly Weekly Report,* February 3, 1996, 313.
24. The twenty-one delegates were congressional district delegates. The nine at-large delegates would be selected in a presidential primary on March 12. Cook, "Dole Suffers," 313; Robert Shogan, "Gramm Upset by Buchanan in Louisiana," *Los Angeles Times,* February 7, 1996; Rhodes Cook, "Gramm's Candidacy Teeters After Loss in Louisiana," *Congressional Quarterly Weekly Report,* February 10, 1996, 363–365; Verhovek, "Strategic Mistakes."
25. The Iowa caucuses were actually nonbinding straw votes with the twenty-five convention delegates to be chosen later in the spring at congressional district and state conventions. Cook, "Gramm's Candidacy Teeters," 363–365.
26. Verhovek, "Strategic Mistakes."
27. Gramm had not endorsed anyone when he dropped out, but he had pointed out that Buchanan's harsh economic nationalism did not fit within the Republican Party and was a "recessive gene" in the American character—"Republicans Battle for Gramm Supporters," Reuters, February 14, 1996.
28. Federal Election Commission, "FEC Announces 1996 Presidential Spending Limits," March 15, 1996, press release.
29. Cook, "GOP Hopefuls Gather," 3159; Cook, "Gramm's Candidacy Teeters," 363–365.
30. Craig Hines, "Forbes Fortune, Ads Rewrite Book on Iowa," *Houston Chronicle,* January 28, 1996, 1. John Connally had forgone federal matching funds in 1980 to avoid being subject to campaign spending limits, but Connally had to raise funds rather than tap personal wealth. Did money translate into votes? Connally spent more than $10 million on his campaign and got one convention delegate, Mrs. Ada Mills of Arkansas.
31. Elving, "Benefits from Powell," 3470–3472.
32. Quotations from Rhodes Cook, "Forbes Candidacy Producing Eye-Opening Poll Showings," *Congressional Quarterly Weekly Report,* December 2, 1995, 3674–3676. Later Dole would admit that Forbes's aggressive television ads in the early states wiped out Dole's lead in preference polls and nearly cost Dole the nomination. See Robert Marshall Wells, "Measuring Forbes' Impact," *Congressional Quarterly Weekly Report,* March 16, 1996, 716.
33. Trial heat Republican presidential preference polls for New Hampshire were obtained from the PoliticsNow Web site *(http://politicsnow.com/resource/polltrak/data/newhdata.htm).*
34. Rhodes Cook, "GOP Faces Uncharted Terrain in Wake of Buchanan Upset," *Congressional Quarterly Weekly Report,* February 24, 1996, 438–442.
35. "White House '96—Buchanan: The Peasants Are Revolting; More Staff Fallout," *Hotline,* February 19, 1996.
36. Alan Greenblatt, "The Struggle for the Soul of a Changing GOP," *Congressional Quarterly Weekly Report,* April 6, 1996, 941–948; "White House '96—Buchanabals: The Establishment GOP Freaks Out," *Hotline,* February 23, 1996.
37. Cook, "GOP Faces," 438–442.
38. Alexander was the favorite in Iowa among caucus-goers who prized electability. See Rhodes Cook, "Dole's Shaky Lead Faces Test in Volatile New Hampshire," *Congressional Quarterly Weekly Report,* February 17, 1996, 399–403.

39. Rhodes Cook, "GOP 'March Madness' May Be Turning Point in Campaign," *Congressional Quarterly Weekly Report,* March 2, 1996, 570–573.
40. Rhodes Cook, "The Nominating Process," in *The Elections of 1988,* ed. Michael Nelson (Washington, D.C.: CQ Press, 1989), 42.
41. Alan Greenblatt, "Lugar, Alexander Withdraw," *Congressional Quarterly Weekly Report,* March 9, 1996, 641.
42. Rhodes Cook, "Dole Supreme in Week of Wins; 'Super Tuesday' Comes Next," *Congressional Quarterly Weekly Report,* March 9, 1996, 636–642.
43. Cook, "Dole Supreme," 636–642.
44. *Congressional Quarterly Weekly Report,* March 23, 1996, 826; Rhodes Cook, "Midwestern Enclaves Suggest Dole Has Work to Do," *Congressional Quarterly Weekly Report,* March 23, 1996, 810–813.
45. Ronald Brownstein, "Worried Dole Campaign, GOP to Accelerate Attack on Clinton," *Los Angeles Times,* April 24, 1996.
46. Haley Barbour, quoted in "Nicholson Tapped to Chair National GOP Task Force on Presidential Primary Schedule," Republican National Committee News Release, February 27, 1996 *(http://www.rnc.org/news release/rel960227.html);* "GOP Task Force Recommends Rules Changes to Encourage Greater Voter Participation," Republican National Committee News Release, July 2, 1996 *(http://www.rnc.org/news release/rel960702.html).*
47. Rhodes Cook, "Some Push for a Change in the Process," *Congressional Quarterly Weekly Report,* August 3, 1996, 10.
48. Except for smaller bonuses (the task force had suggested 10, 15, and 20 percent bonuses, which some thought would change a "front-loaded" process into a "back-loaded" one), these changes were the task force recommendations. Alan Greenblatt and Rhodes Cook, "Nominating Process Rules Change," *Congressional Quarterly Weekly Report,* August 17, 1996, 2299.
49. David S. Cloud, "Tough Campaign Challenges for the Senate Leader," *Congressional Quarterly Weekly Report,* March 30, 1996, 859–861.
50. "Quote of the Day," *Hotline,* May 16, 1996.
51. "White House '96—Veepstakes: Reactions to Dole's Announcement," *Hotline,* May 16, 1996.
52. Brownstein, "Worried Dole Campaign."
53. Rhodes Cook, "Dole's Job: To Convince His Own Party," *Congressional Quarterly Weekly Report,* August 3, 1996, 7–11.
54. ABC News Tracking Poll for August 6, 1996, obtained from PoliticsNow *(http://www.politicsnow.com).*
55. George Hager, "Dole and Taxes," *Congressional Quarterly Weekly Report,* August 10, 1996, 2248.
56. Alissa J. Rubin, "Dole 'Bets the Country' on Tax Cut Package," *Congressional Quarterly Weekly Report,* August 10, 1996, 2245–2249.
57. Rhodes Cook, "Kemp Pops to Top of List on Eve of Convention," *Congressional Quarterly Weekly Report,* August 10, 1996, 2260–2261.
58. *San Diego Union Tribune,* August 11, 1996, as reported in "Platform: Dole Says He Has Yet to Read Draft Document," *Hotline,* August 12, 1996.
59. Rhodes Cook, "Buchanan Will Not Go Gently as He Weighs Next Move," *Congressional Quarterly Weekly Report,* August 3, 1996, 2213.
60. "Dole's Speech Accepting the GOP Nomination for President," *New York Times,* August 16, 1996, A26.
61. ABC News Tracking Poll *(http://www.politicsnow.com/).*
62. Carroll J. Doherty, "With More Prose Than Poetry, Clinton Emphasizes Policy," *Congressional Quarterly Weekly Report,* August 31, 1996, 2457–2458.
63. *Congressional Quarterly Weekly Report,* August 3, 1996, supplement to vol. 54, no. 31, 25.

3

The Election: Turbulence and Tranquillity in Contemporary American Politics

Michael Nelson

H as American politics in the last third of the twentieth century been more like weather or climate?

To say that politics has been more like weather would be to say that it has been basically changeable, even turbulent. To say that it has been more like climate would suggest that it has been mostly tranquil, with change coming only gradually. For example, the weather in Memphis, Tennessee, in November varies from sunny one day to cloudy or rainy the next, from cold to warm and back again. But the climate is more predictable. The day-to-day ups and downs in temperature and precipitation do not change the fact that Memphis is almost always colder and wetter in November than in September and October.

No one can deny the weather-like turbulence of late-twentieth-century American politics, especially the politics of presidential elections. That turbulence is described in the first part of this chapter. But underlying all the rapid changes have been a number of steady and slowly evolving climatic elements in the political system. Because these elements are important, yet less frequently noted in commentaries on contemporary politics, their discussion constitutes the bulk of the chapter. Throughout, emphasis is placed on the general election campaign for president in 1996.

Political Weather: 1968–1996

Political scientists are used to being able to organize American politics into long, coherent eras. In this century, for example, the period from 1896 to 1930 was a Republican-dominated era, during which the Democrats seldom controlled either the presidency or Congress. The two parties' positions were reversed in the aftermath of the Great Depression and Democratic president Franklin D. Roosevelt's New Deal: 1932 to 1964 was a strongly Democratic era.

In some important—and many superficial—ways, American politics became dramatically destabilized in the late 1960s. On March 31, 1968, Lyndon B. Johnson, who only four years earlier had been elected president with the largest popular vote majority in history, announced that he would not seek reelection. In the midst of massive public protests against the Vietnam

War, including serious antiwar challenges for the 1968 Democratic presidential nomination by Sen. Eugene McCarthy and Sen. Robert F. Kennedy, Johnson doubted whether he could be renominated, much less reelected.

Four days after Johnson's announcement, civil rights leader Martin Luther King Jr. was assassinated. Just two months after that, on the night of his victory in the June 6 California primary, Robert Kennedy also was killed. Riots, which had broken out in the nation's urban ghettos after King's death, plagued the Democratic National Convention in Chicago that August.

In November 1968 Republican Richard Nixon was narrowly elected as president against the Democratic nominee, Vice President Hubert H. Humphrey. Former governor George C. Wallace of Alabama won 14 percent of the popular vote, the best showing for a third-party candidate since former president Theodore Roosevelt's in 1912. Wallace's race-based campaign carried five Deep South states and won significant support from white working-class voters around the country. The electorate also chose a Democratic Congress, making Nixon the first president since Zachary Taylor, in 1848, to enter office with a Congress controlled by the opposite party.

In 1972 Nixon was reelected against the antiwar Democratic nominee, Sen. George McGovern. Nixon carried the Wallace vote (Wallace, who had chosen to contest the Democratic nomination, was seriously wounded in an attempt on his life on May 15), and, with it, the electoral votes of every state but Massachusetts. Despite the Republican presidential landslide, however, the voters again elected a Democratic Congress. In early August 1974 the 93d Congress made clear its intention to impeach and remove Nixon from office for abuses of power committed during the Watergate scandal. Rather than become the first president in history to be constitutionally forced out of office, Nixon elected to become the first president in history to resign.

Nixon was succeeded as president by Gerald R. Ford. In 1973 Nixon, with the consent of Congress, had appointed Ford vice president under the Twenty-fifth Amendment, which had been ratified six years earlier. The vacancy in the vice presidency had occurred when Spiro T. Agnew resigned in the face of bribery charges as part of a plea bargain to escape imprisonment. Ford in turn appointed former New York governor Nelson A. Rockefeller as vice president. In 1976 an unelected president and an unelected vice president presided over the nation's bicentennial celebration.

Ford was defeated for president in 1976, the first incumbent to lose an election since Herbert Hoover in 1932. The winner, former Georgia governor Jimmy Carter, was in turn defeated in 1980 by Ronald Reagan of California, also a former governor. (A third-party candidate, Rep. John B. Anderson of Illinois, won 7 percent of the popular vote.) For the first time since the 1920s, Republicans began to hope that they again were becoming the nation's majority party—the voters not only had elected Reagan in the largest electoral-vote landslide ever against an incumbent president (Reagan 489, Carter 49), but they also had broken the Democrats' quarter-century hold on

the Senate. These hopes soon were dashed, however: despite Reagan's personal popularity, the House of Representatives remained Democratic and in
1986 the Democrats regained control of the Senate.

Reagan's vice president, George Bush, was elected president in 1988 by
a comfortable margin. But in that same election, for the first time in history,
the winning candidate's party lost seats in the House, the Senate, the state-
houses, and the state legislatures. In March 1991, in the aftermath of the U.S.
victory in the Persian Gulf War, Bush's public approval rating soared to 90
percent, the highest in the history of presidential polling. Nineteen months
later, he received 37 percent of the popular vote, the lowest total for an
incumbent president since William Howard Taft in 1912, against the Democratic nominee, Arkansas governor Bill Clinton. Ross Perot, a billionaire
businessman, won 19 percent of the popular vote as a self-financed third-
party candidate, exceeding Wallace's total in 1968 and challenging Roosevelt's 1912 record. The Democrats easily retained control of Congress.

Two years later, in 1994, the voters chose a Republican Congress for the
first time in forty-two years. Led by Speaker of the House Newt Gingrich
and, less energetically, by Senate majority leader Robert Dole, the Republicans took such firm control of the legislative agenda that Clinton was forced,
in April 1995, to remind the nation that "the president is relevant here." [1]
When a budget showdown closed the government twice in late 1995, Clinton regained the political high ground. Gingrich rapidly became the most
unpopular political leader in the country.

If historically unique or unusual results are any indication, many aspects
of the elections of 1996 fit the recent pattern of turbulent political weather.
As noted in Chapter 1, Clinton's list of "firsts" was impressive, including first
Democratic president in sixty years to win a second term and first Democrat
in history to be elected along with a Republican Congress. But not all of the
president's firsts were as satisfying. Clinton also was the first two-term president since 1916 not to win a majority of the popular vote in either of his victories and the only one not to receive at least four hundred electoral votes.
As for the Republican Congress, it was the first since 1928 to be reelected and
the first in history to survive at least four years during a Democratic president's tenure.

Political Climate: 1968–1996

The turbulent political weather that has marked the contemporary era
masks the influence of a number of steadier, more tranquil elements in American politics, which are discussed in the remainder of the chapter. Some of
these elements, such as the cycle of politics and policy and the magnifying
role of the electoral college in presidential elections, have deep roots in history. Others have become settled parts of the system only recently. These
include unifying political conventions, the rise of third-party candidates, the
enhanced vice presidential selection process, quadrennial debates between

the presidential and vice presidential candidates, low voter turnout, and divided government.

The Cycle of Politics and Policy

For all their firsts, the elections of 1996 fit squarely into the ongoing history of presidential elections and domestic policy making in the twentieth century. This history can be told in terms of a recurring cycle of electoral politics and government response. The focus of this cycle has been the presidency. The cycle has undergone four complete turns and, with the Clinton administration, has entered into the first phase of a fifth.[2] (See Table 3-1.)

At the heart of the cycle of politics and policy is a *presidency of achievement,* during which great bursts of presidentially inspired legislation are enacted that significantly alter the role of the federal government in American society. Such presidencies become possible only when three conditions are met in the election that brings the president to power: (1) a candidate campaigns for the presidency with promises, however general, of significant reform; (2) the candidate is elected by a strong majority; and (3) the candidate's victory is accompanied by large gains for the party in Congress.[3] (See Table 3-2.) Such gains create a heightened willingness among legislators in both parties to support the president's agenda—copartisans because they want to ride the bandwagon, and members of the opposition because they want to avoid being flattened by it. A president whose election is not accom-

Table 3-1 Twentieth-Century Presidents and the Cycle of Politics and Policy

| | Stages of the cycle of politics and policy | |
Preparation	Achievement	Consolidation
Theodore Roosevelt	Woodrow Wilson	Warren G. Harding Calvin Coolidge Herbert Hoover
	Franklin D. Roosevelt	Dwight D. Eisenhower
John F. Kennedy	Lyndon B. Johnson	Richard Nixon Gerald R. Ford
Jimmy Carter	Ronald Reagan	George Bush
Bill Clinton		

Note: Presidents William Howard Taft and Harry S. Truman were presidents of stalemate.

Table 3-2   Initial Elections of Presidents of Preparation, Achievement, and Consolidation

President	Victory margin over nearest opponent		Gains for president-elect's party in Congress	
	Popular vote (%)	Electoral vote	House	Senate
Preparation				
T. Roosevelt (1904)	18.8%	196	43	0
Kennedy (1960)	0.3	84	−21	0
Carter (1976)	2.1	57	0	1
Clinton (1992)	5.5	202	−10	0
Achievement				
Wilson (1912)	14.4	347	62	9[a]
F. Roosevelt (1932)	17.7	413	97[a]	12[a]
Johnson (1964)	22.6	434	37	1
Reagan (1980)	9.7	440	33	12[a]
Consolidation				
Harding (1920)	26.4	277	63	11[a]
Coolidge (1924)	25.3	246	22	3
Hoover (1928)	17.4	357	30	8
Eisenhower (1952)	10.7	353	22[a]	1[a]
Nixon (1968)	0.7	110	5	6
Bush (1988)	7.8	325	−3	0

[a] President's party took control of the house of Congress.

panied by large gains is more likely to be regarded by members of Congress as tangential to their own political fortunes.

The United States has had four presidents of achievement in the twentieth century. Woodrow Wilson was the first: from 1913 to 1917 his New Freedom program inaugurated a role for the federal government as an umpire that would regulate the excesses of private corporate power. Franklin Roosevelt, in the 1930s, was next. The public philosophy of his New Deal agenda was that, within the bounds of capitalism and private property, the federal government is ultimately responsible for securing the economic foundations of the people's liberty: employment, security, and welfare. In the 1960s Johnson, the century's third president of achievement, extended the helping hand of government to economically deprived minorities and addressed quality-of-life concerns such as education and the environment in pursuit of his vision of the Great Society. Finally, during the early 1980s, Reagan demonstrated that conservative Republicans as well as liberal Democrats can be presidents of achievement by persuading Congress to enact dramatic income tax cuts, social spending reductions, and defense spending increases.[4]

Each presidency of achievement has been followed by a *presidency of consolidation,* in which the reforms of the achievement stage were not rejected but woven into the administrative fabric of government and retired from the roster of divisive political issues. The 1920s presidencies of Warren G. Harding, Calvin Coolidge, and Hoover were of this kind, as were those of Dwight D. Eisenhower in the 1950s, Nixon and Ford in the late 1960s and early 1970s, and Bush in the late 1980s and early 1990s. The election that brings a president of consolidation into office may be marked by an achievement-style landslide and long coattails. But the mandate of such a president comes as the result of campaign promises *not* to push for dramatic domestic policy change.

A presidency of consolidation concludes each turn of the cycle of politics and policy, but it also overlaps with the period in which the seeds of the next turn are planted. New social discontents arise, as they inevitably will in a dynamic society. But presidents of consolidation, empowered only with an electoral mandate not to push aggressively for change and preoccupied with the agenda of their own turn of the cycle, are likely to be unresponsive to these forces.

Eventually, some of the new social discontents become strong enough to dominate presidential politics. A president is elected because of the ability to articulate the new problems and offer new ideas to meet them. The main task during a *presidency of preparation* is for the president to lay the groundwork for the presidency of achievement that will follow. Theodore Roosevelt, John F. Kennedy, and Carter were the century's first three presidents of preparation. Clinton is the fourth.[5]

As with presidencies of achievement and consolidation, the seeds of a presidency of preparation lie in the election. Presidents of preparation run change-oriented campaigns in the manner of a president of achievement. But because their ideas, however appealing, are new and still unfamiliar, they are elected by smaller margins, with shorter coattails, or both.[6]

Could a president of preparation, reelected in a long-coattails landslide, become a president of achievement? None has, but the history of such presidencies is riddled with lost opportunities for achievement status. Theodore Roosevelt almost certainly would have been a president of achievement if he had run for reelection in 1908, but even though he had served only one full term and part of the assassinated William McKinley's, he withdrew in deference to the two-term tradition. Kennedy was consciously laying the political groundwork for a second-term presidency of achievement at the time of his assassination in 1963, a year in advance of the 1964 election.

In 1992 Clinton ran a strongly change-oriented campaign for president. As he declared frequently, the theme of his domestic agenda was neither "trickle down economics" (the standard Republican approach) nor "tax and spend government" (the traditional Democratic solution) but rather "invest and grow"—that is, to channel federal money into new education, training, and infrastructure-development programs designed to enhance American competitiveness in the global economy. Clinton's victory on election day, however, was not overwhelming. His 43 percent of the popular vote was noticeably short of a majority. His 370 electoral votes compared unfavorably with the initial victories of all the century's presidents of achievement: 435 for Wilson in 1912, 472 for Roosevelt in 1932, 486 for Johnson in 1964, and 489 for Reagan in 1980. Equally important, in the 1992 congressional elections, Clinton's party made no gains in the Senate and actually lost ten seats to the Republicans in the House.

Any hopes that Clinton may have had for a second-term presidency of achievement rested on running a bold campaign for reelection and winning a triumphant victory, personally and in the congressional elections. None of these hopes was realized; most were not even attempted.

The seeds of Clinton's reelection strategy were sown in the aftermath of the Democrats' heavy losses in the 1994 midterm election. The president's initial response to the conservative Republican triumph was to proclaim that the voters had endorsed, albeit perversely, his 1992 theme of change: "I think what they told us was, 'Look, two years ago we made one change, now we made another change. We want you to keep on moving this country forward, and we want to accelerate the pace of change.'"[7] This view was reinforced by Clinton's pollster, Stanley Greenberg. He and other liberal Clinton advisers argued that the president should resurrect his invest-and-grow agenda in order to win back the support of lower-middle-class voters. These voters, Greenberg claimed, needed education, training, and jobs-producing infrastructure programs and had grown disenchanted with the president when he decided to stress deficit reduction in 1993.

During the first half of 1995, however, Clinton decided to abandon Greenberg and the change-oriented approach to reelection in favor of a three-pronged strategy, all the elements of which were firmly in place by the end of the year. The first prong was to preempt any challenge to his renomination at the Democratic convention by raising so much money that no serious opponent would dare to take him on. (Senators Bob Kerrey and Bill Bradley and House Democratic leader Richard Gephardt were among those who backed off.) Clinton's success in this effort made him the first Democratic presidential candidate since Johnson in 1964 not to have to fight for his party's nomination.

The other two prongs of Clinton's reelection strategy were aimed more directly at winning the general election against the Republican nominee. One of these was to pursue campaign adviser Dick Morris's goal of *triangulation*. Morris, along with the new polling team of Mark Penn and Doug Schoen and eventually Clinton himself, thought that it was important for the president not only to stake out a position at the political center, midway between liberal congressional Democrats and conservative congressional Republicans, but also to find new issues that would allow him to rise above the conventional left-right political spectrum. The three points of the new political tri-angle would then be occupied by orthodox Democrats and Republicans at opposite ends of its baseline, with Clinton hovering at a point above and between them.

Triangulation explains, for example, Clinton's approach to the defining controversy of his third year as president—the budget battle with the Republican Congress. Fresh from their triumph in the midterm election, the Republicans went beyond the promises of their Contract with America by vowing to balance the budget by 2002 and cut taxes dramatically. Congressional Democrats opposed them on both counts, aiming most of their fire at the spending reductions in many federal programs that would be required to achieve these purposes. In mid-1995 Clinton angered Democrats by boldly embracing the Republican goal of a balanced budget but infuriated Republicans by insisting that Democratic programs such as Medicare, Medicaid, support for education, and environmental enforcement must be left substantially unaltered. The public, prompted in part by $18 million worth of pro-administration television commercials paid for by the Democratic National Committee, supported the president on both counts. Then, when the Republicans tried to impose their own budget on Clinton, he refused to yield.[8] More than that, Clinton persuaded the voters that Speaker Gingrich, Majority Leader Dole, and the Republican Congress, not he, were responsible for the two federal government shutdowns that occurred in late 1995 in the absence of a budget agreement. Public support for Clinton, who had consistently trailed Dole in the presidential "trial heat" polls, increased dramatically: by January he had opened up a double-digit lead against the Republican front-runner, a lead he never lost.

The other prong of Clinton's strategy for winning the general election was to present himself to the voters as a presidential, rather than as a partisan or political, figure. The terrorist bombing of the Oklahoma City federal building in April 1995 gave him his first opportunity after the midterm election to do so. His effort was successful: as one observer recorded in the aftermath of the traumatic bombing, Clinton "exhibited the take-charge determination as well as the on-key rhetoric that Americans expect of their president in times of trouble."[9] In November 1995 Clinton learned something else about presidential behavior. When he overruled public opinion by sending twenty thousand American troops on a peacekeeping mission to Bosnia, the voters' approval of his handling of foreign policy went up. Privately, Clinton likened it to "telling your children to go to the dentist—they don't want to go, but they know you're right."[10]

Clinton's strategy of triangulation and acting presidential had clear implications for the way he conducted his general election campaign in the fall of 1996. In dozens of campaign appearances around the country, Clinton pointed backward with pride to the economic progress of his first term: four consecutive years of low inflation, a drop in the unemployment rate from 7 percent in 1992 to 5 percent in 1996, steady economic growth, and a reduction in the annual budget deficit from $290 billion the year before he became president to $106 billion in the fourth year of his term. He struck unifying presidential poses for the television cameras, signing legislation at the Grand Canyon and presiding over an emergency Arab-Israeli summit conference at the White House. He also celebrated the first-term enactment of laws such as the Family and Medical Leave Act, an increase in the minimum wage, and welfare reform, along with his successful defense of "Medicare, Medicaid, education, and the environment" (a litany that frequent hearers recast as M^2E^2) against alleged Republican assaults.

But Clinton's discussion of the future was hardly the stuff of which achievement-style mandates are made. Riding buses festooned with "On the Road to the 21st Century" signboards or standing under banners that proclaimed "Building America's Bridge to the 21st Century," Clinton repeatedly offered empty "bridge" rhetoric to the voters. He promised (in language later echoed in his inaugural address) a bridge "big enough, strong enough, and wide enough for everybody to walk across" and asserted that "everyone has a right to walk on the bridge." By one count he used the word an average of more than nine times per speech.[11] Aside from some specific promises concerning tax credits for education, Clinton's campaign was short on major proposals for the second term.

Nor did Clinton tie his campaign to the fortunes of congressional Democrats, even when his lead in the polls stretched to fifteen percentage points. Determined to win 51 percent of the popular vote (one campaign aide described that goal as "psychically very important to him")[12] and wary of alienating voters who might fear giving him too cooperative a Congress, Clinton almost never called for the election of a Democratic House and Senate. When endorsing individual candidates, White House press secretary Michael McCurry noted, "The president does not make this appeal solely on partisanship."[13] Only late in the campaign did Clinton raise significant amounts of money for congressional Democrats.

Clinton won 49 percent of the popular vote to Dole's 41 percent and Perot's 8 percent, along with 379 electoral votes to Dole's 159—to that extent his reelection strategy was effective. It certainly was the safest strategy he could have pursued. But the low-risk campaign that Clinton conducted prevented him from winning an achievement-style victory based on a change-oriented agenda and long congressional coattails. Indeed, the Democrats lost two seats in the Senate, outweighing their modest gain of nine seats in the House, and failed to regain control of either legislative body. The Clinton presidency remained stalled at the preparation stage of the cycle of politics and policy, the same stage where it had begun.

Unifying Conventions

In recent years, the politics of presidential nominations has stabilized to such an extent that one can safely include it under the rubric of political climate rather than political weather. Nominations for president in the contemporary era are typically sewn up by the winning candidate long before the national party convention meets in the summer of the election year. The convention, in turn, has become a kind of coronation ceremony, used more to launch the general election campaign from a foundation of party unity than to make any real, and thus potentially divisive, decisions. The result, in almost all cases, is a postconvention "bounce" in the polls for the presidential nominee that gets the campaign off to a strong start.

National party conventions have gone through three eras since their invention in the 1830s. From 1832 to 1952 conventions were the arena in which presidential nominations usually were fought and won. Party leaders from around the country assembled, wheeled and dealed, and decided on a nominee. As one measure of their contentiousness, twenty-eight of the sixty-one Democratic, Whig, and Republican conventions that took place in this period were multiballot affairs. The 1924 Democratic convention needed 103 ballots to choose its nominee; eight other conventions required ten or more ballots.

The second era began with the 1956 election and lasted through 1980. None of the fourteen major-party conventions in this period took more than one ballot to nominate its candidate. The flowering of presidential primaries, which advanced the beginning of the nominating contest to much earlier in the election year, and the presence of live television cameras at the conventions, which rendered closed-door dealing in smoke-filled rooms impossible, invariably led to the emergence of a nominee sometime (often shortly) before the convention met. But the legacy of the convention as an important decision-making body was not entirely lost. Conventions in this quarter-century period were frequently marked by open battles about the party platform, the convention rules, delegate credentials, and other matters. In 1964, for example, conservative supporters of Sen. Barry Goldwater shouted down Nelson Rockefeller, the liberal governor of New York, during a platform debate. In 1980 Sen. Edward M. Kennedy battled President Carter fiercely over a rule that bound the delegates to vote for the candidate they had been elected to support in their state's primary or caucus.

Beginning in 1984, conventions entered a third era, which has lasted to the present. Not only are conventions one-ballot affairs in the contemporary period, but also they are planned and even scripted by the nominee. Such choreography is politically desirable because, as Martin P. Wattenberg has shown, parties that present a united front to the country gain an advantage over parties that place their divisions on display.[14] It is possible because the recent "frontloading" of the delegate-selection process toward the first three months of the election year invariably produces an early winner in the fight for the party's nomination. In 1976, after New Hampshire voted in February, only five states held primaries in March; by 1996 twenty-nine states did. To ensure that a nominee emerges from this blizzard of winter primaries and that the party can unite long before the convention, party leaders and fundraisers rally to the candidate who takes the early lead, rendering effective opposition to the front-runner nearly impossible.

At the convention itself, platform, credentials, and rules fights are either suppressed (under recently adopted party rules, no challenge to a committee's decision is allowed on the convention floor unless at least 25 percent of its members demand it) or shunted into off-hours sessions, outside the gaze of television network programming. Prime time is devoted to speeches, celebrity appearances, and videos whose content is strictly controlled by the nominee. The delegates are little more than a studio audience. In sum, the modern convention is "a huge pep rally, replete with ritual, pomp, and entertainment—a made-for-TV production. From the perspective of the party and its nominee, the convention now serves primarily as a launching pad for the general election."[15] Some of those launches have been spectacular—Democrat Walter Mondale temporarily closed Reagan's long lead in 1984, and Clinton went from trailing Bush by eight percentage points before the 1992 Democratic convention to leading him by twenty-two points afterward.[16]

As Harold Stanley chronicles in Chapter 2, Bob Dole pursued and won an early knockout victory in the frontloaded Republican nominating process of 1996. Aware that presidential nominations in the contemporary era are won or lost by March or early April, Dole spent virtually all of the $37 million that the law allowed for his nomination campaign in the early going. The good news for Dole was that he wrapped up the nomination midway through March; the bad news was that several months remained until the Republican National Convention in August and the $62 million in federal campaign funds that his official nomination would bring. In the meantime, Dole had little money left to try to undo the image that his Republican primary opponents had tarred him with as a tax-raising Washington hack and tool of corporate lobbyists. Clinton, on the other hand, whose nomination was uncontested, had millions of dollars to spend during the spring and early summer—technically for the purpose of becoming the Democratic nominee but realistically to promote his general election campaign against Dole.

Dole's initial plan for the five-month period leading up to the Republican convention was to use his position as Senate majority leader to command the media spotlight and demonstrate his prowess as a mature and effective statesman. When Senate Democrats thwarted this strategy by tying him in legislative knots, causing him to fall further behind Clinton in the polls, Dole made another lunge for the public imagination by announcing on May 15 that he would resign from the Senate. But this action, although briefly accompanied by his swapping a dark suit and tie for a sport coat and open collar shirt, brought only a modest public response. The Democrats attacked him as a "quitter" who, as one television commercial put it, was "leaving behind the gridlock he helped to create." Dole was left with no choice but to invest his hopes for a revived campaign in the convention.

Those hopes were fulfilled, at least temporarily. The Republican convention was all that Dole could have wished. During the ten days before his party gathered in San Diego, he announced a plan to cut taxes dramatically and named Jack Kemp, the former U.S. representative from Buffalo and

Table 3-3 How People Voted in 1996 (percentages)

Voters	Clinton	Dole	Perot
All (100%)	49	41	9
Men (48)	43	44	10
White	38	49	11
Women (52)	54	38	7
Working (29)	56	35	7
Not working (71)	46	43	9
White (83)	43	46	9
African American (10)	84	12	4
Hispanic (5)	72	21	6
Asian American (1)	43	48	8
Other (1)	64	21	9
No high school (6)	59	28	11
High school graduate (24)	51	35	13
Some college (27)	48	40	10
College graduate (26)	44	46	8
Postgraduate (17)	52	40	5
Age			
18-29 (17)	53	34	10
30-44 (33)	48	41	9
45-59 (26)	48	41	9
Over 60 (24)	48	44	7
Family income			
Less than $15,000 (11)	59	28	11
$15-30,000 (23)	53	36	9
$30-50,000 (27)	48	40	10
$50-75,000 (21)	47	45	7
$75-100,000 (9)	44	48	7
Over $100,000 (9)	38	54	6
Protestant (38)	41	50	8
White Protestant	36	53	10
Catholic (29)	53	37	9
Other Christian (16)	45	41	12
Jewish (3)	78	16	3
Other religion (6)	60	23	11
None (7)	59	23	13

(Continued)

Table 3-3   (Continued)

Voters	Clinton	Dole	Perot
Democrat (39)	84	10	5
Republican (35)	13	80	6
Independent (26)	43	35	17
Liberal (20)	78	11	7
Moderate (47)	57	33	9
Conservative (33)	20	71	8
Married (66)	44	46	9
Not married (34)	59	31	9
Gay, lesbian, bisexual (5)	66	23	7
First-time voters (9)	54	34	11
Union member in household (23)	59	30	9
1992 vote			
Clinton (43)	85	9	4
Bush (35)	13	82	4
Perot (12)	22	44	33
Other (1)	24	36	9
Did not vote (9)	53	33	11
Do you think the condition of the nation's economy is			
Excellent (4)	78	17	4
Good (51)	62	31	6
Not so good (36)	34	52	12
Poor (7)	23	51	21
Compared to four years ago, is your family's financial situation			
Better today (33)	66	26	6
Worse today (20)	27	57	13
About the same (45)	46	45	8
Do you think things in the country today are			
Generally going in the right direction (53)	69	24	5
Seriously off on the wrong track (43)	23	51	21

(Continued)

Table 3-3   (Continued)

Voters	Clinton	Dole	Perot
Do you expect life for the next generation of Americans to be			
Better than life today (29)	59	33	7
Worse than life today (33)	34	49	13
About the same (35)	54	36	8
When did you finally decide whom to vote for?			
In the last week (17)	35	41	25
In the last month (13)	47	36	13
Before that (69)	53	41	5
Which candidate quality mattered most in deciding how you voted for president?			
He shares my view of government (20)	41	46	10
He is honest and trustworthy (20)	8	84	7
He has a vision for the future (16)	77	13	9
He stands up for what he believes in (13)	42	40	16
He is in touch with the 1990s (10)	89	8	4
He cares about people like me (9)	72	17	9
Which one issue mattered most in deciding how you voted for president?			
Economy/Jobs (21)	61	27	10
Medicare/Social Security (15)	67	26	6
Federal budget deficit (12)	27	52	19
Education (12)	78	16	4
Taxes (11)	19	73	7
Crime/Drugs (7)	40	50	8
Foreign policy (4)	35	56	8

Source: Voter News Service national exit poll *(http://www.politicsnow.com).*
Note: Percentages may not add to 100 because of rounding.

housing and urban development secretary in the Bush cabinet, as his running mate. Both moves electrified the delegates. The convention itself was a brilliantly choreographed, four-day pep rally, culminating in Dole's forcefully delivered acceptance speech. Postconvention surveys showed that Dole had narrowed Clinton's lead substantially: an August 17 *Newsweek* poll had the race nearly even—Clinton with 44 percent and Dole with 42 percent.[17]

The glow of the Republican convention lasted only a short time. The Democrats held an equally well-scripted, equally unifying and energizing national convention in Chicago two weeks after the Republicans. By Labor Day, the traditional start of the general election campaign, Clinton's lead was again in double digits.

Dole, who in three previous runs for national office had never displayed strong gifts as a campaigner, showed little improvement during the fall of 1996. Lacking a strategy, he lurched from tactic to tactic, stressing variously his economic plan, his support for family values, his opposition to affirmative action and illegal immigration, and several lines of attack on Clinton—that he was responsible for an increase in teenage drug use, that he was too liberal, that his administration was corrupt, that he could not be trusted. In one speech, inadvertently underscoring his campaign's themelessness, Dole proclaimed, "It all boils down to one word. Trust. . . . That's what the election is all about. Trust." He then added: "It's about leadership. It's about family. It's about business. It's about the next century."[18] Dole's speaking skills, whether on television or at campaign rallies, were limited. Departing from carefully crafted speech texts, he often lapsed into shorthand terminology that Washington insiders understood but that left most voters baffled.

To be sure, Dole would have faced an uphill fight under the best of circumstances. With peace abroad and prosperity at home, it was hard for him to make the case, as he tried to do in the first televised debate with Clinton, that the economy had experienced "the slowest growth in the century."[19] Dole's campaign organization, for which he had little respect, was inexperienced, demoralized, and divided. Disastrously, in late October Dole sent an emissary to ask Perot, the Reform Party nominee, to drop out of the race and endorse him, a request that Perot publicly dismissed as "weird and totally inconsequential."[20] Only at the end of the campaign did Dole hit his stride. Four days before the election, playing up published reports of improper foreign campaign contributions that had been solicited by friends of Clinton for the Democratic National Committee, Dole launched a nonstop, ninety-six hour, twenty-state campaign trip. The national exit poll showed that Dole defeated Clinton 41 percent to 35 percent among those who made up their minds during the last week of the campaign. But they constituted only 17 percent of the electorate; those who had decided earlier strongly supported Clinton. (See Table 3-3.)

In addition to late-deciders, the exit poll found that Dole did well with certain groups of white voters—men, Protestants, the affluent, married people, and those for whom taxes, the budget deficit, and the candidates' hon-

Table 3-4 Presidential Election Results by State

State	Clinton Popular	%	Dole Popular	%	Perot Popular	%
Alabama	662,165	43.2	769,044	50.1	92,149	6.0
Alaska	80,380	33.3	122,746	50.8	26,333	10.9
Arizona	653,288	46.5	622,073	44.3	112,072	8.0
Arkansas	475,171	53.7	325,416	36.8	69,884	7.9
California	5,119,835	51.1	3,828,380	38.2	697,847	7.0
Colorado	671,152	44.4	691,848	45.8	99,629	6.6
Connecticut	735,740	52.8	483,109	34.7	139,523	10.0
Delaware	140,355	51.8	99,062	36.6	28,719	10.6
D.C.	158,220	85.2	17,339	9.3	3,611	1.9
Florida	2,545,968	48.0	2,243,324	42.3	483,776	9.1
Georgia	1,053,849	45.8	1,080,843	47.0	146,337	6.4
Hawaii	205,012	56.9	113,943	31.6	27,358	7.6
Idaho	165,443	33.6	256,595	52.2	62,518	12.7
Illinois	2,341,744	54.3	1,587,021	36.8	346,408	8.0
Indiana	887,424	41.6	1,006,693	47.1	224,299	10.5
Iowa	620,258	50.3	492,644	39.9	105,159	8.5
Kansas	387,659	36.1	583,245	54.3	92,639	8.6
Kentucky	636,614	45.8	623,283	44.9	120,396	8.7
Louisiana	927,837	52.0	712,586	39.9	123,293	6.9
Maine	312,788	51.6	186,378	30.8	85,970	14.2
Maryland	966,207	54.3	681,530	38.3	115,812	6.5
Massachusetts	1,571,509	61.5	718,058	28.1	227,206	8.9
Michigan	1,989,653	51.7	1,481,212	38.5	336,670	8.7
Minnesota	1,120,438	51.1	766,476	35.0	257,704	11.8
Mississippi	394,022	44.1	439,838	49.2	52,222	5.8
Missouri	1,025,935	47.5	890,016	41.2	217,188	10.1
Montana	167,922	41.3	179,652	44.1	55,229	13.6
Nebraska	236,761	35.0	363,467	53.7	71,278	10.5
Nevada	203,974	43.9	199,244	42.9	43,986	9.5
New Hampshire	246,166	49.3	196,486	39.4	48,387	9.7
New Jersey	1,652,361	53.7	1,103,099	35.9	262,134	8.5
New Mexico	273,495	49.2	232,751	41.9	32,257	5.8
New York	3,756,177	59.5	1,933,492	30.6	503,458	8.0
North Carolina	1,107,849	44.0	1,225,938	48.7	168,059	6.7
North Dakota	106,905	40.1	125,050	46.9	32,515	12.2
Ohio	2,148,222	47.4	1,859,883	41.0	483,207	10.7
Oklahoma	488,105	40.4	582,315	48.3	130,788	10.8
Oregon	649,641	47.2	538,152	39.1	121,221	8.8
Pennsylvania	2,215,819	49.2	1,801,169	40.0	430,984	9.6
Rhode Island	233,050	59.7	104,683	26.8	43,723	11.2

(Continued)

Table 3-4   *(Continued)*

State	Clinton Popular	%	Dole Popular	%	Perot Popular	%
South Carolina	506,152	44.0	573,339	49.8	64,377	5.6
South Dakota	139,333	43.0	150,543	46.5	31,250	9.7
Tennessee	909,146	48.0	863,530	45.6	105,918	5.6
Texas	2,459,683	43.8	2,736,167	48.8	378,537	6.7
Utah	221,633	33.3	361,911	54.4	66,461	10.0
Vermont	137,894	53.4	80,352	31.1	31,024	12.0
Virginia	1,091,060	45.1	1,138,350	47.1	159,861	6.6
Washington	1,123,323	49.8	840,712	37.3	201,003	8.9
West Virginia	327,812	51.5	233,946	36.8	71,639	11.3
Wisconsin	1,071,971	48.8	845,029	38.5	227,339	10.4
Wyoming	77,934	36.8	105,388	49.8	25,928	12.3
Total	47,401,054	49.2	39,197,350	40.7	8,085,285	8.4

Source: Adapted from "Official 1996 Presidential Election Results," *Congressional Quarterly Weekly Report,* Jan. 18, 1997, 188.

Note: Vote percentages may not add to 100 because of votes for minor-party candidates.

esty and trustworthiness were important considerations. He also won the support (narrowly) of Asian Americans and united his fellow partisans and conservatives behind him—80 percent of Republicans and 71 percent of conservatives voted for Dole. Regionally, he carried most of the South, the Farm Belt, and the Rocky Mountain states. (See Table 3-4 and Figure 3-1.)

Unfortunately for Dole, Clinton did well everywhere and among everyone else. The president's greatest strength, according to the exit poll, was among African Americans, Hispanics, women (especially working women), Catholics, Jews and other non-Christians, gays, lesbians, and bisexuals, the young, the poor and working class, the less educated, liberals, moderates, Democrats, unmarried people, members of union households, and those who regarded Medicare and Social Security, the economy and jobs, and having "a vision for the future" as the most important issues and qualities at stake in the election. Compared with his performance in 1992, Clinton's biggest gains were among women, Hispanics, liberals, moderates, union households, and young voters; he lost support in 1996 among white men, older voters, and Protestants.[21] Clinton carried thirty-one states, including all of the nine largest states except Texas, and the District of Columbia, sweeping the Northeast, the industrial Midwest, and the Pacific West. He won two states that he had lost in 1992 (Florida and Arizona) and lost three others that he previously had carried (Georgia, Colorado, and Montana).

Figure 3-1 1996 Presidential Election

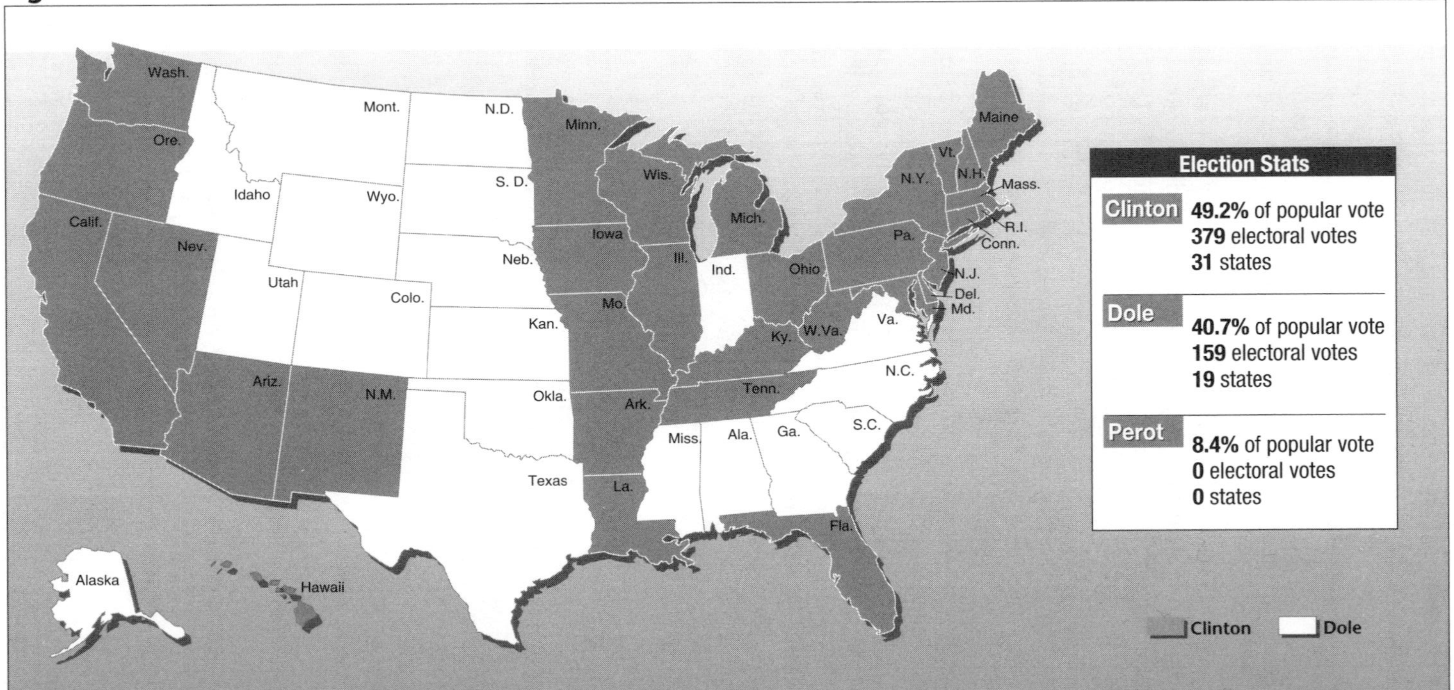

Wash.
Ore.
Calif.
Nev.
Idaho
Mont.
Wyo.
Utah
Colo.
Ariz.
N.M.
N.D.
S. D.
Neb.
Kan.
Okla.
Texas
Minn.
Iowa
Mo.
Ark.
La.
Wis.
Ill.
Mich.
Ind.
Ohio
Ky.
Tenn.
Miss.
Ala.
Ga.
Fla.
S.C.
N.C.
Va.
W.Va.
Pa.
N.Y.
Vt.
N.H.
Maine
Mass.
R.I.
Conn.
N.J.
Del.
Md.
Alaska
Hawaii
Election Stats
Clinton 49.2% of popular vote
379 electoral votes
31 states
Dole 40.7% of popular vote
159 electoral votes
19 states
Perot 8.4% of popular vote
0 electoral votes
0 states
Clinton
Dole

Source: *Congressional Quarterly Weekly Report*, November 9, 1996, 3190.

As in 1992 the voters' perception of the nation's economic health had a great deal to do with the outcome of the election. Seventy-nine percent of the 1992 electorate thought that the economy was in poor or "not so good" condition. Twice as many of them voted for the challenger, Clinton, as for President Bush. In 1996, 55 percent of the voters thought the economy was in good or excellent shape. Clinton, now the incumbent, won more than two-thirds of their votes.

Perot did considerably less well in every state and with every sector of the electorate than he had in 1992. He did best in a diffuse scattering of northern states, ranging from Idaho to Minnesota to Maine. In 1992 he had run strongly throughout New England and the West. In contrast to 1992, when he drew almost equally from voters at all education and income levels, Perot's support in 1996 was concentrated among the less educated and less prosperous. More of Perot's 1992 voters supported Dole (44 percent) than Perot (33 percent) in 1996. Once again, however, Perot did best among the discontented, such as those who thought the economy was in bad shape and those who thought life will be worse for the next generation.

Clinton's 379 electoral votes and 49 percent of the popular vote, although disappointing in light of his hopes for a landslide, were an improvement on his 370 electoral votes and 43 percent of the popular vote in 1992. Dole's 41 percent exceeded Bush's 37 percent in 1992; his 159 electoral votes were slightly fewer than Bush's 168. As in 1992 Perot carried no states and won no electoral votes. His share of the popular vote declined from 19 percent in 1992 to 8 percent in 1996.

Third-Party Candidates

Since 1968 significant third-party candidates have become a familiar part of the presidential landscape.[22] Four of the past eight presidential elections, including three of the past five, have featured such candidates: 1968, when George Wallace received 14 percent of the popular vote and 46 electoral votes; 1980, when John Anderson won 7 percent of the popular vote; 1992, when Perot received 19 percent of the popular vote; and 1996, when Perot won 8 percent of the popular vote. The average share of the popular vote received by minor-party candidates in this period has been 7.5 percent per election, more than a dozen times higher than the 0.6 percent that such candidates averaged in the four preceding elections of 1952 through 1964.

To be sure, there have been extended periods of significant third-party activity before, notably the twelve years from 1848 to 1860 and the thirty-two years from 1892 to 1924. The contemporary era of third-party presidential politics may last longer, for three main reasons: some of the historical barriers to third-party candidacies have been weakened, many voters have become detached from the major parties, and Perot has independently altered the political landscape.

Weakened historical barriers. Three main barriers traditionally have stood in the way of third parties: the high hurdles to ballot access that many state legislatures, controlled by a two-party duopoly of Republicans and Democrats, have imposed on them; the difficulties, reinforced by the Federal Election Campaign Act of 1974, of raising enough money to wage a credible national campaign; and the legal and constitutional biases that inhere in a system of single-member district, simple-majority elections and, in particular, in the electoral college.

Each of these barriers has been eroded to some extent in recent years. A number of lawsuits by Wallace, McCarthy (who ran in 1976), and Anderson successfully challenged onerous ballot access laws. Perot and other third-party candidates needed 716,000 signatures to get on all fifty state ballots in 1992, but that was considerably fewer than the 1.2 million that Anderson required in 1980. Perot was on every ballot in 1992 and 1996, as was the Libertarian Party candidate. Perot's success in 1996 made the path to the ballot much easier for his Reform Party in 2000.

As for the campaign finance law, although it places limits on the fundraising ability of third-party candidates and denies them federal funding unless they win 5 percent or more of the popular vote (and even then only after the election), it also guarantees timely and ample funding in the next election for candidates and parties who cross that threshold. Anderson would have had federal funding if he had run again in 1984, as will the Reform Party nominee in 2000.

The bias against third parties that inheres in the election system is less mutable. As Maurice Duverger argued in the 1950s when promulgating Duverger's law ("the simple-majority, single-ballot system favors the two-party system"), the winner-take-all system of elections discourages third parties because even a large number of votes, if it is less than a plurality, does not win their candidates any offices.[23] The consequence is that talented political leaders, eager for victory, shy away from third parties, as do many voters, who fear that a third-party vote would be wasted on a candidate who cannot win.

Perot fell prey to Duverger's law in some ways but not others in 1992. His 19 percent of the popular vote, for example, carried no states and therefore yielded no electoral votes. He was unable to attract the support of established political leaders. Nearly one-fourth of the voters who thought Perot was the best candidate cast their ballots for either Bush or Clinton as (in their minds) the lesser of the two evils who had a real chance of winning.[24] Yet Perot's support actually increased during the general election campaign from 8 percent in early October to 19 percent on election day. His strong finish stood in contrast not only to Duverger's law, but also to the pattern of declining third-party support that Wallace and Anderson had experienced late in their own campaigns.[25]

Independent voters. Third parties have their greatest opportunity to do well when there is a large pool of voters who are not strongly attached to either of the two major parties. Such a pool has existed throughout the last third of the twentieth century. During the 1950s and early 1960s only about one-fifth of voters were classed as independents in the National Election Studies; by 1992 nearly two-fifths were.[26] From 1988 to 1996 more new voters registered as independents than as Democrats and Republicans combined.[27]

Historically, voters' ties to the major parties grow weaker—and their potential openness to third parties may grow stronger—the longer ago the realigning election took place that defined the era of party competition in which they live. The source of the dividing line between the parties, whether slavery in 1860 or the economy in 1896 and 1932, becomes less relevant with the passage of time, especially to new generations of voters who do not remember what the original controversy was all about.

Although every era of party competition has shown this sort of fraying toward the end, none has become more attenuated than the contemporary era. In the past, party realignments occurred roughly every thirty years: 1800, 1828, 1860, 1896, 1932. Yet the most recent realignment took place more than sixty years ago, and many scholars wonder whether another ever will occur.[28] Dealignment, the word usually used to describe the contemporary era, creates a fertile field in which third parties may flourish.

Ross Perot. Perot is unlike any third-party candidate in history. A few comparisons make the point. Historically, most third-party candidates have run once, then either exited the political stage or affiliated with a major party. Perot has run twice and drawn a substantial number of votes each time. Historically, popular third parties have expired when the issues they raised were addressed by the two major parties. Yet even though both the Republicans and Democrats rapidly placed Perot's two main issues from the 1992 election—the federal budget deficit and political reform—high on their agendas, he returned to run again in 1996. Historically, only former presidents who campaign as third-party candidates win 19 percent or more of the popular vote, as Roosevelt did in 1912 and Millard Fillmore did in 1856. Perot, who has never held public office of any kind, won 19 percent in 1992. Historically, as James Q. Wilson has shown, third parties have fit into one of four categories—ideological parties, such as the Libertarians and the Socialists; one-issue parties, such as the Know Nothings and the Prohibitionists; economic protest parties (the Greenbacks, the Populists); or factional parties (Roosevelt's "Bull Moose" Party in 1912, the States' Rights Party in 1948).[29] Perot lies completely outside that taxonomy.

Further evidence of Perot's distinctiveness is found in the work of Steven Rosenstone and Roy Behr. Their model of third-party formation revealed that, although conditions were ripe in 1992 for a strong third-party candidate, that candidate should have received about 6 percent of the popular vote. Perot was able to triple that figure because of what he brought to the campaign: massive campaign spending (nearly $73 million) from his own fortune, successful participation in the presidential debates, and intensive media coverage.[30]

Perot kept the apparatus of his 1992 campaign alive after election day in the form of fifty state chapters of United We Stand America—technically a nonprofit public policy organization but in reality a political network. In the eight months after the election he spoke at more rallies than in the eight months before. Not everything went smoothly for Perot: on November 9, 1993, he participated in a nationally televised debate with Vice President Al Gore on NAFTA (the North American Free Trade Agreement), which Perot opposed, and was badly beaten. Nonetheless, on September 25, 1995, Perot appeared on CNN's "Larry King Live" to announce that he was forming a new Independence Party and launching an effort to get it on the ballot—as an enduring political party, not as a vehicle for a one-time candidacy—in every state. Finding that the "Independence" name already was taken in some states, Perot changed it to the Reform Party.

As described in Chapter 2, Perot devised an elaborate process to select the Reform Party candidate for president. He insisted that he did not want to run, claiming that he was seeking "George Washington II" to head the Reform ticket, and reportedly asked former Oklahoma governor and U.S. senator David Boren to be the party's presidential nominee. But when Richard Lamm, the former governor of Colorado, announced his candidacy, Perot immediately jumped into the race, raising doubts that he had ever intended to pursue any other course. After receiving the Reform nomination in August, Perot announced that he would finance his campaign not with personal funds, as in 1992, but with the $29 million in federal campaign funds to which his 1992 finish entitled him. His main issues in 1996 were those for which he was already widely known: campaign finance reform, the budget deficit, and foreign trade.

Perot's campaign strategy also was familiar: a few speeches, a few appearances on "Larry King Live," but mostly a series of paid thirty-minute infomercials on prime-time network television. The audience for Perot's television appearances was much smaller in 1996 than in 1992, however. He limped along in the polls, drawing 4 percent to 7 percent in the late summer and early fall trial heats against Dole and Clinton. "When we ask people to use one word to describe him," reported pollster Andrew Kohut, "the words are just awful—'rich,' 'crazy,' 'idiot,' 'egotistical.'"[31] The Commission on Presidential Debates, declaring that Perot had no "realistic chance" to be elected, chose not to include him in the presidential debates. Perot's exclusion denied him access to a forum that he had used to good effect in 1992—indeed, voters had judged him the winner of his debates with Bush and Clinton.[32] It also undercut Perot's rationale for choosing economist Pat Choate as his running mate—namely, that Choate, an experienced interlocutor on televised public affairs programs, would shine in the vice presidential debate.

Perversely, Perot got a small political lift from his exclusion from the debates—he regained the media spotlight and won a certain measure of sympathy from the strong majority of voters who thought he should have been invited. He really hit his stride late in the campaign when the reports of improper foreign contributions to the Democratic Party hit the front pages and airwaves. Perot had been aiming most of his attacks at Dole, whom he blamed for keeping him out of the debates. Now, combining his long-standing themes of corrupt election campaigning and excessive foreign political influence with assaults on Clinton's character, Perot directed his rhetorical fire at the president. Evoking Clinton's reputation as a womanizer, he said at a rally on October 31, "Here's one for all the dads in the audience. Which of the candidates would you be very comfortable having your daughter work for?"[33]

Perot's late surge to 8 percent of the popular vote on election day ensures that the Reform Party's presidential nominee will have a place on most states' ballots in 2000 and will receive federal campaign funding at half the level of the major-party nominees, perhaps as much as $35 million. The national exit poll revealed that Perot did best (25 percent) among those who decided whom to vote for during the last week of the campaign. As in 1992, he drew votes about equally from each of the major-party candidates, with many of his supporters saying they would not have voted if Perot had not been on the ballot. Young voters were more likely than any other generation to support Perot in both 1992 and 1996, which may augur well for his party's future.

The main issue confronting Perot and the Reform Party is whether the former will ever let go of the latter. The contemporary era is ripe for a lasting third party that does the things political parties do—runs candidates for state and local offices, has open presidential nominating contests, and prepares itself to accept the responsibilities of governing. But such a party cannot sink deep roots and grow if its existence continues to depend on one person. Perot already has made history. As Kevin Phillips notes, "He's the first independent presidential candidate able to score in double-digits who has come back to run again four years later, and he's the first to launch a successful new national party in the same period."[34] In 1996 Perot showed every sign of knowing that he needed to let the Reform Party develop in its own way but was unwilling to act on that knowledge. Between now and 2000, when he will be seventy years old, he will either bring his actions into conformity with his words or see his hopes for an enduring political legacy evaporate.

Vice Presidential Selection

Careful selection of vice presidential nominees is another feature of the late-twentieth-century political climate. Winning votes on election day is still as much the goal as it always has been when candidates for president choose their running mates. What has changed is that modern presidential candidates realize that the voters now care more than they did in the past about competence and loyalty—a prospective vice president's ability to carry out a departed president's policies capably and faithfully if the need should arise.[35]

During the nineteenth century, vice presidential nominations were used almost exclusively to balance the ticket, partly to heal the party's divisions and partly to win additional support in the general election. Old-style ticket balancing usually paired candidates from different and often opposing factions of the party, all but guaranteeing that the president would not trust the vice president in office. In addition, those who were elected as vice president could expect to be replaced after one term, when an altered political setting would dictate the choice of a different vice presidential candidate who could provide the ticket with a new set of electoral balances. (Until 1912 no vice president was nominated for reelection by a party convention.) The prospect of spending four years drearily presiding over the Senate, only to be unceremoniously dumped from the ticket, dissuaded most talented political leaders from accepting a vice presidential nomination. Daniel Webster, declining the Whig Party's second spot in 1848, said, "I do not propose to be buried until I am dead."

The situation improved somewhat in the early twentieth century, when the rise of national political campaigning and a national media made the vice presidency a more visible and appealing office to a better class of politicians. In fact, every elected first-term vice president in this century has been nominated to run for a second term, beginning with James S. Sherman, in 1912. But the seeds for a real transformation were planted in 1945, when Harry Truman succeeded to the presidency after Franklin Roosevelt died. The combination of Truman's lack of preparation (he was at most dimly aware of the existence of the atomic bomb, for example), the subsequent development of an ongoing cold war with the Soviet Union, and the proliferation of intercontinental missiles armed with nuclear warheads heightened the voters' concern that the vice president should be someone who is ready and able to step into the presidency at a moment's notice. Good government—namely, the selection of competent, loyal vice presidential candidates—became good politics.

Little is left to chance in modern vice presidential selection. Carter established a precedent in 1976, when he conducted a careful, organized preconvention search for a running mate. A list of four hundred Democratic officeholders was compiled and scrutinized by aides, then winnowed down to seven finalists who were investigated and, ultimately, interviewed by Carter. (He tapped Sen. Walter F. Mondale at the convention.) Mondale, Gov. Michael S. Dukakis, and Clinton followed similar procedures as the Democratic presidential nominees in 1984, 1988, and 1992, respectively. Reagan did nothing so elaborate in 1980 because he hoped to lure former president Ford onto the ticket, but he and his aides gave considerable thought to the kind of running mate they wanted. Bush searched widely before choosing Indiana senator Dan Quayle in 1988.[36]

The fruits of the new emphasis on loyalty and competence and of the care that is invested in the selection process can be seen in the roster of postwar vice presidential nominees. The modern era has been marked by an almost complete absence of ideologically opposed running mates, and those vice presidential candidates who have differed on certain issues with the heads of their tickets have loyally hastened to gloss over past disagreement and deny that any would exist in office. The record is even more compelling with regard to competence. In recent years, as the office has been given a significant range of responsibilities and resources and has developed into the main political stepping-stone to the presidency, a vice presidential nomination has become attractive to nearly all political leaders. From 1948 to 1992 the vice presidential candidate as often as not was more experienced in high government office than the presidential candidate, including Mondale in 1976, Lloyd Bentsen in 1988, and Gore in 1992.

To be sure, no guarantee exists that reasoned, responsible vice presidential nominations will be made on every occasion. Politicians do not always see their interests clearly. In 1984, for example, many observers thought that Mondale was too eager to placate feminist groups within his party when he selected Rep. Geraldine A. Ferraro, a three-term member of the House with no notable experience in foreign affairs, as his running mate. Four years later, Bush erroneously convinced himself that Quayle's youth and good looks would attract the votes of young and female voters.

What seems certain, however, is that the presidential candidate who pays insufficient attention to competence and loyalty in choosing a running mate pays a price in the election. The news media present critical stories, the other party runs harsh commercials, and the now traditional televised vice presidential debate may reveal the nominee as an unworthy presidential successor. Quayle reduced Bush's margin of victory in the popular vote by as much as four to eight percentage points in 1988.[37] In contrast, although the nomination of Gore in 1992 defied all the conventions of ticket balancing—like Clinton, he was a southerner, a Baptist, a moderate, and a baby boomer—Gore's obvious intelligence and ability appealed to many voters.

In light of this history, Clinton's choice of Gore for renomination as the Democratic vice presidential candidate in 1996 was, as with almost all incumbent vice presidents in the contemporary era, virtually automatic. Perot was unable to find a running mate whom the voters would regard as being of presidential caliber. Turned down by Boren and by representatives Marcy Kaptur, an Ohio Democrat, and Linda Smith, a Republican from Washington, Perot settled on the media-savvy economist Choate, with whom he had coauthored an anti-NAFTA book in 1993, in the hope that Choate would be sure-footed in the vice presidential debate. Although Dole was rebuffed by his first choice for a running mate, former general Colin Powell, he had a wide range of impressive contenders from which to choose.

Long before the Republican convention, Dole constructed an elaborate screening process to identify politically appealing vice presidential candidates and scrutinize their lives for any hint of scandal. The process generated a long list of Republican politicians, most of them governors and senators who, it was presumed, would carry their own states for the party ticket. But Dole, way behind in the polls, decided to make a more dramatic choice—"a 10," as he frequently put it. Despite his long-standing dislike of "the quarterback" (Dole's preferred name for Kemp) and his irritation at Kemp's decision to endorse Steve Forbes near the end of the Republican primary season, Dole held a lengthy preconvention meeting with him. Kemp, who was the party's leading advocate of supply-side economic policies and had long nursed presidential ambitions of his own, agreed to support Dole and his agenda in the role of a loyal "blocking back."

Dole's selection of Kemp excited and united the convention delegates. Many voters also liked the choice: few doubted Kemp's competence to become president if the need should arise, no small matter in view of widespread public concern about Dole's advanced age. In addition, Kemp seemed to balance the ticket in ways that were no less important for being intangible: he was energetic and visionary where Dole was laconic and pragmatic, smiling and articulate where Dole was dour and cryptic. In view of his long commitment to cutting taxes, Kemp presumably could sell Dole's economic plan more credibly and enthusiastically than the presidential nominee himself, a recent convert to dramatic tax cuts.

Nevertheless, Kemp proved to be a disappointing candidate in the general election. Although he brought his own publicly expressed views into conformity with Dole's, he was a poor campaigner. Kemp spent much of his time on a futile quest for minority votes, appearing before sparse crowds in solidly Democratic inner-city neighborhoods. He refrained from the sort of hard-nosed partisan attacks on the opposing ticket that vice presidential candidates traditionally are expected to make. "I am not an attack dog," he said.[38] In the October 9 vice presidential debate, for which he had prepared only casually, Kemp explicitly rejected an invitation from moderator Jim Lehrer to criticize Clinton's ethics. "It looked like a fraternity picnic there for a while," Dole commented sourly.[39] Postdebate polls revealed that viewers regarded Gore as the winner by a two-to-one margin.

In recent years, a vice presidential nomination often has prefigured a run for the presidency. Of the past five unsuccessful candidates for vice president, three sought their party's nomination for president in the next election: Edmund Muskie, Sargent Shriver, and Dole. Kemp has already run once for the Republican presidential nomination. (He was badly defeated in 1988.) Two years before the 1996 election, he decided not to run again when advisers told him what would be required, beginning with about 250 fund-raising events in the following eighteen months. His nomination as Dole's running mate revived Kemp's national political career, but his weak performance during the campaign disturbed many Republican activists. Still, the national exit poll showed Kemp running only four percentage points behind Gore in a hypothetical presidential match in 2000.

Election as vice president is an even more certain path to a presidential candidacy—and nomination. Six of the past nine vice presidents—Nixon,

Johnson, Humphrey, Ford, Mondale, and Bush—went on to win their party's presidential nomination. The roles modern vice presidents perform as party builder (campaigning during election years, raising funds between elections) and as public advocate of the administration and its policies uniquely situate the vice president to win friends among party activists. The growth in diplomatic travel and other high-level vice presidential activities has made it a more prestigious office and thus a more plausible stepping-stone to the presidency. Second-term vice presidents are freed by the Twenty-second Amendment's two-term presidential limit to spend much of the four years preceding the election campaigning on their own behalf. In the aftermath of his first term and reelection, Gore is well positioned to seek the Democratic presidential nomination in 2000.

Presidential Debates

A fifth element of the contemporary American political climate is the routine occurrence of live, prime-time, nationally televised debates between the presidential and vice presidential candidates. The first presidential debates took place in 1960.[40] One reason they occurred then was the rapid diffusion of television sets throughout the nation: in 1950 only about one-tenth of American homes had a television; by 1960 only about one-tenth did not. Another was the strong incentive that both of the major-party candidates had to debate, Nixon because he fancied himself (in error, as it turned out) the stronger debater and Kennedy because he wanted a forum in which he could overcome the widespread public perception that he was too young and inexperienced to be president.

No debates occurred in the next three elections because one of the candidates in each contest did not think he had anything to gain from debating his opponent. Johnson in 1964 and Nixon in 1968 and 1972 each held a strong lead over the other party's nominee and saw no reason to give him an opportunity to cut into it. Nixon also was chastened by his disappointing experience against Kennedy and, in 1968, was wary of sharing the stage with Wallace, the third-party candidate.

The political motivations that animate presidential candidates did not change in 1976 and 1980, but political circumstances did. In each election, an unpopular incumbent president—Ford in 1976 and Carter in 1980—faced a popular challenger, Carter and Reagan, respectively. The president wanted to debate so that he could overcome the challenger's lead; the challenger wanted to debate so that he could, by sharing the platform with the incumbent, appear "presidential." Debates took place in both elections, but each had a unique feature. The 1976 election introduced the first debate between the vice presidential candidates, Mondale and Dole. In 1980 one of the two presidential debates included the third-party candidate, Anderson. Carter refused to participate in that debate, arguing that Anderson was really a Republican.[41]

The 1984 election was a landmark in the history of presidential and vice presidential debates. As Sidney Kraus has argued, 1984 marked the "institutionalization" of debates as a standard part of the general election campaign.[42] From 1960 to 1980 debates had taken place only when the political interests of both major-party candidates coincided. In 1984, for the first time, a popular incumbent president, Reagan, debated his opponent even though he had nothing to gain by doing so, and he instructed his running mate, Bush, to do the same.

The fruits of institutionalization became apparent in 1988. By then, voters had come to take debates for granted; a candidate who chose not to participate would pay a high political price. Although Bush had no desire to debate Dukakis or allow Quayle to debate Bentsen, he did so. In 1992, almost as a matter of course, Bush and his running mate debated Clinton, Perot, and their running mates. Similarly, in 1996 Clinton debated Dole, and Gore debated Kemp.

To say that debates have become institutionalized is not to say that they are self-executing or devoid of controversy. Every four years, arguments take place between the candidates about the number, timing, and format of the debates—the aptly named "debate about the debates." In 1996 Dole, who was trailing, wanted four presidential debates, with the last of them taking place close to election day. Clinton, seeing no need to take unnecessary chances, wanted only two debates, one of them with his preferred town hall format and both of them well before the voting. Dole conceded every point in return for Clinton's agreement not to include Perot or his running mate, Choate, in the debates. Dole feared that Perot and Choate's presence would help the third-party ticket to divide the anti-Clinton vote.

Dole acquitted himself reasonably well in both the October 6 and October 16 debates, but Clinton had the easier task. Resting on a double-digit lead in the polls, the president needed only to present a sunny view of his record and policies and avoid reacting angrily to Dole's attacks. He performed so successfully that even though most viewers thought Dole did better than they had expected, they overwhelmingly judged Clinton the winner. Yet the audience for the 1996 debates was dramatically lower than that in any previous election: 35–45 million viewers per debate, as compared with 80–100 million viewers in, for example, 1992.[43] This falloff occurred partly because, as noted in Chapter 1, interest in the election was much lower than usual and partly because most voters—69 percent, according to the national exit poll—had already made up their minds before the first debate took place.

The most important unresolved question concerning presidential debates is the role of third-party candidates. This question is tightly interwoven with another—that of sponsorship. Until 1988 debates were sponsored by either the television networks or the League of Women Voters. In 1988 the newly formed Commission on Presidential Debates, a privately funded organization co-chaired by the heads of the two major-party national committees, took charge. The ten-member commission, which consists entirely of Republicans and Democrats, promulgated a number of criteria to be used in deciding who should be invited to debate, including whether a candidate had a "realistic chance of election" in the opinion of journalists and political scientists. In 1992 both Clinton and Bush insisted that Perot be invited, forcing the commission's hand. But in 1996 the commission judged Perot to have no realistic chance, and the major-party candidates were divided. Perot sued in Washington's federal district court, but on September 30, six days before the first debate, Judge Thomas F. Hogan ruled that the courts lack jurisdiction to resolve the issue.

Perot's failure to be included in 1996 will not end the matter. He has other legal avenues to pursue: in March 1996, for example, the Federal Election Commission issued a regulation stating that organizations sponsoring debates may accept corporate contributions only if they use objective criteria to determine who is to be invited to participate. Perhaps more important is the political pressure that voters may bring to bear in the future, especially if significant third-party candidates remain a familiar part of the political scene.

Low Voter Turnout

Low voter turnout is another feature of the late-twentieth-century American political climate. The percentage of the voting-age population that casts ballots has fallen in every presidential election but two since 1960, when the turnout rate was 63 percent. In 1996 only 49 percent voted, the lowest share of the electorate since 1924, a year when many women, newly enfranchised by the Nineteenth Amendment, were unfamiliar with voting and many states had registration laws that discriminated against recent immigrants and African Americans.

The steady decline in voter turnout in the contemporary era has occurred despite several developments that, according to a considerable body of research by political scientists, should have led to greater turnout. Since 1960 it has become much easier for people to register to vote. The poll tax was eliminated in 1964 by the Twenty-fourth Amendment; discrimination against African Americans and other minorities was ended by the Voting Rights Act of 1965; residency requirements have been greatly eased in response to Supreme Court decisions; and the states have instituted procedures such as mobile registrars, postcard registration, and, in some cases, election day registration. In 1993 the National Voter Registration Act, the so-called motor-voter bill, required all the states, in preparation for the elections of 1996, to allow registration by mail and at motor vehicle, welfare, unemployment, and other state offices.

Voting also has become easier in recent years. Most states allow people to vote at their leisure during the weeks preceding the election. More important, education levels have been rising steadily in American society. Nothing correlates more strongly with voting than education: the more of it citizens have, the more likely they are to vote. The reason, as Raymond Wolfinger and Steven Rosenstone observe, is that education "imparts information about politics . . . [and] increases one's capacity for understanding and working with complex, abstract, and intangible subjects, that is, subjects like politics."[44] The real puzzle is not why voter turnout has been declining since 1960, but why it has not been rising.

The solution to this puzzle is complex and, among scholars, much contested, involving elements as diverse and seemingly nonpolitical as the age, marital, and religious structure of American society.[45] Evidence shows that young people, single people, and people who do not attend church regularly—all of whom have been growing in number since 1960—are less likely to vote than those who are older, married, and churchgoers. Certainly the 1971 enactment of the Twenty-sixth Amendment, which reduced the minimum voting age from twenty-one to eighteen, contributed to the six percentage point falloff in the voter turnout rate that occurred between 1968 and 1972.

But the more important explanations for declining voter turnout are profoundly political. As noted earlier, voters in the contemporary era of dealignment tend to be less strongly committed to a political party than in the past. The consequences for turnout are clear: just as strong party attachments typically increase one's psychological involvement in politics and reduce the time and effort needed to decide how to vote, weak attachments tend to distance one from politics and raise the costs of voting. Equally important, Americans' sense of their own political effectiveness has been in steep decline since 1960. Fewer people see a connection between what the voters do on election day and what the government does afterward.[46]

The Electoral College "Magnifier"

During the 1980s much was heard about a supposed "Republican lock" on the electoral college that all but guaranteed victory in presidential elections to the Republican nominee regardless of what happened in the national popular vote.[47] The lock theory simply took note that the Republican candidates for president had carried twenty-one states with 191 electoral votes in each of the six presidential elections from 1968 to 1988, and the Democrats had consistently won only the District of Columbia, with three electoral votes. Broadening the standard to include states that had supported the same party in at least five of these elections only widened the disparity: 318 electoral votes (thirty-three states) for the Republicans and 13 electoral votes for the Democrats (the District and Minnesota). With 270 votes needed for victory, the electoral college seemed to some to be so imbued with a Republican bias as to practically rig the election.

Clinton's victory in the election of 1992 laid the Republican lock theory to rest: the Democrat carried eighteen states with 198 electoral votes that had gone Republican either five or six times since 1968. His reelection in

1996, however, gave birth to a new lock theory, this one Democratic. Noting that Clinton carried twenty-nine states with 346 electoral votes both times he ran, White House political director Douglas Sosnik claimed, "We are seeing the beginning of a Democratic electoral college advantage, making us better positioned for a generation of presidential campaigns to come."[48]

Sosnik is as wrong as his Republican predecessors were. Rather than bias the outcome of presidential elections in any systematic way (such that the disadvantaged party's candidate may get the most popular votes but lose the election), the electoral college "magnifies" the margin of victory received by the popular-vote winner. The reason is that the unit, or winner-take-all, rule for casting electoral votes, which is used by every state except Maine and Nebraska, translates even a modest popular-vote plurality in a state into a sweep of its electoral votes. Thus, every electoral vote tally since the election of 1892 has magnified the popular vote winner's margin. In the twenty-six presidential elections that took place from 1892 to 1992, the average 53 percent of the popular vote for the winning candidate became 76 percent of the electoral vote. In 1996 Clinton's 49 percent of the popular vote yielded 70 percent of the electoral vote, just as the Republican Bush's 54 percent of the popular vote in 1988 won him 80 percent of the electoral vote.

Still, the possibility always exists that someone will be elected president with fewer popular votes than the opponent, as happened when Benjamin Harrison received 65 more electoral votes than Grover Cleveland in 1888, even though he trailed by ninety thousand in the popular vote. In the late-twentieth-century era of constant political polling, candidates who are far behind—McGovern in 1972, Mondale in 1984, and Dukakis in 1988—typically give up trying to win a national popular-vote plurality and run campaigns aimed at carrying just enough states to eke out a narrow majority in the electoral college.[49] Dole pursued this strategy in 1996, writing off all but twenty-nine mostly small and medium-sized states that, taken together, had 278 electoral votes, eight more than he needed to win.[50]

Such a strategy may someday succeed. But if the electoral college ever does select the popular-vote loser as president, the winning candidate's administration will be seriously tainted, especially if seeking victory in the face of public rejection is revealed to have been a conscious campaign strategy. Indeed, such an outcome might doom the electoral college, converting Americans' long-standing but passive support for a direct-election constitutional amendment into active support.

Divided Government

The recent pattern of divided government is the final aspect of the contemporary political climate to be discussed in this chapter. United government, with the same political party in control of both the presidency and Congress, was until recently the norm in twentieth century American politics. From 1900 to 1968 united government prevailed 79 percent of the time.

Since then, it has prevailed only 20 percent of the time—the four years of Carter's presidency and the first two years of Clinton's first term, when the Democrats controlled both of the elected branches.

During most of the contemporary era, divided government has meant a Republican president and a Democratic Congress; indeed, from 1968 to 1992 that was the only form that divided government took. A number of theories arose to explain this pattern. For example, one theory held that many voters regarded a Democratic Congress as the best safeguard of their desire for an active federal government and a Republican president as insurance against their corresponding dread of higher taxes.[51] Another looked to the nature of the two parties: a heterogeneous Democratic Party that satisfied a variety of constituencies at the congressional level but seldom could unite behind a single presidential candidate, and a homogeneous Republican Party that found it easy to rally to its standard-bearer for president but difficult to tailor its appeals to a wide range of states and congressional districts.[52]

But since 1994 divided government has meant a Democratic president and a Republican Congress, a condition that is certain to last through 1998 and, in view of the nearly unbroken pattern of midterm losses for the president's party, very likely to last at least two years beyond that. Theories to explain the new pattern are in shorter supply. It may be, as Gary Jacobson suggests in Chapter 7, that the "southernization" of the Republican Party has simultaneously made it harder for the Republicans to win the presidency and, joined with the decennial reallocation of House seats from the North to the more conservative South, easier to win Congress. Or, perhaps, the obvious explanation is the accurate one: the voters elect a divided government because they do not wish to entrust complete control to either major party.[53] To be sure, only a minority—about 20 percent in 1996, according to the national exit poll—split their ticket between a presidential candidate of one party and a congressional candidate of the other, and nearly half of them were Perot voters. Nevertheless, a plurality said they hoped divided government would be the election's outcome. Republican strategists even played to this desire during the final weeks of the campaign, when it became obvious that Clinton was going to win the presidential election. The National Republican Congressional Committee ran television ads urging voters not to give the president a "blank check" in the form of a Democratic Congress.[54]

The consequences of divided government are mixed. After studying federal lawmaking from 1946 to 1990, David Mayhew concluded that divided government is as productive of "major statutes" as united government.[55] Paul Quirk and Bruce Nesmith, although cautious in their argument, suggest that on "autonomy issues"—that is, issues such as foreign aid and entitlement reform in which public opinion conflicts with elite conceptions of the public interest—a divided government may act more responsibly than a united government, in which the incumbent party would have to bear the entire burden of political blame for taking principled but unpopular actions.[56]

In at least two areas of fundamental importance to a constitutional system, however, the effects of divided government are corrosive. One is democratic accountability. Voters need to know who is responsible for what the government is doing if they are to render an effective judgment on election day. Yet divided government confuses the matter by allowing both the Republicans and the Democrats to evade responsibility, blaming the other party and the branch of government that it controls for whatever is going wrong in Washington. During the 1980s and early 1990s, Republican presidents and Democratic Congresses did little more than point accusatory fingers at each other as the annual federal budget deficit ballooned to nearly $300 billion. The voters, not knowing which party to believe, believed neither. Serious deficit reduction came only in 1993, the first year since 1980 that the same party controlled both the presidency and Congress.

The other clearly corrosive effect of divided government is on the judiciary, which has become a political football in the partisan battle between presidents and Senates of different parties. From 1900 to 1968, during the era of united government, only three of forty-five (7 percent) Supreme Court nominations were rejected by the Senate. Two of these rejections came in 1968, a year of de facto divided government because the Republicans firmly expected to win control of the presidency but not the Senate in that year's elections. Since 1969 four of seventeen (24 percent) Supreme Court nominations have been rejected, including four of twelve (33 percent) of those made when the president and Senate were of different parties. Even worse, as John Anthony Maltese has shown, the "selling of Supreme Court nominees" has recently become indistinguishable from overtly (and appropriately) partisan battles about public policy.[57] Consequently, the legitimacy of the courts, dependent as it is on public trust in their nonpartisanship, has been called into serious question.

The late twentieth century is not the nation's first era of divided government: the periods 1848–1860 (the years leading up to the Civil War) and 1874–1896 (the "Gilded Age") were, too. Few historians celebrate the government's performance during those eras. Not surprisingly, the contemporary era of divided government has been undistinguished as well.

Conclusion

American politics has experienced weather-like turbulence during the last third of the twentieth century. The years since 1968 have been rich in dramatic moments—assassinations, scandals, resignations, riots, and a host of rapid oscillations in fortune for political parties and political leaders. Many observers regard this period as a confusing welter of wild fluctuations and almost random changes.

Yet underlying the stormy political weather have been steadier, more slowly changing elements in the political climate of the contemporary era. This chapter has looked at several such elements, with particular attention to the general election campaign for president in 1996. The cycle of politics and policy helps to explain the victory that brought Clinton to power in 1992, as well as the likely second-term frustration engendered by his reelection strategy. Dole's nomination was shown to be emblematic of the unifying conventions that characterize contemporary politics. The persistence of Perot and the creation of the Reform Party manifest the late twentieth century's openness to third-party candidacies. Other aspects of the 1996 elections—the now-institutionalized presidential and vice presidential debates, the all too familiar low voter turnout, the magnifying effect of the electoral college, and the persistence of divided government—also embody the contemporary political climate.

Not every aspect of *fin de siècle* American politics has been charted in this chapter, but some are treated in the chapters that follow. In Chapter 4, for example, Matthew Robert Kerbel describes the misdirected coverage of election campaigns that the mass media now routinely offer. In Chapter 5 Jean Bethke Elshtain and Christopher Beem argue that what Alexis de Tocqueville called "small party" politics—that is, the politics of narrow interests and personalities—characterizes the contemporary era at the expense of "great party" passions and principles. Paul Quirk and Sean Matheson, writing about the presidency in Chapter 6, rue the public's shrinking concern about suitable presidential qualifications. Jacobson suggests in Chapter 7 that a natural Republican majority may have replaced the long-existing natural Democratic majority in Congress. Finally, John DiIulio assesses the growing importance of uncontroversial "valence issues" in presidential politics.

Notes

1. "Clinton Lays Down Challenge on Welfare Reform Bill," *Congressional Quarterly Weekly Report*, April 22, 1995, 1140.
2. The cycle theory is explained in greater detail in, for example, Erwin C. Hargrove and Michael Nelson, *Presidents, Politics, and Policy* (Baltimore: Johns Hopkins University Press, 1984); and in Michael Nelson, "The Presidency: Clinton and the Cycle of Politics and Policy," in *The Elections of 1992,* ed. Michael Nelson (Washington, D.C.: CQ Press, 1993), 125–152.
3. The other conditions for a presidency of achievement are described in Hargrove and Nelson, *Presidents, Politics, and Policy,* chap. 3.
4. Presidencies of achievement usually run out of domestic policy steam during the president's first term, for reasons described in ibid.
5. The severity of the Great Depression, and the enormous public demands for action by the federal government that it spawned, obviated the need for a presidency of preparation in 1932.
6. A *presidency of stalemate* occurs when the president wants to lead the country in an unpopular direction. William Howard Taft sought consolidation when the pub-

lic wanted achievement; Harry S. Truman pursued achievement when the public wanted consolidation.

7. Bob Woodward, *The Choice* (New York: Simon and Schuster, 1996), 23.
8. Clinton understood Morris's triangulation strategy better than its author—Morris strongly urged the president to reach a budget agreement with Gingrich and Dole. For Morris's account of triangulation, see Dick Morris, *Behind the Oval Office: Winning the Presidency in the Nineties* (New York: Random House, 1997).
9. "Victory March," *Newsweek*, November 18, 1996, 48.
10. Woodward, *The Choice*, 368.
11. "A Bridge Too Far," *New York Times*, October 16, 1996. Pollsters Penn and Schoen test-marketed several "building a bridge to" slogans—including "the year 2000," "a second term," and "the next four years"—before deciding that "the twenty-first century" resonated best with voters. Richard Stengel and Eric Pooley, "Masters of the Message," *Time*, November 18, 1996, 90.
12. "Clinton Opens Hard Charge in Drive for Majority of Vote," *New York Times*, October 31, 1996.
13. "Clinton Buoys His Party in Capitol Hill Visit," *New York Times*, September 27, 1996.
14. Martin P. Wattenberg, *The Rise of Candidate-Centered Politics: Presidential Elections in the 1980s* (Cambridge: Harvard University Press, 1991), chap. 3.
15. Stephen J. Wayne, *The Road to the White House 1996: The Politics of Presidential Elections* (New York: St. Martin's, 1996), 150.
16. Ibid., 178.
17. Dole had trailed by twenty points in the same poll a week earlier, just before the convention. See Howard Fineman, "Bring on the Baby Boomers," *Newsweek*, August 26, 1996, 20.
18. "Dole, in 3–Prong Effort, Seeks to Add Spark to His Campaign," *New York Times*, September 11, 1996.
19. "A Transcript of the First Televised Debate Between Clinton and Dole," *New York Times*, October 8, 1996.
20. "Perot Turns Down Dole Plea to Quit, Calling It 'Weird,' " *New York Times*, October 25, 1996.
21. For 1992 data, see Paul J. Quirk and Jon K. Dalager, "The Election: A 'New Democrat' and a New Kind of Presidential Campaign," in Nelson, *The Elections of 1992*, 78, 81.
22. In this chapter, the term *third-party candidates* also includes independent candidates. The distinction is nicely drawn in Steven J. Rosenstone, Roy L. Behr, and Edward H. Lazarus, *Third Parties in America*, 2d ed. (Princeton: Princeton University Press, 1996), 48, 81.
23. Maurice Duverger, *Political Parties: Their Organization and Activity in the Modern World*, trans. Barbara North and Robert North (New York: Wiley, 1963).
24. John H. Aldrich and Thomas Weko, "The Presidency and the Election Campaign: Framing the Choice in 1992," in *The Presidency and the Political System*, 4th ed., ed. Michael Nelson (Washington, D.C.: CQ Press, 1995), 255.
25. Wallace fell from 21 percent to 14 percent during the 1968 campaign; Anderson fell from 24 percent to 7 percent in 1980. Hargrove and Nelson, *Presidents, Politics, and Policy*, 161.
26. Paul R. Abramson, John H. Aldrich, and David W. Rohde, *Change and Continuity in the 1992 Elections*, rev. ed. (Washington, D.C.: CQ Press, 1995), 368.
27. Rhodes Cook, "Third Parties Push to Present a Respectable Alternative," *Congressional Quarterly Weekly Report*, July 13, 1996, 1986.
28. See, for example, Sidney M. Milkis, "The New Deal, the Modern Presidency, and Divided Government," in *Divided Government: Change, Uncertainty, and the*

Constitutional Order, ed. Peter F. Galderisi (Lanham, Md.: Rowman and Little-field, 1996), 135–171.

29. James Q. Wilson, *American Government: Institutions and Policies,* 2d ed. (Lexington, Mass.: D.C. Heath, 1983), 149–151.
30. Rosenstone, Behr, and Lazarus, *Third Parties in America,* chap. 8.
31. "The Third Dimension," transcript of segment on "The NewsHour with Jim Lehrer," August 19, 1996.
32. Abramson, Aldrich, and Rohde, *Change and Continuity in the 1992 Elections,* 56–61.
33. "Trying a Different Approach, Perot Takes to the Campaign Trail and Goes on the Attack," *New York Times,* November 1, 1996.
34. "Is Clinton Safe?" *Washington Post National Weekly Edition,* September 2–8, 1996.
35. Most of the historical material in this section is from Michael Nelson, *A Heartbeat Away* (Washington, D.C.: Brookings Institution, 1988).
36. Michael Nelson, "Choosing the Vice President," *PS: Political Science and Politics* 21 (fall 1988): 858–868.
37. Michael Nelson, "Constitutional Aspects of the Elections," in *The Elections of 1988,* ed. Michael Nelson (Washington, D.C.: CQ Press, 1989), 190.
38. "Kemp Backers Still Seeking Pit Bull, but He's Not Biting," *New York Times,* October 17, 1996.
39. Dan Goodgame, "Jack Kemp: From Savior to Scapegoat," *Time,* October 21, 1996.
40. Actually there were three, if one includes Congress's temporary suspension of Section 315 of the Federal Communications Act, the so-called equal-time rule. In 1976 and 1983 the Federal Communications Commission reinterpreted Section 315 in ways that effectively eliminated it as a legal barrier to televised debates.
41. Anderson, a longtime Republican member of the House of Representatives, had unsuccessfully sought the Republican presidential nomination in 1980 before breaking with the party.
42. Sidney Kraus, *Televised Presidential Debates and Public Policy* (Hillsdale, N.J.: Lawrence Earlbaum Associates, 1988).
43. The 1996 figures are from "The Ratings," *New York Times,* October 18, 1996. The 1992 figures are from Anthony Corrado, *Let America Decide* (New York: Twentieth Century Fund Press, 1995), 85.
44. Raymond E. Wolfinger and Steven J. Rosenstone, *Who Votes?* (New Haven: Yale University Press, 1980), 18.
45. An excellent discussion of the literature on voter turnout may be found in Abramson, Aldrich, and Rohde, *Change and Continuity in the 1992 Elections,* chap. 4.
46. Ibid., 117–120.
47. See my discussion of this matter in "Constitutional Aspects of the Elections," 192–195.
48. Quoted in "Power of Geography Taking Root," *USA Today,* November 7, 1996, 43.
49. Nelson, "Constitutional Aspects of the Elections," 194–195.
50. "Threading the Needle, State by State," *Washington Post National Weekly Edition,* September 30–October 6, 1996. In mid-October, Dole decided to add California, with its fifty-four electoral votes, to his list of targeted states and to write off Ohio, Michigan, and New Jersey, which together have fifty-four electoral votes.
51. Gary C. Jacobson, *The Electoral Origins of Divided Government* (Boulder, Colo.: Westview Press, 1990), chap. 6.
52. Nelson, "Constitutional Aspects of the Elections," 195–201.

53. For evidence to support this argument, see Morris P. Fiorina, *Divided Government* (Boston: Allyn and Bacon, 1996), chap. 5. For an argument that the voters do not create divided government intentionally, see John R. Petrocik and Joseph Doherty, "The Road to Divided Government: Paved Without Intention," in Galderisi, *Divided Government*.

54. "GOP Seems to Gear Ads to Dole Loss," *New York Times*, October 28, 1996.

55. David R. Mayhew, *Divided We Govern: Party Control, Lawmaking, and Investigations, 1946–1990* (New Haven: Yale University Press, 1991). For a different view, see Sean Kelly, "Divided We Govern? A Reassessment," *Polity* 25 (1993): 475–488.

56. Paul J. Quirk and Bruce Nesmith, "Divided Government and Policymaking: Negotiating the Laws," in Nelson, *The Presidency and the Political System*, 531–554.

57. John Anthony Maltese, *The Selling of Supreme Court Nominees* (Baltimore: Johns Hopkins University Press, 1995).

4

The Media: Viewing the Campaign Through a Strategic Haze

Matthew Robert Kerbel

L ate in the winter of 1996, four candidates for the Republican presidential nomination gathered in South Carolina to debate the issues. Over the course of ninety minutes they discussed a range of topics from trade to taxes to abortion rights. That evening Dan Rather told the national *CBS Evening News* audience about the event:

> They were the hottest quartet to come out of Columbia, South Carolina, since Hootie and the Blowfish. Four Republican presidential candidates today made a joint appearance to talk about the issues in advance of the South Carolina primary Saturday, the first primary in the South. As Phil Jones reports, none of the candidates was likely to take home a Grammy for this performance.[1]

The scene shifted to a familiar debate set, in which the candidates acted like children in a sandbox. Steve Forbes shouted at Bob Dole, "You voted for tax increases across the board." Dole growled back, "Not rate increases, no." Forbes: "Now, now, now, now senator, now senator—." Dole: "Don't malign my integrity here." Then Phil Jones stepped in and reminded viewers how disgusted they should feel about what he was showing: "At high noon, just as South Carolinians were sitting down to the best chicken wings in the South, the spectacle they saw on TV was anything but appetizing." Cut to a restaurant with the debate droning, largely unnoticed, from a television in a far corner. A male patron, presumably speaking on behalf of all citizens, said of the debate, "It seemed like an elementary school playground, sniping back and forth taking cheap shots at each other." Then cut to Lamar Alexander, who was shown saying to no one in particular, "You should be ashamed of yourself."

Alexander could have been talking to Phil Jones, whose coverage of this event downplayed its substantive content in order to send the cynical message that politicians are children who attack and posture. Jones was covering politics as theater, or "performance," as Dan Rather called it. Meanwhile, in the real world, a campaign was under way. There were theatrics at the South Carolina forum, of course, but there were also attempts at reasoned discourse. Citizens asked the candidates questions about issues; sometimes the candidates responded. But for those in the national audience who relied on the CBS version of events, it would be hard to disagree with the restaurant patron who closed the Jones piece by saying—not having attended or watched the debate—"I'm not impressed with any of them. I'd like a ballot that says, 'none of the above.'"

The CBS account was a harbinger of things to come in the media's coverage of the 1996 campaign and a symptom of the tunnel vision often displayed by political reporters. While candidates trawled for votes by shaking hands, refining campaign themes, giving speeches, airing commercials, granting interviews, traveling great distances, and eating too much bad food, reporters noticed little more than the tactics and strategy of getting elected. At the South Carolina debate, amid a fair amount of shouting, candidates were talking about issues and were eager to meet voters who, for their part, had substantive questions to ask. But reporters were inclined to see participation in the debate and other similar issue forums as tactical maneuvers to enhance political credibility or as distractions to avoid answering reporters' hard-hitting questions about "important" matters—like strategy.

For reporters, election coverage was approached as if the only purpose of the electoral process was to pick a winner. Speeches were covered more for their political relevance than for content. Policy proposals were portrayed as tactical elements of a broad electoral strategy. And in a self-referential gesture that bordered on the absurd, reporters made themselves the object of their own news as they covered how effectively the media were covering how well the candidates were playing the political game.

The resulting image was of a campaign skewed to its basest political characteristics. According to S. Robert Lichter and Richard Noyes of the Center for Media and Public Affairs, half of the airtime apportioned during the primary season by the major networks to candidate sound bites addressed electability, strategies, and tactics. The candidates, however, devoted most of their advertisements and speeches to policy issues.[2] Moreover, the media were far more negative about the candidates than the candidates were about one another. Lichter and Noyes found that the candidates had positive things to say about one another in three-quarters of the candidate evaluations contained in stump speeches and advertisements. Yet almost two-thirds of network television news coverage was negative.[3]

The negative tone befits "horse race coverage," which focuses inordinately on the electability and relative positions of the candidates. After all, an election must be portrayed as a fight to the political death if it is to warrant so much attention. So, despite what candidates were saying and doing on the streets of Manchester or Miami, and regardless of the real electoral prospects of Pat Buchanan, Steve Forbes, and Bob Dole, reporters portrayed the nominating process as a heated battle, depicting candidates in the roles of fallen front runner and long-shot challenger as if they were casting a performance, which, in fact, they were.

In fairness to reporters, they did not create the horse race. The quest for power is inherent in the presidential campaign, and the 1996 version featured a compressed primary schedule with built-in benchmarks for evaluating the candidates' political prowess. Assessing winners and losers is one way to understand a campaign, although it is not the only way or even the most useful way. But media coverage of the 1996 campaign was mostly about winning, and as such it asked the electorate to undervalue policy debate, trenchant analysis of the candidates' records, and related aspects of the process that strengthen democratic foundations, while asking it to overvalue strategy, posturing, and other manifestations of winning at all costs. Those citizens who were paying attention to the media surely learned a lot about the campaign of 1996. But they were poorly informed.

This chapter will explore the surreal media coverage in 1996, a campaign season in which information was tightly controlled by political operatives, candidates struggled to stay "on message," allegations from opposing campaigns were countered within one news cycle, negative advertisements were employed by challengers against front runners to level the playing field, and campaign aides continually anticipated how everything the candidate said and did would look on the evening news. We will consider how viewers and readers are invited to think about politics when the campaign is diminished to these lowest terms, when information is reduced to information about information control.

Framing Election News

"Election as strategic game" typifies how the mainstream media chose to frame election news in 1996. Frames provide the context for understanding political coverage, directing or deflecting our attention to or from political actions and issues and packaging facts to provide us with a basis for understanding politics. Frames shape the story lines that give election news continuity and meaning. Consequently, frames are the mechanism through which readers and viewers interpret the motives and actions of political actors and make judgments concerning everything from the viability and attractiveness of particular candidates to the larger meaning and purpose of politics and elections.

The concept of framing—following Erving Goffman's work and its application by other scholars to news reporting[4]—is a useful analytical tool for understanding how political information is communicated to the mass public. Gaye Tuchman likens a news frame to a "window on the world" that, like any window, offers a panorama that varies with the size and pitch of the window and where the viewer is situated in relation to it.[5] Similarly, elections—and individual campaign stories—may be framed by the media in a variety of ways, depending on what information is emphasized and how it is packaged by reporters. An election may, for instance, be framed as a contest about issues, a clash of ideologies, a choice among campaign promises, an assessment of an incumbent's performance,[6] or an encounter between alternative political styles. How it is framed is a matter of choice and context, of where reporters decide to place the window and where they direct us to stand.

Frames are important because they are, fundamentally, our model for experiencing and evaluating the campaign.[7] Frames are a factor in political agenda setting, inviting the public to think about certain substantive concerns more than others.[8] When reporters emphasize the horse-race aspects of American elections, as Thomas Patterson and other scholars have argued they do,[9] they create a context for understanding politics that emphasizes delegate counts, poll results, endorsements, and financial viability. When reporters play up the character flaws of politicians, they increase the public significance of private conduct and, in political scientist Larry Sabato's words, "strip the candidates naked on the campaign trail."[10]

Frames are also a factor in "priming," defined as offering a set of criteria by which issues and politicians are evaluated. Experimental studies strongly support the argument that the manner in which stories are framed affects the standards by which people evaluate public figures.[11] In 1992 television news coverage of the economy emphasized George Bush's responsibility for the recession—a plausible perspective but also a matter of choice by journalists that invited viewers to assess the incumbent in terms of his inability to handle important domestic affairs.[12] Like all frames, this perspective was both justifiable (given poor economic indicators early in the year) and arbitrary (given the availability of alternative viewpoints, such as the complex forces beyond the president's control that contribute to an economic downturn).

Because of the links among frames, agenda setting, and priming, the most distressing characteristic of how journalists portrayed the 1996 election was their relentless tendency to characterize events in a fashion that invited the voters to draw antisystemic conclusions about politics. Stories depicting candidate debates as exercises in mudslinging carried such a message. A different frame, one that placed substantive give-and-take among debate participants in the context of ongoing policy dilemmas, might have summoned viewers to experience the debates as issue oriented or ideological rather than petty and partisan. Such a framework was rare, because substantive stories, when they occurred, were generally disjointed or unrelated. But strategic, horse-race coverage, with its continuing story lines and clear thematic content, offered accessible guidelines for explaining the election. It was the Muzak of campaign coverage, anonymous by virtue of its ubiquity, providing an easy way for reporters to organize voluminous political information.

The abundance of stories about tactical and strategic maneuvers provided a perspective on politics as a self-serving, cynical venture in which candidates battle each other and reporters for control of the political agenda. Experimental studies suggest this is precisely the perspective adopted by subjects exposed to strategic news.[13] To the extent that such framing provides a filter for understanding politics, it invites us to doubt the motives of those involved in the political system. We are summoned to view politics in a way that undermines the legitimacy of political actors, leaving readers and viewers at a loss for where to find responsible political behavior.

Strategy Past and Present

The cynical, strategic frame is the product of a shared cultural environment in which journalists, living on the road with the candidates for long stretches of time, develop a consensus about what constitutes news. Their reporting reflects the partisan contest for power that encompasses their daily routine, in which they are engaged by candidates and their handlers in a constant battle for control of the news agenda. Lacking an external frame of reference, reporters become absorbed in the strategic struggle for message control. This battle overwhelms other aspects of the campaign, other experiences, and other meanings. Reporters describe their hermetically sealed experience on the campaign trail as life in "the bubble." [14] An ABC News producer who worked on the 1992 campaign summed up the experience this way:

> We all live in this cocoon, in a completely different world from anyone else, those of us who are covering the campaign. You're there all the time, morning to night you live together in this strange world. You see crowds and outside people, but you live in your own community. It swells and it decreases, but basically there's a core of people who are always in this community. [15]

Similarly, writer Timothy Crouse showed how isolation from outside forces and competitive pressures produce stories that resemble each other both on a daily basis and over the course of the campaign. [16] In this closed environment, correspondents develop commonly held perspectives about the motives and goals of the candidates and the meaning of political events that encourage them to frame politics as little more than a high-stakes game.

Content data from recent national campaigns suggest that the strategic frame for election news has become more prevalent in recent years, as lengthening campaigns have intensified the bubble culture. Journalists who once reported elections as equal parts substance and game now squeeze most campaign news through the strainer of political competition. Patterson examined a random sample of *New York Times* front-page political stories on the nine national races between 1960 and 1992 for occurrences of "game" and "policy" frames. Coverage of the Kennedy-Nixon contest in 1960 included slightly more policy than game stories. A similar pattern held through 1968. But the policy frame declined dramatically at the expense of strategic accounts in *Times* stories starting in 1972, as proliferating primaries transformed the election contest from dash to marathon. By 1992, Patterson found, more than 80 percent of *Times* articles interpreted candidates' words and actions in terms of how they were calculated to advance electoral prospects. [17]

Accordingly, reporters began analyzing more, describing less, and permitting candidates fewer opportunities to speak in their own words about matters of concern to them. In 1960 nearly every story in Patterson's sample was descriptive in nature, offering accounts of what the candidates did or said. By 1992, 80 percent were analytical, offering a rationale for why the candidates did or said something.[18] To use Michael Robinson and Margaret Sheehan's phrase, news had become more "mediated," as reporters took hold of the agenda and imposed their interpretation of events on readers and viewers.[19] It is telling that Patterson found such an effect dominating the coverage of so staid a vehicle as the *New York Times*, because the analytical approach to reporting originated as a feature of television news, which by design is better suited to relaying a story than simply to listing facts.

Network television shifted rapidly from being a video clipping service in its early days to its current incarnation as a storytelling forum for reporters who use brief video clips to emphasize their themes. In 1968, when the thirty-minute network evening news format was just five years old, the average campaign sound bite was longer than forty seconds. Candidates were featured speakers, imparting political news in their own words. By 1992 the average sound bite had shriveled to less than ten seconds—window dressing, really, for a tale told by the correspondent.[20] Although candidates remained the focus of campaign news, the point of view had shifted from candidate to reporter.

Because reporters live the horse race and live with the candidates, it is not surprising to find gamesmanship and character attributes among the most commonly related themes in campaign news. One study of the 1992 campaign found that the *Times* was hardly alone in featuring stories about the candidates' political prospects, strategic plans, and tactical maneuvers; these topics far outpaced items about the candidates' issue positions on network and local television broadcasts and in an array of local newspapers.[21] My study of CNN and ABC News coverage of the 1992 campaign bears this out. Horse-race themes shaped about half the political stories on CNN's *Prime News* and more than one-third of the campaign reports on *ABC World News Tonight*. One-quarter of the stories addressed the candidates' character and image manipulation, including references to how they crafted issue positions to garner electoral advantage. About one-fifth included references to the media as objects of the candidates' manipulative efforts.[22]

Collectively, the 1992 coverage amounted to a personalized, politicized, self-interested account of the election, running like a narrative through the campaign. To be sure, there were also accounts of policy matters that did not invoke a horse-race theme, but because reporters tend to cover issues idiosyncratically, it is difficult to argue that their presence amounted to a competing issue frame.[23] Absent an ongoing discussion of the interrelationship of, say, health care policy, entitlement reform, and deficit reduction, periodic references to each appeared like static boulders in a fast-flowing river of strategic news.

Consequently, as in other recent elections, reporters in 1996 asked viewers to think about the political process in terms of its most manipulative features. Continuing a generation-long trend, they framed the election in their own words and from a bubble-wrapped perspective that portrayed the campaign as a cynical power quest in which candidates do what they must to snare the big prize. If this viewpoint is self-serving, by virtue of repetition it is also self-fulfilling.

In the pages ahead we will look closely at the news framework that night after night invited voters to peer into the ugly abyss of American politics in 1996. The examples in this chapter invite a qualitative assessment of coverage from five sources representing television, newspapers, and news magazines: *ABC World News Tonight, NBC Nightly News, CBS Evening News,* the *Washington Post,* and *Newsweek.* Although this assessment reveals patterns of coverage borne out by earlier quantitative analysis,[24] it does not represent a scientific sample of election coverage, just as the media portrayed here are a prominent but incomplete subset of respected mainstream sources of political information. That the same themes appear among all five news sources is intriguing because it suggests broad acceptance of the strategy frame among political journalists. But a systematic account of campaign frames will have to wait for another day.[25]

Coverage of the Strategic Game

Journalism textbooks still quaintly assert the importance of balance and neutrality to correspondents who value fairness in reporting. Such dispassionate qualities speak of another era. Coverage of the 1996 campaign could more accurately be described as having balance and neutrality tempered by ego, as in this *Washington Post* account of a Dole visit to California. It has, shall we say, attitude:

> Call it the Bob Dole Sword of Damocles tour. The featured players are the presumptive Republican nominee, dressed in a dark blue suit and looking grim, and the governor of the nation's most populous state, also in a dark blue suit and looking even grimmer. Backdrops include a super-secret bomb factory, a rusty fence that fails to keep out illegal Mexicans, an execution chamber in which a murderer was killed last month, and a sweet-faced, bomb-sniffing golden retriever named Peggy Sue. The script for Senate Majority Leader Robert J. Dole's campaign swing through California this weekend seemed written to exploit the insecurities of non-Latino whites who, like the Greek Damocles, feel themselves in imminent danger—not from a dangling sword but from political forces out of their control. . . . With Governor Pete Wilson as his guide, Dole appeared to be trying to plug into voter anxiety about lost defense jobs, illegal aliens, and the handling of criminals by a justice system reluctant to put convicted murderers to death.[26]

This is not merely an account of what happened in the Dole campaign on March 24, 1996. It is analysis with a vengeance, a chronicle of a performance seen through the eyes of an observer intent on finding thematic significance in mundane political acts. It is as much about the observer as the observed.

In one respect, the *Post* account incorporates all the elements of a traditional "inverted pyramid" print story. The first few sentences tell us who was involved (Dole and Wilson), where they were (at a California bomb factory and prison and at the Mexican border), when the events took place (this weekend), even details about what the principals were wearing. But the traditional print story would feature these facts rather than use them to support a thematic tale of why Dole was in California. This story makes it clear that the senator was engaged in a media event staged for reporters in order to exploit the fears of Anglo whites in California for political gain. Dole and Wilson are not candidate and governor but "featured players" who are in character ("looking grim"). Locations are "backdrops." Events follow a "script." As the intended target of the action, the reporter-narrator is an integral part of the play, making this not simply a story filed by the journalist but a story involving the journalist.

This sort of story is a far cry from what Robinson and Sheehan found when they compared print accounts of the 1980 campaign with their television counterparts and pronounced the former to be a tame, traditional reflection of their edgy, thematic electronic cousins.[27] In 1996 thematic coverage was hardly exceptional in print or on the air. Moreover, the same themes emerged repeatedly from an array of reporters working for news magazines, newspapers, and competing networks. Some called the election a play, others a contest or a war, but the frame remained the same: like the account of Dole's weekend on the coast, political stories repeatedly filtered the election through the prism of strategic maneuvers.

Accounts of the horse race provide the most obvious forum for strategic coverage, and reporters in 1996 supplied abundant news about the machinations of front runners and long shots. But strategy also framed less obvious material. As in 1992, reporters were wont to find familiar strategic motivations in the positions taken by political candidates. Whenever budgetary issues and economics assumed a place on the news agenda, stories appeared to suggest that the best way to decipher the complex fiscal debate was to apply the calculus of electoral politics to what otherwise could have been news about, say, the costs and benefits of various economic proposals. Even the ubiquitous Clinton scandals could not escape strategic analysis. When Whitewater flared, some reporters eschewed the details of FBI files and suspect business dealings to explain how the president intended to contain the political damage.

Horse Race as Strategy

With horse-race stories dominating news coverage of the nominating process, it was not surprising to find in this fertile field a wealth of strategic information, featuring material on how to wage commercial air wars, "spin" reporters, stay on message, and, whenever necessary, drive up the opponent's negatives. It is not exaggerating to say that an attentive reader or viewer could have compiled a handbook on how to run for president while concluding that most if not all of what a candidate does is politically self-serving.

On the air and in print, the horse-race-as-strategy framework shared the same familiar elements: money and television. The players were portrayed as either (1) cash-starved candidates who spent millions on television commercials in order to (a) buttress a shaky claim to front-runner status (Dole) or (b) convince the pundits who confer front-runner status to take them seriously (Alexander); or (2) political oddballs turned momentary contenders who complicated the efforts of mainstream candidates by (a) spending a personal fortune on negative ads in order to undermine the front runner (Forbes) or (b) applying television savvy and a colorful screen-ready persona honed on talk shows to remain a political presence despite limited funds (Buchanan).

Above all, money (or the lack thereof) figured in coverage of the strategic fortunes of the players. Long before the expansion of primaries supplied an orgy of benchmark elections to assess the progress of the race, reporters identified cash reserves as *the* measure of competitive prowess. Even after the expansion of the primary season, ready funds remained an important benchmark. In a series for *ABC World News Tonight* almost one month before Iowans cast the first caucus votes of the year, Peter Jennings left no doubt about what fuels the political engine:

> At this point in the presidential campaign of 1996 there is no more important goal for presidential candidates than filling their campaign bank accounts with enough money to make the rest of the race possible. Sen. Phil Gramm may have explained it best for politicians as a class when he said a candidate's best friend is ready money. And so the men who want to be president have spent virtually all of 1995 trying to raise staggering amounts of money. The Republican pollster Frank Lutz puts a successful campaign in context: "The three most important ingredients are money, money, and more money."[28]

In this vein, part two of the ABC series *The Greenback Primary* educated the audience on how legally to circumvent campaign finance restrictions through techniques such as raising "soft money"—something Jennings called "an art form."[29]

Other stories made it clear that money matters because it puts the candidate on the air in an age when television appearances define political viability. When Forbes bankrolled a relentless commercial barrage against Dole in Iowa, the front runner was forced to abandon the high road and respond in kind, a strategic fact that reporters felt worthy of coverage on the evening news. ABC reported:

> Senator Dole has an immediate problem on his hands. After months of ignoring Steve Forbes, the millionaire magazine publisher who is challenging him for the Republican presidential nomination, Senator Dole has decided that looking the other way isn't working. And so today the

Dole campaign began airing a television commercial in Iowa, a month
before the Iowa caucus, which is directly attacking Mr. Forbes.[30]

The same day, CBS news reported:

> Until now, Dole has virtually ignored all his opponents, but this
> change in strategy [running negative ads against Forbes] is a clear sig-
> nal that Dole has decided he'd better deal with Forbes now or these
> charges [that Dole is a Washington insider] could cause long-range
> political damage.[31]

Not just changes in strategy but any change in direction warranted coverage. Personnel changes were particularly interesting to reporters, sending
them scrambling to find clues to future political moves. As the Dole campaign struggled from the New Hampshire primary through the general election, reporters looked for signs that fresh blood would yield better tactics for
the beleaguered candidate. In March, *Newsweek* treated the Kansan's strategic dilemma this way:

> Despite his disappointing showing in New Hampshire and broad crit-
> icism of his lackluster campaign there, Bob Dole didn't lose his cool in
> defeat. Instead, the senator is quietly dealing with his difficulties. Dole
> sources say adman Stuart Stevens, who honchoed Dole's negative TV
> spots, is being eased aside for media consultant Don Sipple. And the
> search is on for someone to help refine Dole's message.[32]

Six months later, the *Washington Post* ran almost the same story, albeit with
a harsher edge, on the occasion of Sipple's early departure:

> Don Sipple and Mike Murphy, who have sparred for some time with
> top campaign officials over strategy, left the [Dole] campaign today
> after [campaign manager Scott] Reed ordered a reorganization
> designed to integrate the media team more directly into the cam-
> paign. . . . One source said Murphy, who earlier this summer lost an
> internal power struggle, had privately complained that the Dole effort
> was embarrassingly weak.[33]

The idea that Dole's campaign was sinking under the weight of an infe-
rior strategic effort was a mainstay of political coverage throughout the year.
Reporters locked on to the candidate's difficulties with communication and
message control, generating a slew of repetitive stories about how Dole's
shortcomings as a speaker placed him at a strategic disadvantage at a
moment in history when voters expect politicians to be glib and articulate.
The following excerpt from a *Newsweek* story typifies the strategic detail
that filled magazines, newspapers, and television reports during the spring
and summer of 1996:

> Advice poured in—from [former president George] Bush, from allies
> of the former president, from Senate colleagues. . . . His friends told
> him: don't be buffaloed by handlers, but heed them. If they tell you to
> stand somewhere for a photo op, stand there. Connect the dots. Make

it clear how leadership—just how enacting something as abstract as a balanced budget—would actually help real people. Drop the legispeak about bills you've sponsored. Don't just say you're for "values." Enumerate them—hard work, faith, service—and explain how your life exemplifies them. Voters *know* you're a leader. Say *where* you want to lead them. For once, the famously intractable Dole listened. He still mumbles droll asides. He's still a diffident man irked at having to sell himself. But he has begun to make the sale.[34]

Of course, Dole really had not begun to make the sale, certainly not when this piece appeared in early March, not during the summer doldrums or the long march to the Republican convention in San Diego, or ever. But the strategic angle would not die. Rather than dampen reporters' interest in tactical maneuvering, the dismal reality of the Dole campaign actually created a market for more strategic stories, with each one speculating anew about what Dole would need to do to make himself viable and many suggesting that time was running out. Every real or potential Dole setback fueled a new round of strategic analysis. How was the campaign responding to his offhand assertion that he did not know if cigarettes are addictive? Will Dole's summer run-in with Katie Couric on the *Today* show reopen questions about the pit bull side of his character? How much will his prospects be hurt by the lackluster public response to his tax cut proposal? Can his aides hold the Republican Party together despite deep differences on abortion and an enduring rift with Buchanan? Will the choice of Jack Kemp as a running mate close the gender gap? Should Dole aggressively raise questions about Clinton's character in the debates? How will he deal with the suspicion that he's too old?

In fact, these questions had been rendered moot by a stream of polling data suggesting that months had passed without any movement in the horse race. It hardly seemed to matter what Dole did or did not do. Yet, even as reporters privately began wondering whether the Dole campaign was a lost cause, even as they blistered him in print as "far behind in the polls and dogged by an image as a dull speaker,"[35] they scrutinized the candidate's every move. In the fall campaign's waning moments, as Dole desperately tried to contest California, the *Washington Post* reported that "Dole's advisors hope their abrupt shift in strategy will throw President Clinton on the defensive," even as it labeled the candidate's prospects "forbidding."[36] Others called the Dole strategy "similar to that of a gambler hoping to draw to an inside straight."[37] But they kept reporting about it. In the absence of a real contest, the strategic story intensified as November 5 approached.

Had an issue stalled as the Dole campaign had, it would have disappeared from the news entirely. Reporters contend that once a policy statement is issued and covered, it loses its news value,[38] which contributes to the disjointed quality of substantive news. But reporters had no difficulty reiterating the strategic machinations of a disabled presidential campaign as it failed to gain traction during a period of many months.

Accordingly, issues need to masquerade as props for the horse-race story to maintain a stable news presence. The above litany of strategic items includes a number of topics—among them nicotine regulation, tax policy, and abortion rights—that offered clues to where the candidates might lead the country and that lent themselves to substantive analysis. But thoughtful consideration of these matters tended to be episodic; as a consistent thematic presence in the news, issue information was more likely to be filtered through the familiar framework of political winners and losers.

Economics as Strategy

A case in point is the coverage afforded economic policy during late winter and early spring 1996, as the Republican field debated the merits of a flat tax and Congress and the president struggled over a budget resolution, and during the fall, when Dole proposed a sweeping tax cut plan. Reporters could have used their analytical skills to dissect the merits of the budget deal or tax initiatives. Instead, they succumbed to the temptation to cast substantive discussion in the language of politics, describing the calculations underlying policy development and portraying policy statements as weapons. Although offering a fine primer on the intricacies of political gamesmanship, this coverage also implied that any connection between a politician and a deeply held belief is purely coincidental. More important, it deflected attention from the consequences of the economic debate.

For the duration of the campaign, coverage of the economy echoed the themes established in an early NBC piece from "the front lines in Iowa," in which Republican hopefuls were, according to reporter Brian Williams, struggling to "make . . . the economy a point of attack."[39] Gwen Ifill of NBC explained that "Republicans hoping to replace President Clinton cannot figure out how to address the economic anxieties that still linger, especially when interest rates are down and unemployment has improved." Absent a winning political angle, "they're more likely to attack each other than to talk about the unfocused anxieties that seem to plague so many Americans."[40] The point made by the media is that candidates bicker about issues as they jockey for position. But what happens when someone comes along with an idea? Reporters cover the political ripples created by the idea more intensely than the idea itself. Bickering and jockeying enjoy the media spotlight, while only a dim light is periodically cast on the issue.

So it was in January, when Forbes became a credible contender by waging a single-issue campaign for tax simplification. Forbes's meteoric rise in the polls posed a dilemma for his more established counterparts, and reporters were quick to cover the strategic moves necessitated by the political fluidity Forbes's presence produced:

> Tom Foreman (ABC News): In a weekend debate, everyone thought Dole would be the target, but instead other Republican contenders

went after Forbes, who is now second in some polls, challenging the centerpiece of his campaign, the 17 percent flat income tax.

SOUND BITE OF LAMAR ALEXANDER: I think it would be a disaster for America, a truly nutty idea. And most economists who've looked at it think it would be a middle income tax increase.

FOREMAN: Forbes has reportedly spent $15 million of his own money to spread his flat tax message. The latest *Fortune* magazine estimates his worth at a half-billion dollars, all of which is helping other candidates promote an image of Forbes as a pampered rich boy trying to buy the White House. . . . Other candidates do not necessarily oppose a flat tax. Several of them have their own versions. What they do not like is one candidate getting all the credit for the idea.[41]

What Foreman and other reporters did not emphasize in all this is exactly what the flat tax would do—would it hurt the middle class, for example, as Alexander claimed?—and whether the economic assumptions on which it was based are sound. Although these questions were addressed elsewhere in the news, the overall debate was trivialized because thematic coverage of strategic concerns cast the flat tax as a political football. Taken as a whole, coverage of the flat tax asked voters to think about the policy implications of tax reform in terms of the political implications of tax reform. It may indeed be a nutty idea, as Alexander suggested, but the audience was invited to assess a different claim, namely, the effectiveness of the tax as a campaign tactic.

Meanwhile, in Washington, a budgetary debate between Democrats and Republicans with significant policy implications was portrayed as political posturing with significant electoral implications, contributing to the sense that governing is first and foremost about politicians' self-interest. On this count, reporters with a penchant for finding war in politics missed the lead. What could have been a story with the headline-grabbing appeal of a battle about the role and scope of the federal government was turned into the story of a protracted set of skirmishes in which differences about the role and scope of the federal government served only the strategic positions of politicians staking out electoral high ground. Months of policy debate were portrayed in political terms, with the usual array of military imagery: carefully mapped positions, crushing retreats, divisions in the ranks, and delight in an opponent's failed tactics.

In early January 1996, President Clinton said he would balance the budget and promote key programs. How would he do it? Which programs would he protect? It was hard to tell from Brit Hume's account on ABC. But viewers did learn something about the president's tactical considerations:

> Try as he might [to negotiate a budget deal], it's very hard, and not just because of disagreements with the Republicans with whom he's been negotiating. The president is not free simply to make a deal with them.

Any compromise budget that actually gets to balance in seven years, using the conservative estimates of the Congressional Budget Office which Mr. Clinton has agreed to, will likely mean accepting much of what the Republicans have proposed. But the president, up for reelection, needs to maintain the support of his own party. Getting congressional Democrats to go along with any of that Republican budget will be difficult.[42]

The question, according to Hume, seemed to be: Would there be a deal, and, if so, who would get the political credit? Accordingly, viewers learned the day after Clinton's well-received State of the Union address that "Behind the scenes White House officials are ecstatic, because they believe Republicans have now realized their hardball tactics and constant attacks on President Clinton have backfired, and that the public supports the president's call for a compromise."[43] But they did not learn much about the fiscal desirability of the budget compromise.

As the campaign progressed into the fall, the economic debate centered on Dole's proposal to cut income taxes across the board by 15 percent. Like its earlier counterparts, the Dole plan unleashed a stream of strategic analysis concerning the likelihood that the plan would "jump-start his candidacy and reshape the political debate."[44] At times this analysis linked the Dole plan to the earlier budget battle: "Dole has sought to avoid a re-run of last winter's budget fight by providing relatively little detail on what programs he would cut."[45] The *Washington Post* noted that Dole's effort to convince voters the economy is stagnating "is an essential part of the Dole strategy, crucial to his call for a 15 percent cut in income tax rates."[46]

Like coverage of the budget debate, coverage of the Dole proposal framed it in strategic terms but left vital questions unaddressed: Is the tax plan sound? Is it feasible? Are there reasons to believe a tax cut this large would not be worthwhile? Who would benefit and who would not?

Building election news around questions such as these would permit reporters to continue to analyze winners and losers, as they are fond of doing in their strategic coverage, while framing matters in a far more useful way to the readers and viewers who eventually will be asked to make an informed electoral choice. Such an approach would invite reporters to frame economic matters as an evolving series of ideas rather than tactics, some better than others and with a range of policy ramifications. This approach would invite the audience to conclude that an important contest was occurring during the economic debate but that the debate was not a game.

Scandal as Strategy

In the mediated world of political self-preservation, even scandalous news is reported in the language of damage control, emphasizing the concerted efforts of the accused to contain the fallout from harmful accusations rather than assessing the severity and meaning of the alleged transgressions.

Several times prior to the election, the Clinton White House faced a feeding frenzy about Whitewater-related incidents: missing records that mysteriously surfaced in the White House residence, the unauthorized use of FBI files, the conviction of the president's close business associates on fraud charges. At each juncture, press coverage featured episodic news of the details set against thematic accounts of how the administration was trying to minimize the political damage caused by news of the details.

Take, for instance, coverage of the allegations that Hillary Rodham Clinton may have been involved in the disappearance and subsequent discovery of potentially incriminating records subpoenaed by Congress. Complementing a flurry of items on what may or may not have happened were stories about the strategic ramifications of what may or may not have happened. If the first lady is the subject of politically volatile allegations, will the White House keep her under wraps? Apparently not, said NBC: "The White House dismisses any suggestion that Mrs. Clinton plans to lower her public profile, saying the first lady plans to resume her full schedule next week." [47] Will the Republicans take advantage of her newfound vulnerability? Apparently so, according to ABC: "Republicans believe the public has always been skeptical about Hillary Clinton, so they have felt free to go after her with the zeal usually reserved for attacks on the president himself." [48]

Among the more blatant efforts to cover Whitewater as a strategic inconvenience was a piece on NBC that Tom Brokaw billed straight-faced as "in-depth reporting [on] damage control"—as if the American public needed a hard-hitting inside account of spin doctoring. It opened with Jim Miklaszewski recounting Clinton's remark that if he were not president he would enjoy punching out *New York Times* columnist William Safire for calling his wife a "congenital liar." Miklaszewski put the comment in strategic perspective:

> It's all part of the new White House strategy to launch an aggressive counterattack against Mrs. Clinton's critics. First, deny the allegations. . . . Second, attack the investigations as political witch hunts. . . . Then attack the chief accusers, like Republican senator Alfonse D'Amato, who has been the target of an ethics investigation himself. Mrs. Clinton will also play a key role in the defense strategy. She'll take on reporters' questions during an upcoming tour to promote her new book.[49]

What did viewers learn from this? They learned that the White House was fixated on political damage control. They learned that the Clintons were on the defensive, which meant they likely had something to hide. They learned that the Clintons' greatest accusers, being politicians, were none too clean themselves.

What they did not learn is what Whitewater is about. Is it about incompetence or abuse of power? Were any laws broken, and, if so, were they felonies or misdemeanors? Were ethical issues at stake—and, if so, what were they? Was the president involved, and, if so, to what extent? How much of Whitewater is allegation, how much is supported by fact?

Opinion polls taken in late spring 1996, following a period of weeks in which Whitewater dominated campaign news, indicated that most people were at a loss to address these meaningful questions. But they had learned precisely the lessons that strategic coverage communicated. Majorities felt that the Clintons did something wrong and possibly illegal because they were obviously covering their tracks, and most felt the president was lying about whatever he did in order to cover it up.[50] But few could say what that was, admitting they did not understand what Whitewater was about. Most also felt that, despite their conviction that the president was guilty of something, the press was making too much of the story.

That last point bears repeating: even though people believed the president had committed a crime and lied about it, they thought the story was overplayed. On the surface, these seem to be contradictory beliefs, but they are entirely consistent with the message communicated by the scandal-as-strategy story. By covering the scandal as a public relations problem for the Clintons, reporters sent the message that Whitewater is serious business. Viewers and readers attentive to this political message during saturation coverage learned correctly that the president was doing everything he could to stem the tide of negative coverage. Since he would not work so hard (or receive so much attention) if Whitewater were simply a minor annoyance, it stood to reason that something big was going on.

But what? In the absence of a clear thematic news account of the evolution and meaning of Whitewater events, it was hard for people to know. So they reacted to the volume of coverage and to the explosive language of scandal that pervaded the news. They responded to Whitewater as it was reported, in terms of the *idea* of scandal, written in the now familiar language of cover-up and spin control, certain that something big was going on but without a clear sense of what it was. Deprived of a framework for understanding Whitewater as a well-developed, internally consistent series of meaningful events, people related to it in the context provided by strategic news—as scandalous and problematic but lacking a substantive core and therefore overblown by the media.

The scandal-as-strategy theme supplied reporters with an opportunity for egotism they could not refuse: when commenting on Clinton's strategic responses to Whitewater coverage, reporters were essentially covering themselves. Jim Miklaszewski may have spoken of the Clinton spin-control efforts as if they were not aimed at him, but the framework of his story was tacit admission that more than just the Republicans were the target of White House opposition.

Denial of participation and use of third-person detachment are the signatures of the self-reference that pervades political coverage. Reporters know they are writing about themselves when they write about spin control. Sometimes they try to hide their awareness, although often they are quite direct about it. Election news assumes an eerie quality as reporters emerge from behind the cameras and notepads and make themselves stars in the political constellation.

Covering Coverage of the Game

Who better than a reporter to explain that reporters interfere with the democratic process by shoving a wedge between candidates and voters? And what better way to illustrate the point than by devoting precious minutes on the evening news to a report about how reporters create obstacles to democracy? With a hint of self-importance masking any sense of irony, Tom Brokaw devoted a portion of a pre–New Hampshire edition of *NBC Nightly News* to a primer on how his medium had turned campaigns into freak shows:

> If this were a popularity contest, I think I know who would finish last among New Hampshire voters this year: we would—the news media, especially television. There was a time when New Hampshire voters went eye to eye with the candidates. No more.[51]

Under the self-referential title "Feeding Frenzy," the NBC story continued with pictures of reporters mobbing a candidate. Brokaw explained: "If you're a presidential candidate, this is your view of New Hampshire. If you're a New Hampshire voter, this is your view of the candidate."

FEMALE VOTER: I see a bit of him. I would love to shake his hand.

MALE VOTER: More reporters than voters. It's chaotic.

BROKAW: It's a kind of traveling electronic stockade. Everyone is a hostage.

BEAT REPORTER (AS SOURCE): It's the worst I've ever seen. I covered O. J. and [this is] definitely more vicious.

BROKAW: Never have so many cameras come so far to cover a few candidates.[52]

Speaking over an image of shoving cameramen and security personnel, Brokaw asked: "Is this really necessary? In a word, no. It's become a kind of mindless video game. Television has transformed the American political campaign. This year it is in danger of running it off the road." The knowing anchor shook his head slightly, thereby claiming enough distance to appear scornful, and concluded, "There is no easy solution, but common sense, discretion, and a few manners would be a beginning."[53]

Where exactly these manners will come from is an open question; Brokaw offered nothing concrete to challenge the media coverage he ostensibly disdained. To the contrary, NBC's decision to run a story about how television was ruining democracy is indicative of how the medium is better suited to judge its influence than to change it. In Brokaw's world, the news *is* a popularity contest for a diminishing share of viewers, and if that means flaunting the media circus for dramatic effect, then so be it.

NBC was not unusual on this count—every network was running self-referential stories about the dreaded press. About the time of Brokaw's lament, CBS peddled the same theme in multiple reports. First Bob Schieffer noted that "New Hampshire sets up an obstacle course for candidates, then invites the media in to watch them navigate it."[54] Days later, Dan Rather echoed the sentiment: "There's already a lot of talk about the nature of this New Hampshire primary—is too much attention paid to it, has it changed, and how has it changed? Case in point: the transformation of politics from the small-town personal visits by candidates to the global village of mass campaigning by television."[55]

Such talk is problematic because simply mentioning the dangers to democracy posed by turning elections into video games reinforces a difficult condition but does nothing to improve it. So a peculiar dynamic takes over: reporters, aware of their intrusiveness but unable to alter circumstances that make them obstacles to an edifying campaign dialogue, simply alert the audience to the fact of their intrusiveness and thereby compound it. Even reporters who might wish to overcome their situation do little more than subvert the dialogue by talking about themselves; self-reference substitutes for deliverance.

It therefore becomes acceptable if not inevitable for news reports to mention other news reports in the context of discussing how coverage of the political game influences the political game, even as self-referential stories define the destructiveness they address. With the lengthening shadows cast by stories about stories, reporters assume a detached, third-person relationship to one another. Reporters begin to pop up as sources in stories about reporters, as in the Brokaw piece. Correspondents refer to the media as "they" and "them," as if disavowing group membership. Newspapers build stories around reports from other media. The result is news accounts like the following analysis of the State of the Union address from the *Washington Post*, which views the strategic ramifications of Dole's response to Clinton from the standpoint of what other reporters have said:

> On the evening news, Sen. Robert J. Dole's lackluster response to the State of the Union Address was played as a major blunder. "A nightmare," said CBS's Phil Jones. "Many thought he looked older than usual," said ABC's John Cochran. "He did look like a grumpy old man," Paul Gigot said on PBS's "NewsHour with Jim Lehrer." A day later, the Republican presidential front-runner was widely described as in trouble. "Did Bob Dole just have a bad outing?" NBC's Brian Williams asked. "This is for real, Brian. . . . Bob Dole is going to have to fight and fight hard for this nomination," Tim Russert replied.[56]

Because self-references and strategic stories abounded, the former were naturally found in the latter. Readers and viewers did not have to search hard to find accounts of how the media figured in strategic considerations, stories that placed self-interested reporters at the center of the action. Self-references easily infiltrated strategic news because reporters devoted so much attention to tactical considerations and because candidates devoted so much tactical consideration to how their actions would play in the media. Of course, this had the peculiar effect of injecting reporters and their concerns into the news itself. As in this *Newsweek* story, the agenda of the press corps became as important as the candidate's schedule:

> In Pierre [South Dakota], the smallest state capital, [Dole] was greeted like a brother. The national press corps had not followed him. . . . But presidential politics isn't Pierre. It's a digitized national feedback loop of handlers and pundits. And back in Washington, everyone wanted to know: what happened on television last week?[57]

Of course, they did. But what happened on television last week matters only when the campaign is perceived as a strategic horse race. Viewed through a different lens, campaigns are about candidates gauging voters' concerns and voters assessing candidates' positions. Even if the sepia-tinged hyperbole about voters who once met the candidates a dozen times is simply the stuff of television reporters' nostalgia, the imperfect bonding process between citizen and candidate remains fundamental to the political process. This does not preclude the importance of the handlers and their digital gadgetry—reporters are correct to point out that much of today's bonding occurs on a mass scale over the air—but it does illuminate an aspect of the campaign that eludes the work of journalists in a Washington culture in which "everyone wanted to know what happened on television last week": political choice occurs in the world of policy agendas and issues qua issues as much as it transpires in the realm of careful posturing and issues qua weapons.

Alter the reporters' perspective of politics as a horse race and issues as tools, and the press can begin to make headway into what Brokaw suggested was the media's popularity problem. Reporters did not do much in 1996 to alter their perspective because of a lack of willingness to make the effort or a lack of awareness that it was possible. Either way, the result was coverage of coverage of the game that served to reinforce its own antisystemic message.

Making Coverage Work

Early in 1996, with some bravado, Howard Kurtz wrote in the *Washington Post:*

> Finally, in the wake of the Iowa caucuses, one all-important group is having its say in the presidential campaign. The media. We make the rules. Sure, the voters play a walk-on role. But the real stars are those who read the electoral tea leaves. Forget about who gets the most votes in the early primaries. That's for wimps. The question is who tri-

umphed in the arcane game of expectations, and therefore can be said
to possess 'Big Mo,' as George Bush once called it.[58]

Truer words could not be penned—from a horse-race standpoint. But the
readers of tea leaves are hardly useful if in the course of their pontificating
they lure people away from an edifying discussion of their future.

Ideally, we would like to think that the press is useful. Surely it could be
an institution that helps us to fathom the complexities of issues, rather than
a necessary evil or, worse, a hindrance to understanding. But it is hard to
make a case that the press serves an educational purpose when coverage
bears down on the media-obsessed process of winning the political game.
Consequently, doubts that are troublesome by their very nature are raised
about the usefulness of the press as an instrument of democracy.

I do not suggest that we disregard the news. It is one thing, as political
tactics go, for candidates to circumvent reporters by producing infomercials,
appearing on talk shows, maintaining a home page on the Web, and otherwise exploiting the possibilities of alternative media. It is quite another thing,
as democracy goes, for the public to have to circumvent press accounts in an
effort to be better informed. But when reporters contend with campaign
information-control methods by describing each tactical turn—when they
deal with the adversarial candidate-reporter relationship by recounting the
ugly details—it becomes hard to see how they perform a public service. Laying bare the ugly underbelly of a troubled system does nothing to improve it.
But it can give people reason to reach for the remote control.

Reporters have claimed that horse-race coverage provides valuable
insight into how we elect our presidents. Some, in self-defense, have contended that it is better for the public to be told about the manipulative efforts
of campaign organizations than for those efforts to go unscrutinized or,
worse, pass undiluted into the evening news. These may be reasonable asser-
tions, but they do not justify accepting the status quo.

Even if we believe that only the most noble intentions motivate reporters
to adopt the horse-race framework, it is hard to see how anyone's interest is
served by portraying the campaign as a horse race and the horse race as a
media-candidate struggle for supremacy. Doing so has not produced better
campaigns, nor has it diminished the importance of the information-control
strategies regularly featured in campaign news. But it does cast doubt on the
candidates who, as we are constantly and graphically reminded, do whatever it takes to win our sympathies. Eventually, one of those candidates is elected president. And he or she is supposed to govern with something resembling
popular support.

Even if we regard self-referential strategic coverage as a strategy in its
own right adopted by reporters who otherwise face the prospect of being
tools of spin, it is hard to see how the fruits of their efforts educate the electorate. Such coverage clouds journalist Tom Rosenstiel's fundamental
requirement for meaningful reporting, namely, that the press "provide peo-

ple with information they need to live their lives."[59] Reporters may avoid being taken in by acknowledging the strategic maneuvers designed by campaign organizations to manipulate them. But by emphasizing the battle between campaign organizations and the media, reporters ask us to think about what candidates do in the most self-serving terms. This is indeed one way to think about politics. But it is not the only way. It certainly is the most cynical way, and there are enough cynical Americans already.

In true self-referential fashion, columnists and reporters often write of their struggle to be more responsible, which generally translates into covering issues more and the horse race less. If we accept these proclamations at face value (overlooking, for now, how much fun political reporters have covering their role in the horse race), it would be difficult to argue that the 1996 campaign was a model of improvement. This is partly because real improvement requires reporters to challenge the competitive perspective that pervades campaign news. Dan Rather went through a period in which he worked the word *substance* into election stories whenever possible, as if using the word would make it so. But he said "substance" when he really meant "horse race": "Some substance is already emerging based on CBS News exit polls,"[60] he said, when reporting New Hampshire primary results; "there is a shifting in the substance of the Republican presidential campaign, including the widely expected drop-out today of Senator Phil Gramm";[61] a commentary on the electoral implications of the conservative vote is "part of our continuing emphasis on the substance of the campaign."[62] Nice try, but a bit empty.

A more fruitful direction for coverage might entail something political reporters understand well: a change in strategy. Reporters in the political trenches are correct to note that there is something deeply disturbing about the political battle to control information. They can offer a constructive assessment of this matter by covering the problem rather than the tactics that are symptoms of the problem. They can focus on the elements of the system in which they feel the problem lies rather than on the individuals in the system who, after all, are only acting according to their self-interest, given how the rules of the game are written.

This shift in focus would make campaign coverage relevant and accountable to the democratic process. In keeping with the goals of the recent "public journalism" reform movement, the new focus would enable the press to facilitate the public dialogue it now self-consciously obstructs, to provide what public journalism advocate Jay Rosen calls "a space where the public can do its work."[63] The objective would be to sustain a dialogue on what is wrong with a process in which candidates must go to great lengths to control the media, rather than narrowly framing such efforts in terms of the candidates' short-term strategic self-gain. Far from saying "look at how we in the press undermine democracy," such a context would enable and impel reporters to think seriously about what works, what does not, and what can be done to improve matters beyond exercising common courtesy.

In a concurrent tactical adjustment, the press could consider offering a more diverse set of messages than is allowed by the cool detachment of self-reference. To do so would require acknowledging that press reports are more than information: they are information in a package, stories that give meaning to information and structure how we think about it. If greater substance is the goal, routine coverage might adopt as an ongoing theme that elections are about evaluating policy differences. This means more than simply offering stories that recite issue positions, although arguably we would benefit from more of these—it means providing a different thematic representation of politics through stories suggesting that candidates take positions for reasons other than mere political expediency. It means initiating an issue frame that might lead people to think about campaigns in a more useful, system-affirming way.

Reporters need not challenge their deeply held beliefs about what constitutes election news in order to reconsider how they frame events. But they do need to expand their views, to be aware that context matters in the presentation of information and that more than one suitable context exists for understanding politics. Otherwise, the best predictor of what coverage will look like in the next election is what it looked like in this one; inevitably, sadly, coverage will reflect the experience of Henry Burton, the harried political aide in the season's best-selling, anonymously penned novel *Primary Colors,* who was charged with the thankless job of fending off the relentless media horde:

> [Reporters] were all over me, and the questions—it was weird—were about *process:* How would we be able to soldier on with the press all over us about [a scandal involving the candidate]? How would we be able to get our message out? Wouldn't we just be on the defensive now? The press was asking this. It was surreal. . . . The [reporters], dumb animals, came with that: How you gonna get his message out with us all over you?[64]

The accuracy of this fictional observation is proved by a hundred real stories, including this one from a CBS News report circa January 1996: "During the next couple of weeks Steve Forbes is going to have his skin removed by his opponents and also by those of us in the media."[65] Precisely the point of the novel, and fittingly so, because both passages were written by the same man, erstwhile CBS analyst Joe Klein.

For a brief moment in mid-1996, self-referential strategic coverage was interrupted by outbursts of introspection as the journalistic community reacted to the long-withheld news of the novelist's identity. And an unusual phenomenon occurred. Klein faced a firestorm of criticism from his colleagues for furtively writing about figures he covers in his day job and for blatantly lying about his authorship of the book. In a fit of press criticism of the kind usually reserved for politicians, reporters raised important issues about the meaning of journalistic integrity, the obligation of the reporter to the reader, and the incompatible perspectives offered by fact and fiction. Reporters may have been in a frenzy, but they were asking the right questions, and, for a change, they were asking them about themselves. Evidence, perhaps, that it can be done.

Notes

1. *CBS Evening News,* February 29, 1996.
2. S. Robert Lichter and Richard Noyes, *Media Monitor* (Washington, D.C.: Center for Media and Public Affairs, 1996).
3. S. Robert Lichter and Richard Noyes, *Campaign '96: The Media and the Candidates* (Washington, D.C.: Center for Media and Public Affairs, 1996).
4. Erving Goffman, *Frame Analysis: An Essay on the Organization of Experience* (Cambridge: Harvard University Press, 1974). For a discussion of the application of frame analysis to media coverage, see Gaye Tuchman, *Making News* (New York: Free Press, 1978); Mark Fishman, *Manufacturing the News* (Austin: University of Texas Press, 1980); and Michael Schudson, *Discovering the News* (New York: Basic Books, 1978).
5. Tuchman, *Making News,* 1.
6. This follows the retrospective voting tradition. See Morris Fiorina, *Retrospective Voting in American National Elections* (New Haven: Yale University Press, 1981).
7. In this respect, frames may be understood similarly to an anthropological view of culture as publicly shared systems of meaning that provide accounts of—and guide—action. See Clifford Geertz, "Thick Description: Toward an Interpretive Theory of Culture," in *The Interpretation of Cultures,* ed. Geertz (New York: Harper TorchBooks, 1973), 8–30; and Robert A. LeVine, "Properties of Culture: An Ethnographic View," in *Culture Theory: Essays on Mind, Self, and Emotion,* ed. Richard A. Schweder and Robert A. LeVine (Cambridge: Cambridge University Press, 1984), 67–87.
8. For a good discussion of the agenda-setting function of the mass media, see Donald L. Shaw and Maxwell E. McCombs, *The Emergence of American Political Issues: The Agenda-Setting Function of the Press* (St. Paul: West Publishing Company, 1977); and Benjamin I. Page, Robert Y. Shapiro, and Glenn R. Dempsey, "What Moves Public Opinion?" *American Political Science Review* 81 (March 1987): 23–43.
9. Thomas E. Patterson, *The Mass Media Election: How Americans Choose Their Presidents* (New York: Praeger, 1980); and Michael J. Robinson and Margaret A. Sheehan, *Over the Wire and on TV: CBS and UPI in Campaign '80* (New York: Russell Sage Foundation, 1983).
10. Larry J. Sabato, *Feeding Frenzy: How Attack Journalism Has Transformed American Politics* (New York: Free Press, 1991), 4. A similar argument is made in Thomas E. Patterson, *Out of Order* (New York: Knopf, 1993).
11. Shanto Iyengar and Donald R. Kinder, *News That Matters: Television and American Public Opinion* (Chicago: University of Chicago Press, 1987); Shanto Iyengar, *Is Anyone Responsible? How Television Frames Political Issues* (Chicago: University of Chicago Press, 1991); Shanto Iyengar, "Television News and Citizens' Explanations of National Affairs," *American Political Science Review* 81 (September 1987): 815–831.
12. Matthew Robert Kerbel, *Edited for Television: CNN, ABC, and the 1992 Presidential Campaign* (Boulder, Colo.: Westview Press, 1994), 60–63.

13. Joseph N. Cappella, June W. Rhee, and Kathleen Hall Jamieson, "Cynical Reactions to Strategic and Issue-Based News: Experimental Tests and Social Cognitive Explanations" (Paper delivered at the annual meeting of the International Society of Political Psychology, Vancouver, June 30–July 3, 1996).
14. See Kerbel, *Edited for Television*, 151–180.
15. Quoted in ibid., 157.
16. Timothy Crouse, *The Boys on the Bus: Riding with the Campaign Press Corps* (New York: Random House, 1972).
17. Patterson, *Out of Order*, 72–74.
18. Ibid., 81–82.
19. Robinson and Sheehan, *Over the Wire and on TV*.
20. Kiku Adatto, "Sound Bite Democracy: Network Evening News Presidential Campaign Coverage, 1968 and 1988," Research Paper R-2, Joan Shorenstein Barone Center on the Press, Politics, and Public Policy, John F. Kennedy School of Government, Harvard University, 1990.
21. Marion R. Just et al., *Crosstalk: Citizens, Candidates, and the Media in a Presidential Campaign* (Chicago: University of Chicago Press, 1996), chap. 5.
22. The study encompasses the period January 1, 1992, through election day. Stories could include references to multiple frames. See Kerbel, *Edited for Television*, 15–34.
23. Horse-race coverage has a thematic quality that differs from the episodic way television frames issue coverage. See Iyengar, *Is Anyone Responsible?*
24. See Lichter and Noyes, *Campaign '96*.
25. The author is working on a longitudinal analysis of campaign frames from 1984 to 1996.
26. Blaine Harden, *Washington Post*, March 24, 1996, A8.
27. Robinson and Sheehan, *Over the Wire and on TV*.
28. *ABC World News Tonight*, January 17, 1996.
29. Ibid., January 18, 1996.
30. Ibid., January 12, 1996.
31. *CBS Evening News*, January 12, 1996.
32. *Newsweek*, March 4, 1996.
33. Dan Balz and Howard Kurtz, "Two Top Media Advisors Quit as Dole Operation Suffers Another Shake-up," *Washington Post*, September 6, 1996, A18.
34. Howard Fineman and Thomas Rosenstiel, "The Last Insider," *Newsweek*, March 11, 1996. Emphasis in original.
35. Blaine Harden, "Dole Steps Up Attack on Clinton," *Washington Post*, May 4, 1996, A1.
36. Dan Balz, "Dole Shifts Strategy for the Stretch Run," *Washington Post*, October 20, 1996, A1.
37. Ronald Brownstein and Gabe Martinez, "Dole 'Betting the Campaign' on California," *Los Angeles Times*, October 22, 1996.
38. See Doris A. Graber, *Mass Media and American Politics* (Washington, D.C.: CQ Press, 1984), 200–204.
39. *NBC Nightly News*, January 6, 1996.
40. Ibid.
41. *ABC World News Tonight*, January 15, 1996.
42. Ibid., January 5, 1996.
43. *CBS Evening News*, January 24, 1996.
44. Blaine Harden, "Tax Cut Speech Takes a Populist Approach," *Washington Post*, August 6, 1996, A1.
45. Ronald Brownstein, "Big Government Is Critical Issue for Clinton, Dole," *Los Angeles Times*, October 1, 1996.

46. Thomas B. Edsall, "Dole Tells the Tale of Two Economies," *Washington Post,* October 23, 1996, A17.
47. *NBC Nightly News,* January 27, 1996.
48. *ABC World News Tonight,* January 10, 1996.
49. *NBC Nightly News,* January 9, 1996.
50. The CNN/*USA Today*/Gallup poll of May 30 reported that 60 percent felt Clinton was "hiding something regarding his role" in Whitewater. Two weeks later (June 12–13), the same poll reported that 52 percent felt "suspicions against the Clintons" were "serious or very serious," and a plurality of 45 percent felt the president had done something illegal.
51. *NBC Nightly News,* February 20, 1996.
52. Ibid.
53. Ibid.
54. *CBS Evening News,* February 17, 1996.
55. Ibid., February 20, 1996.
56. Howard Kurtz, "TV Coverage Setting the Tone for Voters," *Washington Post,* January 29, 1996, A5.
57. Howard Fineman, "Last Call," *Newsweek,* February 5, 1996.
58. Howard Kurtz, "Forget the Final Tally. The Media Declare the Real Winner," *Washington Post,* February 13, 1996, C1.
59. Tom Rosenstiel, *The Beat Goes On: President Clinton's First Year with the Media* (New York: Twentieth Century Fund, 1994), 3.
60. *CBS Evening News,* January 20, 1996.
61. Ibid., January 14, 1996.
62. Ibid., January 11, 1996.
63. Jay Rosen, *Getting the Connections Right: Public Journalism and the Troubles in the Press* (New York: Twentieth Century Fund, 1996), 1. See also Jay Rosen and Paul Taylor, *The New News v. the Old News* (New York: Twentieth Century Fund, 1993).
64. Anonymous, *Primary Colors: A Novel of Politics* (New York: Random House, 1996), 116–117.
65. *CBS Evening News,* January 21, 1996.

5

Issues and Themes: Economics, Culture, and "Small-Party" Politics

Jean Bethke Elshtain and Christopher Beem

A re we moving from presidential elections as political events to elections as collective Rorschach tests? To judge from much of the media coverage and the words of political pundits, the 1996 election demonstrated that we are. Would Americans go for the baby boomer Clinton or the sturdy veteran Dole? What would the choice say about us as a people and as a culture as we near century's end?

One story (call it "scenario no. 1") held that once upon a time Americans were stalwart sorts—embattled farmers who stood their ground "by the rude bridge that arched the flood"; pioneer women who, with their families, forged into a wilderness and carved out settlements, giving birth and returning to the plow; immigrants who worked long hours, learned a new language, and brought their distinctive cultures to the vast mix that was America. Stump preachers and stump politicians; school marms and suffragists; protesters and peacemakers—these and others like them epitomized the American ethos. The reigning view was that because of this ethos, Americans could rise to new challenges, could somehow shape vast forces to democratic purposes.

From this vantage point, we have suffered a rather distressing decline. We have redefined what counts as vulnerability and requires special attention from government to include all of the people some of the time, some of the people all of the time, and, according to some, all of the people all of the time. No longer resolute and self-reliant, we have become big children who want tending. When government governs according to certain open, shared standards and civic criteria, we are constituted as citizens. When government acts as a well-meaning parent, or watchful baby sitter, we are infantilized and turned into needy kids. In this scenario, therefore, our presidents should once again help us to take the strong medicine and compel us to act like grown-ups rather than treating us in a condescending or overly familiar manner. We don't require presidents to share our woes. Sturdy democrats respond instead to calls to civic duty.

But there is, of course, another perspective, a "scenario no. 2," that decries the stalwart tale of brave pioneers as a myth used to cover a vast array of social inequities and political perfidies. In fact, this alternative story goes, government has always played a big role in framing and guiding the American story, through programs as diverse as public education and the Homestead Act.[1] There have always been at least as many losers as winners in our society, and government rightly took on a more capacious role to chasten the winners and ease the burdens of the losers. Indeed, one could hope that government might hasten the day when there would be no winners or losers at all. But certainly it was meet, right, and necessary for government to take on a more explicit, direct, and complex role as America grew into a twentieth-century constitutional republic and, in the international arena, a superpower. To tell tales of the heroic past is to romanticize and to forget the troubles of that past and the real achievements brought about by government in its caring role.

In this second scenario, it makes sense that the president is now as much a facilitator as a leader in the old, hierarchical sense. Revolutionary changes in media coverage alone guaranteed the transformation. The president is bound to be more familiar to us than he used to be, and we are right to ask with whom we feel most comfortable as our leader. Presidents must act as friendly parents serving the "American family." All the talk of "character" is beside the point unless it encompasses elusive dimensions of personality that have palpable effects. That Bill Clinton feels our pain is no joke. We want someone familiar to us to share our troubles and our woes.

Each of these scenarios is overdrawn for heuristic purposes but not by much. Consider that conservative politicians and pundits are more likely to sign on with the first scenario, offering sweeping and doleful judgments based on the results of the 1996 presidential election. They will argue that never before has an electorate been so willing to overlook a candidate's ethical failings, so willing to ignore issues of personal character. They will conclude that the election reveals the moral decline of American society. Rejoinders from the liberal end of the political spectrum will likely outline judgments that are equally facile, dismissing these claims as so much sour grapes. For them, the candidate with the better ideas won: end of story.

We believe that the truth of the matter is somewhere in the middle. To be sure, neither of us celebrates the condition of contemporary American culture. But we are not willing to assign unique and wholesale condemnation to the moral acumen of the 1996 electorate. In the first place, such an accusation could be challenged on historical grounds. After all, despite a crescendo of corruption and evidence of poor or lax judgment, Americans reelected U. S. Grant and Richard Nixon. Just as important, sweeping lamentations fail to acknowledge that in any election the choice before the electorate is merely and simply that. That one candidate wins and the other loses does not necessarily mean that voters wholeheartedly support the personal profile of the winner or condemn that of the loser. It simply means that the majority thinks that the winner will execute the office of president better than would the opponent(s). To this extent, then, the too simple conclusions proffered by those in the liberal camp have got it at least partially right.

But it is equally true that there is still plenty of room to form judgments about the thinking of the American electorate and the condition of American society. Elections are more than just a timely opportunity for reflection; they focus and magnify the spirit of the time. What can be said with certainty about the election of 1996 is that Americans elected Clinton over Bob Dole despite their widespread, considered belief that the former's personal and professional ethical conduct was significantly less admirable than the latter's.[2] Why? What is it about Clinton or his administration that made his election preferable despite the doubts? Alternatively, what is it that made Dole a less desirable option despite Americans' almost universal admiration for his life of public service? Surely answers to these questions would tell us a great deal about the condition of American democracy and American culture as we near century's end.

The Cultural Context

If one focuses on the cultural context for the 1996 election, one quickly concludes that the conservative Jeremiahs have a strong case. Less than a month before election day, researchers at Fordham University released their "Index of Social Well-being." The report looked at 1994 federal government statistics concerning sixteen social problems—including rates of unemployment, homicides, poverty, and infant mortality. It concluded that the nation's aggregate social well being is at its lowest level in twenty-five years. (The report also noted that "of the six problems concerning Americans younger than 18, four of them—child abuse, teen-age suicide, drug abuse and the high school dropout rate—worsened in 1994.") Even more disconcerting, this aggregate rating has been falling more or less precipitously and more or less continuously since the survey began. The index level in 1973 was 77.5. By 1994 it had shrunk to 37.5. These findings, the report concludes, "suggest that despite a range of stated differences in philosophy and policy, neither political party has been able to achieve significant progress in social health over 25 years."[3]

Whatever else one can say, then, it is clear that the election took place within the context of long-standing and serious social decay that neither party appears able to ameliorate. Most Americans are not aware of the Fordham report. Nor are they cognizant of the specific data on problems like teen suicide or growing income disparity. Nevertheless, they are both aware of and concerned about the deteriorating condition of American culture. And the long-standing and widespread inability of government to address these problems meaningfully has had a profound effect on the public's confidence in the institutions of the federal government.

A groundbreaking survey of American political culture produced by the Post-Modernity Project of the University of Virginia notes that in 1996, only 13 percent of Americans had "a great deal of confidence" in the presidency, and only 5 percent expressed a similar level of confidence in Congress. (In 1966 these figures stood at 41 percent and 42 percent, respectively.)[4] Of course, this precipitous decline is also tied to the media's coverage of every "gate" scandal and to the almost chronic accusations of malfeasance and corruption emanating from inside Washington's beltway. But while much of this loss of confidence is attributable to perceptions of corruption and incompetence, it is important to recognize that the two failings are not identical. The latter is more directly tied to people's perception that government is ineffective than the former. Rather than conclude that the nation's problems are insoluble, the Hunter and Bowman study discovered that 66 percent of the population agrees with the statement "Our system of government is good, but the people running it are incompetent."[5]

This abiding feeling of unease and dissatisfaction, inchoate and inarticulate though it may be, has also been clearly captured in the "direction of the country" poll. In various iterations, the poll asks one simple question: "Do you think the country is generally moving in the right direction, or do you think it's generally on the wrong track?" Traditionally, the poll's results were tied to economic performance. That is, if the economy was rolling, Americans would tend to believe that the country was moving in the right direction. If the economy was suffering from some combination of high unemployment, runaway inflation, and recession, the mood would reflect this condition as well. Yet, although the latest economic turnaround began in 1992, this fact was slow to translate into increased feelings of optimism. Despite several years of consistently encouraging economic news, Americans continued to profess grave misgivings about the direction of the country. In April 1996, just months before the election, an ABC/*Washington Post* poll showed that more than 70 percent of the American public was pessimistic, concluding that the country was basically on the wrong track.[6] This disconnect does not necessarily mean that concern about the condition of American society was overriding thoughts about one's own economic prospects, but it does reveal a rather unusual condition: a surfeit of good economic news was unable to produce the expected widespread optimism.

Yet, as the 1996 campaign rolled on, that condition slowly began to reverse itself. For all the pronounced fluctuations in responses that one might expect with a question of this sort, during 1996 there was a slow and steady growth in the numbers of people expressing optimism and an equally significant decline in respondents expressing pessimism. In fact, the last poll before the election by NBC and the *Wall Street Journal* showed that the trend had actually, and for the first time, reversed. By a slim margin (42–39 percent), those who counted themselves generally optimistic about the country's future outnumbered the pessimists.[7] Exit polling on election day confirmed this trend. More than half of all voters said the country was on the right track.

What is one to make of these changes? Some might conclude that the turnaround was a result of the campaign itself: a distracted and gullible populace changed its mind only because it had been bombarded by campaign rhetoric encouraging it to do so. Could be. But we are inclined to attribute the turn to the established political barometer: economic numbers on key indicators supporting the notion that ours is a growing but stable economy with low inflation, low unemployment, and a shrinking deficit. These numbers have been so good for so long that they appear to have worn down the resistance built by a deteriorating social climate. It took much longer than usual, but over an extended period of time, good economic news achieved a critical mass that turned around many people's assessments of our nation's future. It is instructive to note that on the same day that Fordham released its report on social indicators, the Dow closed above 6000 for the first time. For this election, anyway, the second story overwhelmed the first.

At least some of the credit for the sustained recovery, and the apparently successful quest for a "soft landing," must go to Clinton—or so the voters clearly concluded. While those on the right routinely talk about Clinton's lurch to the left during the first two years of his administration—citing issues such as health care reform and gays in the military—they appear to have forgotten that he adroitly steered the General Agreement on Tariffs and Trade (GATT) and the North American Free Trade Agreement (NAFTA) into law. What is more, the deficit-reduction package of 1993 will likely be seen as a watershed event in the attempt to restore our nation's fiscal equilibrium. As any incumbent loser will happily tell you, the appearance of a healthy economy in time for a reelection campaign is often a matter of dumb luck. Similarly, many claim that Clinton succeeded in large part because he took credit for the good side of the economy and because he appropriated many choruses from the Republican songbook, including its central refrain that "the era of big government is over." But at the very least, Clinton—the inveterate "hearts" player—appears to have played his cards very well.

At the same time, it must also be said that the economy is far from perfect. There is growing evidence that the economy is splitting in two—one for the haves and the other for the have nots. A joke making the rounds during the election speaks to deep economic anxiety. Clinton, so the story goes, approached a voter, his arms outstretched. After pumping the guy's hand, the president solicited his vote. "Why should I support you?" queried the voter. "Well, because I've created millions of new jobs on my watch," the president replied. The rueful voter shoots back: "Yeah, and I've got three of them." The joke speaks to an undercurrent of anxiety seething just beneath the sunny statistics on low unemployment. Workers now find themselves in an economy generating low-pay, service-sector jobs with precious few prospects for long-term security, reliable benefits, and opportunities to hone and to use developed skills over the course of a working lifetime.

This condition may well be the inevitable result of a globalizing economy, but it has serious implications for our democratic culture. It is critical in part because work has been and remains so central to the American identity. Immigrants came here in search of jobs and opportunities. They dreamt of owning a bit of land or a home, of passing something on to their children and grandchildren. They counted on hard work being rewarded with reciprocal loyalty between employee and employer. No more. You're a sucker if you believe these things, or so those calling the economic shots are, in effect, telling people (or, more likely, showing them, often in the crassest ways). What is rewarded now is maximum "flexibility," which means, in practice, no particular commitment to a job, a skill, or a place. In this "dynamic economy" employees come and go, quickly moving on to the next of the many jobs they will likely occupy over the course of their working lives.

But while Robert Reich, secretary of labor during Clinton's first term, and others in the administration celebrated these changes, they take a severe toll on an individual's need for self-identity and a sense of permanence through time. For many of us, therefore, our sense of self, including our sense of citizenship, is not what it used to be. Similarly, the notion that a corporation is built on a shared commitment to a common enterprise is now sullied and obsolete, a fact that spills over into all aspects of our lives: family, neighborhood, and society. Finally, globalization means that while income disparities between nations decline, income disparities within nations grow. In our brave new world, the middle class—the undisputed backbone of a stable democracy—continues to shrink, while those at the very top and very bottom of the economic ladder multiply. A smaller middle class means the poor and the rich are left isolated, holed up with those in similar economic straits. With fewer opportunities for the classes to associate, fewer occasions in which the identity of everyone present centers on the common and egalitarian notion of citizenship, the public world declines. Distrust and animosity are the inevitable results.

Although these issues were virtually ignored by both major party candidates,[8] they have hardly gone away; instead, we infer that the bad news and heretofore inveterate bad feelings associated with the changing economy were temporarily swamped by consistent reports of good news. Yet the undercurrent remains. When parents are asked to give their version of today's discontents, they point to the coarsening of the social fabric, the loss of community, the fear that they are losing their children to a violent and materialistic culture. Frequently, they add "economic insecurity" to the list as well. All sorts of people in today's economy live with the gnawing anxiety that their jobs will disappear, their companies or factories will be downsized or relocated, their hopes for their children's futures will come to naught. They understand that corporations can more readily than ever before shift operations "south of the border"—any border—and engage in "outsourcing," getting higher profits by paying foreign workers less than they would pay American working men and women. In the meantime, those who remain in the American work force are working longer and harder and seeing less for it. Juliet Schor, professor of economics at Harvard University, estimates that the average American worker "has been working a progressively longer schedule for twenty-five years, with increases in overtime, moonlighting, weekly hours, weeks of work each year, and a dramatic decline in vacations and paid holidays. Compared to the late 1960s, the average worker is working about an extra month of work per year." Schor adds that we have "gotten more things, but there is growing evidence that consumerism is not giving us satisfaction and peace of mind. Americans are neither happier nor more satisfied."[9]

And yet, for all this, there was enough good economic news in 1996 to make people forget, at least temporarily, that clouds without silver linings loom on the horizon. As well, despite half-hearted and murky military forays into Haiti, Somalia, Bosnia, and Iraq, the nation, in 1996, was at peace. To a large degree, then, the reelection of Bill Clinton was fairly straightforward and predictable. In conditions of peace and prosperity, the incumbent usually wins.

But this argument, as stated, is facile. It fails to recognize that the peace and prosperity the nation now enjoys is tenuous and thin. More important, it also fails to acknowledge the skillful, even masterful political positioning by which Clinton sought to address this uneasy climate of good and bad news. In Alexis de Tocqueville's terms, Clinton was reelected because of his mastery of small-party politics.

The Tocquevillian Thesis

In the mid-nineteenth century, in *Democracy in America,* Tocqueville draws a distinction between great and small parties. Tocqueville's words cannot be improved on, so we quote them at length:

> What I call great political parties are those more attached to principles than to consequences, to generalities rather than to particular cases, to ideas rather than to personalities. Such parties generally have nobler features, more generous passions, more real convictions and a bolder and more open look than others. . . . On the other hand, small parties are generally without political faith. And they are not elevated and sustained by lofty purposes, the selfishness of their character is openly displayed in all their actions. They glow with a factitious zeal; their language is violent, but their progress is timid and uncertain.[10]

For all his apparent distaste for small parties, Tocqueville believed that America's success and stability were directly connected to the fact that small parties had come to dominate the political scene. Small-party politics allowed American society to creep along, contesting greatly over minor and self-interested matters (Tocqueville calls them "wretched trifles") but leaving untouched the most basic features of government and society. America thereby avoided the class warfare and ideological struggles that Europe had been subject to.

Tocqueville is correct to argue that truly revolutionary politics has been, for the most part, blessedly absent from American history. (The Civil War and to a lesser degree the civil rights movement stand as stark counterexamples.) But it is also true that our political history is marked by a succession of more or less controlled upheavals in which the peaceful transfer of power has taken on many of the features of great-party politics. The elections of

Abraham Lincoln in 1860, Franklin Roosevelt in 1932, and Ronald Reagan in 1980 signaled dramatic if not revolutionary changes in the American body politic. The congressional elections of 1994 fall into this category as well. The revolutionary rhetoric of the freshman Republicans, the ideological fervor of Speaker Newt Gingrich and other House leaders, and the constant attention to the "angry white male" all evoke a contest more closely attuned than usual to great-party politics.

The 1996 election was very different. To be sure, we have identified issues on the horizon that have the potential to evoke great passion and split the electorate. But if people's satisfaction with the status quo, as well as their satisfaction with their president, was demonstrably thin in 1996, enough satisfaction remained to allow them to bracket those concerns. More precisely, they were willing to accept and even demand small policies that addressed their cultural unease without rocking the economic boat or addressing the hard choices facing the country. The economy has eased concerns about the culture to the point that people accepted—even demanded—small-party politics as a way of dealing with great-party issues.

Clinton: The Campaign of Small-Party Politics

Clinton understood the mood of the electorate and exploited it brilliantly. During the campaign, Clinton would repeatedly tout each of his most minuscule policy proposals as an event of profound cultural significance. He was particularly wont to do so if the policy in question spoke to our feelings of cultural unease: "More effective 911 service? I'm here for you. School uniforms? You bet. Youth curfews? Good idea." [11] These and other small, even cosmetic, proposals created a veneer of action and purpose that simultaneously legitimated the electorate's deep anxiety and affirmed voters' conservatism about the political and economic status quo.

Something else about Clinton's strategy is worth noticing. Consider his proposals for V-chips, to allow parents to control their children's television viewing; school uniforms; and drug testing for driver's licenses. In every instance, the constituency affected by these proposals was children. None of the proposals required any significant behavioral changes—let alone sacrifices—from any member of the electorate. For the voters, this was cultural reform on the cheap. And that, apparently, is just the way they wanted it.

What might be called, somewhat unkindly, the political idolatry of the child trumped most other concerns in 1996. The Republican and Democratic National Conventions gave ample evidence of that: never have so many babies and toddlers been kept up past their bedtimes for the edification of the "feeling" electorate. Similarly, at the conventions we saw far more victims of individual tragedy than we did politicians, especially in prime time. Sentimentalism triumphed. Clinton thrives in this venue and played his role to the hilt. And even though Dole was clearly uncomfortable talking about his war injury and his arduous recovery, he felt obliged to join in: the campaign as talk show.

This evocation of a kind of instant intimacy effaces the distance between us and others. One wonders what is happening to politics when political issues get transformed into psychological or behavioral tragedies and triumphs. Certainly much of what got talked about, and the way it got talked about, in 1996 was neither civic nor political. Instead, the prevailing rhetoric effaced distinctions between parenting and political leadership, between intimacy and justice, between hard choices and feeling good about ourselves. But, again, this seems to be the way voters wanted it. Not only is this small-party politics, it is often a depoliticized politics.

Let us be clear. We are not arguing that all political action, to be meaningful, must respond in a big, dramatic way to serious, overarching concerns. Certainly a liberal democracy is given to piecemeal, incremental reforms. But even by that standard, the policies and proposals outlined by Clinton were minimalist—glancing blows at what were, by the administration's own accounts, grave problems. Yet to judge the matter by Clinton's rhetoric alone, his proposals were sturdy walls against the cultural siege. This strategy of appearing tough without really changing anything is the essence of small-party politics. And it was the centerpiece of Clinton's campaign.

Consider the following: In 1996 the swing group *du jour* was the "soccer moms." The term was meant to highlight the gender gap between men and women voters. Indeed, pollster Daniel Yankelovich argues that the most important legacy of the election is that it "institutionaliz[ed] the gender gap." [12] But the singling out of soccer moms as representative of the electorate is itself significant. What are soccer moms concerned about? To a large degree, their issues were identified with what are commonly considered "women's issues"—health care, welfare, education, and the environment. But it is also fair to say that these and other issues were articulated in ways that reflected their interests not just as women but also as moms—that is to say, they manifested the maternal focus on hearth and home. The operative question, then, was how the issues of the campaign affected their families—their kids' education and moral climate, their kids' environment, their parents' retirement.

Personal economic concerns were embodied here as well—most important, the time pressures associated with two working parents—but the fact that the media represented moms almost exclusively as parents who take their kids to soccer practices indicates that this particular cohort is a mostly suburban, fairly well-to-do group. The economic status quo may have them running from sunup till long past sundown, but it is also putting food on their tables and a roof over their heads. One suspects that whatever public policy can do to address their fears and concerns, soccer moms will not tolerate any proposal that jeopardizes their somewhat precarious sense of well-being. Their desire for small-party politics is thus born of, and driven by, their sense of underlying vulnerability regarding the economy. The lower the boat sits in the water, the more concerned the passengers are with rocking.

Much has been made of Clinton's ability to present an image that has visceral political appeal—especially to women. The "I feel your pain" line captures this aspect of his campaign, and perhaps of his persona. It is difficult to evaluate such analyses. Continued references to Clinton as the great seducer contain the clear implication that women are more easily taken in than men; moreover, such analyses fail to take seriously the singular achievement of the president's campaign. Clinton quickly discovered the dynamics of the contemporary unease and cannily outlined policy initiatives that addressed it, however superficially. In short, he fastidiously and skillfully walked the line between the voters' feelings of unease and their desire for governmental abeyance. Because this appears to be what a majority of Americans wanted, they were likewise willing to overlook Clinton's own moral failings.[13]

We think this is the only way satisfactorily to explain the results of a Marist poll conducted just weeks before the election. Potential voters were asked whether the candidate's character or his stand on the issues was most important. By an overwhelming percentage (71–29), they said issues.[14] But what issues? Many of the serious issues were not debated at all in 1996; they were at best ignored and often were the focus of demagogy—campaign finance reform, the future of entitlements, the condition of the inner city. What issues were part of the campaign? Crime, education, and the pervasive sense of moral decline seemed to garner the most attention. If these issues secured the American public's preference for Clinton, if these subjects were more important to voters than character, it confirms our belief that Americans wanted small-party politics. Clinton addressed the issues that people were concerned about but not so concerned about that they actually wanted to do something dramatic (one might well say meaningful) about politics and culture.

There is another issue. The results of the Marist poll challenge much democratic theory. To be sure, the issues of government are complex and time-consuming. Regardless of their inclination or abilities, soccer moms and dads do not have the time to examine the niceties of the telecommunications bill, or the Mexican financial bailout (discussion of this issue during the vice presidential debate would seem to confirm the point). But if the people cannot be "trusted" to make decisions on complex matters like these, they can, so the story goes, be trusted to pick a candidate whom they can rely upon to decide for them.

But if this is so—indeed, if this is the most salient justification for democratic government—then is not character a crucial reference point for choosing one candidate over another? And how does one reconcile the Marist poll results with that? Maureen Dowd of the *New York Times* offers an explanation that makes the political analyst squirm. Clinton is trusted not because he is trustworthy, she suggests, but because he reflects ourselves. "When he was first in office, Mr. Clinton tried being a leader, with disastrous results. Now he settles for being a mirror. The role suits him. He perfectly reflects the confessional, narcissistic, cynical, opportunistic, personality-driven times."[15]

Dole: Good Athlete, Wrong Sport

The Republicans, of course, had to operate within the same cultural and economic context. To some degree, therefore, Dole was similarly constrained to run a campaign of small-party politics. Yet despite the desires and efforts of the campaign, great-party themes repeatedly intruded. Dole's campaign thus reflected the tensions within the Republican Party—tensions between small- and great-party politics.

Even though many of its most vocal spokesmen became almost invisible during the campaign, the strongly ideological conservative strain that came to power in 1994 was still present within the party. The force of great-party politics dictated the terms of the highly ideological Republican platform, for example. But by the time the conventions were concluded, it was already apparent that this more strident brand of conservatism was not going to appeal to a majority of the electorate. The soccer moms in particular ran headlong from right-wing rhetoric. So Dole ignored the platform—indeed, he came close to repudiating it—and tried instead to find issues that would appeal to a cross section of the electorate.[16]

Probably against his better instincts, and almost certainly against his personal inclinations, Dole chose tax relief as the central theme of his campaign. The strategy was meant to uncover a broad base of support: almost all Americans want their taxes lowered. What's more, the message offered Dole the opportunity, as he put it, to "be Reagan if that's what you want." For clearly that is exactly what the Republicans wanted in 1996: a candidate who, through personality and charm, could unite the disparate and contesting wings of the party and appeal to crucial swing voters. The idea of tax relief, of helping working families make ends meet, was intended to connect Dole vicariously to that kind of magical, Reaganesque appeal.

Dole's 15 percent tax-cut proposal was much more dramatic than Clinton's call for school uniforms or the installation of V-chips. Nevertheless, Dole's campaign touted this proposal in terms that identified it as small-party politics. Dole argued that his tax-cut proposal was a way to address both the crisis in the American family (by making it financially possible for one parent to stay home) and the crisis in American education (by making it financially possible for more parents to send their children to private schools). Under Dole's plan, a family of four with an income of $35,000 would have seen a reduction of $1,400 in their federal tax.[17] This is not an insignificant amount of money, but it is nowhere near enough to make these options truly viable. Like Clinton's, Dole's proposals were explicitly associated with Americans' great cultural unease. And, like Clinton's, his proposals could not carry the weight of his rhetoric.

What's more, the tax issue did not achieve the broad-based support Dole sought. In the first place, Ross Perot's campaign in 1992, and the budget battles of 1993 and 1995, had placed budgetary control squarely on the agenda of American politics. Americans knew about the deficit, believed (rightly in our judgment) that it was associated with the tax cuts of the Reagan years, saw it and the debt as an unacceptable burden to their children, and demanded that the problem be addressed. The nation's hawkish mood about the deficit could not be distracted by appeals for tax relief. Indeed, in this context, Dole's tax-cut proposal came off as an unabashed appeal to crass self-interest: "Vote for me and I will give you money." Lewis E. Platt, chairman and C.E.O. of Hewlett-Packard, captured the point. Platt noted that although he was "ordinarily a Republican," concerns about the deficit drove him to vote for Clinton. "I like a tax cut as much as the next guy, but not if it doesn't fit with deficit reduction." [18] In the vice presidential debate, Clinton's running mate, Al Gore, exploited this sentiment by sounding the phrase "a risky scheme that will blow a hole in the deficit" to the point of self-parody. Gore's words were the product of focus group testing, but there was clearly a reason why they resonated: Americans had seen for themselves the budget battles, seen the fierce objections to the elimination of federal mohair subsidies and the like, and, although they may have trusted Dole more than Clinton, they were not willing to accept his word that major tax relief and budgetary reform could be undertaken together.

At the same time, Dole's appeal was willy-nilly connected to some great-party themes of the Republican Party. The demand for lower taxes resonated strongly with the ideological and divisive idea that government is the enemy, the autocrat, and that the people, the real rulers, had been subverted. As was so often the case in the campaign, Dole tried this rhetoric on for size, then quickly discarded it. Yet as long as he clung to the tax-cut theme, Dole was unable to escape the revolutionary rhetoric of the most ideological wing of the party and thus was unable to mollify the swing voters who clung uneasily to the status quo.

Yet the fact that Dole's campaign was a strange amalgam of small- and great-party politics does not sufficiently explain its failure. As Tocqueville notes, small-party politics is endemic to American politics. And if anyone understands the endemic features of American politics, it is Dole. Although he had little to say about it in the campaign, Dole's long and undeniable record of achievement in Congress manifestly illustrates that he too could play the game. But as many have noted, the presidency and the Senate are two different beasts, and success in one venue does not guarantee, and perhaps even hinders, success in the other. [19] Almost every skill and trait that served Dole well as Senate majority leader, indeed, many of the same traits that caused him to be universally liked and admired by his Senate colleagues, were of little use to him in the glaring, sentimental, and bombastic world of presidential politics.

After his campaign had been put out of its misery, Dole appeared on the *Late Show with David Letterman*. After his appearance, Letterman and guest Ted Koppel went on at length about Dole's genuine charm and humor—qualities, they noted, that were almost completely absent during the campaign. But whatever Dole's future as a good talk show guest, it is, as the Marxists say, no accident that his personality was given something less than free rein during the campaign. In dramatic contrast to the Reagan years, not once did we hear Republicans demanding, "Let Dole be Dole."

Dole faced other fundamental problems. He apparently did not fit the contemporary idea of what Americans want to see in their president. Americans have come to rely on their president as a national pastor. Since Franklin Roosevelt, and surely since Reagan, the president has taken on the priestly responsibilities of bringing meaning to national tragedies, bringing dynamism and focus to the signs of the times, and bringing a unifying voice to the nation's troubles.[20] Dole is a rhetorical minimalist. He does not like to call attention to himself, and broad-gauged displays of emotion were not his métier. In some ways, Dole's very effort to associate himself with the Reagan legacy only intensified the unflattering comparison between himself and the Great Communicator.[21]

Dole also did not fit the forward-looking dynamism of Americans—the ethos that came naturally to Reagan. The election of 1992 was, for good or ill, a passing of the generational torch—America's leadership moved, in a real if symbolic way, from the World War II generation (represented by George Bush) to the baby boom generation—as exemplified by the pot smoking (if not inhaling), draft avoiding (if not dodging), sax playing (if not well) Clinton. These milestones are not passed lightly, but once passed, it is extremely difficult to go back. Dole's efforts to highlight his experiences before and during the war (while virtually ignoring his decades of service on Capitol Hill) only increased the difficulties.

Rhetorical failings aside, Dole did strive to offer himself as a morally superior man and as one who could better address the rumblings of cultural discontent than Clinton. Surveying a long litany of claims regarding impropriety in the Clinton administration, Dole asked, with apparently genuine dismay, "Where's the outrage?" He spoke continually of "trust" and "character" and of wanting to build a bridge to a time when these cultural problems were not apparent. But he had already compromised his standing by appearing to change his position on supply-side economics in order to be elected. In addition, his claims were often poorly formulated, even contradictory. The repeated charge that the president is "Slick Willie"—that is, an official who has no guiding principles, a political chameleon able and willing to alter his position on any issue to fit the results of the latest focus group—is difficult to make stick if one is simultaneously presenting Clinton as a political liberal of single-minded consistency. As well, Dole was so concerned that he would be tagged "mean" that he thought it imprudent to attack the president's personal failures. One also suspects that even when he finally decided to address the issue in the second debate, he had no stomach for it.

Yet the character argument was surely there to be made. In the last two weeks before the election, third-party candidate Perot finally found a voice. Responding to a round of media accusations regarding Democratic campaign financing and influence peddling, Perot fiercely attacked the president and his administration, recounting what he regarded as a legacy of arrogance and greed. This denunciation cut into Clinton's lead, especially among voters who had not yet made up their minds. But although Perot's efforts, unlike Dole's, were both forceful and effective, he began these attacks far too late in the game to have any significant effect. It is an open question whether a more focused and sustained barrage would have changed the outcome. But one must reiterate that deemphasizing character was, at least for the Dole campaign, a deliberate choice. It is more than a little ironic that even as he continually berated the American public for their insouciant lack of outrage, Dole was acting much as they were. Just like the public, Dole evaluated his own self-interest and gave Clinton a free ride. Clinton's election was thus the drama-less end to a drama-less campaign.

But the problems remain. As Tocqueville notes, we are "daily advancing toward an unknown future," [22] and the strains on American culture are severe. If the economy perks along, Clinton's policy of small steps will continue to enjoy moderate support. But the inevitable cycles of free market economics mean that eventually the economy will go south. And when it does, the viability of small-party politics will go with it. At that point, big ideas will be necessary. For all of Clinton's astonishing abilities of self re-creation, it seems unlikely that he could have succeeded had a poor economy been the context in 1996.

Notes

1. The Homestead Act, passed in 1862, was intended to make available western land to farmers.
2. More than half of those who voted for Clinton expressed "serious reservations" about doing so. See David Broder, "Power to Both Parties," *Washington Post National Weekly Edition*, November 1–17, 1996, 7. Exit polling also showed that the majority of voters (54 percent) said they do not believe the president is honest. Thomas B. Edsall and Richard Morin, ibid., 12.
3. Nick Ravo, "Index of Social Well-Being Is at the Lowest in 25 Years," *New York Times*, October 14, 1996, A14.
4. James Davison Hunter and Carl Bowman, *The State of Disunion: 1996 Survey of American Political Culture* (Ivy, Va.: In Media Res Educational Foundation, 1996), 27.
5. Ibid., 26.
6. ABC/*Washington Post* poll, April 4–5, 1996. Data were taken from the Politics-Now Web site *(http://www.politicsnow.com)*.
7. NBC/*Wall Street Journal* poll, October 19–22, 1996. Data were taken from the PoliticsNow Web site *(http://www.politicsnow.com)*.
8. Republican primary candidate Pat Buchanan sought to exploit people's misgivings about the condition of the economy. But that effort clearly was not able to garner levels of support anywhere near sufficient to run a successful national campaign.
9. Juliet Schor, "A Sustainable Economy for the 21st Century," available from *Open* magazine, Westfield, N.Y.
10. Alexis de Tocqueville, *Democracy in America*, trans. George Lawrence, ed. J. P. Mayer (Garden City, N.Y.: Anchor Books, 1969), 175.

11. See, for example, "Bill Clinton's Itsy-Bitsy Frontier," *U.S. News and World Report*, August 5, 1996, 8.
12. Quoted In Bob Herbert, "In America," *New York Times*, November 18, 1996, A15. A *Wall Street Journal* editorial argues, to the contrary, that the gap was not related to gender but to marriage. The *Journal* quoted a Wirthlin Worldwide poll which showed that married women voted for Clinton and Dole in even numbers (44–44 percent). The women who voted overwhelmingly for Clinton were widowed, single, or divorced. The editorial suspects that these women possess a more general feeling of insecurity than married women and see the government as a form of insurance. "The Marriage Gap," *Wall Street Journal*, November 15, 1996, A14.
13. We suspect (in contrast to many others) that Clinton does indeed possess a moral vision. His best performances—Oklahoma City, the address before African American ministers in Memphis, the 1992 convention speech—reflect a substantive and even laudable moral vision and a moral compass. Nevertheless, as David Maraniss and others have shown, Clinton would rather be loved than be right. As a result, even if his rhetoric is not wholly factitious, effectively speaking, it is exactly that.
14. Bob Herbert, "In America," *New York Times*, November 4, 1996, A15.
15. Maureen Dowd, "The Man in the Mirror," *New York Times*, September 12, 1996, A13.
16. This quest has become something of a sine qua non for the modern presidential campaign. In a discussion of the 1992 campaign, Donald E. Stokes and John J. DiIulio Jr. define it as the search for "valence issues"—that is, ideas, conditions, or goals that have a universal appeal. See "The Setting: Valence Politics in Modern Elections," in *The Elections of 1992*, ed. Michael Nelson (Washington , D.C.: CQ Press, 1993). The connection between that concept and small-party politics is certainly worth exploring, but we will not take it up here.
17. Paul Blustein, "A Sweetener for Families with Kids," *Washington Post National Weekly Edition*, August 12–18, 1996, 19.
18. *Wall Street Journal*, November 7, 1996, B1.
19. In a lecture given at the University of Chicago in 1946, Sen. William Fulbright had this to say about the distinction: "The great executives have given inspiration and push to the advancement of human society, but it is the legislator who has given stability and continuity to that slow and painful progress." Cited in *Political Quotations*, ed. David B. Baker (Detroit: Gale Research, 1990).
20. See Richard V. Pierard and Robert D. Linder, *Civil Religion and the Presidency* (Grand Rapids, Mich.: Academia Books, 1988).
21. The comparison between Dole and Reagan reveals the positively eerie similarities between the election of 1996 and that of 1984. Both campaigns featured a contest between an effective, but rhetorically hamstrung, senator and a slick, well-packaged, and carefully insulated great communicator. See Wilson Carey McWilliams's chapter on the 1984 election in his *Politics of Disappointment: American Elections from 1976–1994* (Chatham, N.J.: Chatham House, 1995).
22. Tocqueville, *Democracy in America*, 174.

6

The Presidency:
Elections and Presidential Governance

Paul J. Quirk and Sean Matheson

Elections shape the presidency in more ways than merely installing a
Democrat or Republican, a liberal or conservative, in the Oval Office.
The campaigns and outcomes in the presidential and congressional elections
shape the president's capabilities for leadership, opportunities and constraints, and prospects for success. Stated very broadly, as presidents are
elected, so will they govern.

In this chapter, we look at three ways that elections shape the presidency, with special attention to the elections of 1996. First, a presidential election chooses an individual with particular skills, experience, and personality.
These traits, or qualifications, affect a president's performance. Some presidents have been poorly suited to the office in important respects. Richard
Nixon, for example, was driven by deep-seated anger and suspicion; his
aggressive illegality provoked the constitutional crisis of Watergate. Jimmy
Carter disdained politicians and often had difficulty dealing with them.

Second, the rhetoric of the campaign, especially that of the winning
presidential candidate, creates commitments that carry weight after the election. Such commitments may help establish a popular mandate for the president's program. They may also, however, bind the president to an unwork-
able strategy for governing. After making an unusually categorical campaign
promise to oppose new taxes when he was running for president in 1988,
George Bush was politically devastated by having to reverse his position two
years later and tell voters in effect to re-read his lips.

Third, the elections measure and ultimately define the support for the
president and his or (in the future) her initiatives. The tenor of debate
in both the presidential and congressional elections, the balance of partisan
and ideological power in Congress, and the president's margin of victory
all affect the support for his agenda and his prospects for effective governance.

In short, elections shape the presidency through qualifications, commitments, and support. To shed some light on these effects, we first explore the
general considerations: For each of our three categories of effects, how do
elections matter? What would we like elections to accomplish or to avoid
doing? We then look closely at the elections of 1996. We examine their implications, which are generally positive, for Bill Clinton's second term. We also
consider what the nature of electoral politics in the contemporary era bodes

for presidential governance in the foreseeable future—on the whole, a more disturbing prospect.

Meanings of Success

How the elections (or anything else) affect a president's prospects for success depends on what kind of success one is talking about. Presidents have at least three kinds of goals, each with its own forms of success and failure. First, presidents want public support. They want high approval ratings and, above all, electoral success. After the first term, they hope to be reelected for a second; and after the second term, they hope for the further vindication of being succeeded by a president of their own party. Second, presidents have policy preferences that they want to enact. In most cases, they have significant changes in public policy that they want to accomplish; in other cases, they are more interested in resisting changes sought by their partisan or ideological opponents. Finally, presidents want to govern effectively. Quite apart from any policies that they put in place, they want to make progress in resolving the principal problems facing the country. Among the reasons for their concern, such accomplishment is critical to the verdict of historians. Policy success and governing success, although related, are different. A president could enact his policies, but they could fail to work—policy success without governing success. Or he could collaborate with the opposition, adopt policies that he had not preferred initially, and help solve national problems—governing success without policy success.

As one moves down this list of presidential goals—from popular support, to policy achievement, to governing achievement—judgments of success become more complex and controversial. In particular, reasonable people often disagree about whether a president's policies benefited or harmed the country. Yet the harder judgments about policy and governing success are also the most important from the public's standpoint. Thus we want to know: Do elections make it possible for presidents to achieve their policy goals? Above all, do they help presidents serve the nation's interests?

Qualifications

The campaign and election determine what manner of person will occupy the White House. The skills, experience, and personality of the victorious candidate will shape his or her performance in office. The voters should not be oblivious, therefore, to whether a presidential candidate is reasonably qualified for the presidency.

Defining Qualifications

The main difficulty with asking voters to consider candidate qualifications is that the traits that constitute "the right stuff" for the presidency are highly uncertain and controversial. There are in fact several ways to look at the question.

Public expectations. One approach is to consider what qualities the voters want in a president. Unfortunately, they have a variety of partly contradictory notions. Donald Kinder and his associates asked survey respondents to identify the most important desirable and undesirable traits for a president. They found that Americans want above all for the president to be honest, with 91 percent selecting that trait.[1] They also expect the president to be knowledgeable (88 percent) and open-minded (79 percent). They are most opposed to someone who is power-hungry (76 percent); and they also want to avoid a president who is unstable (66 percent), weak (51 percent), prejudiced (49 percent), or reckless (47 percent). Americans expect the president to provide strong leadership (75 percent), appoint good advisers (64 percent), and solve the country's economic problems (63 percent). The president also should avoid unnecessary wars (74 percent), refrain from using the presidency for personal gain (62 percent), and stand up for the country in foreign affairs (54 percent).

In explaining their findings, the authors suggested that people get these notions from their cultural values, their own observation of presidents, and the messages they receive from journalists and politicians about what a good president is and does.[2] Two of the public's strongest attitudes—the demand for honesty and aversion to power seeking—seem to reflect cultural values concerned with judging people in everyday life. It is unlikely that sophisticated journalists or politicians would argue that presidents should always tell the truth or that they should not have a desire for power. In fact, the public's concerns about a president's or candidate's "character," in the sense of personal morality, is rarely connected to any specific concern about performance in the presidency.

In some respects, the public appears to demand opposite things. As George Edwards and Stephen Wayne have argued, Americans expect their president to be a leader who can take stands on issues even if his position is contrary to public opinion; however, they also expect the president to be responsive to their wishes. Americans want an open-minded and flexible leader, yet one who will take firm and consistent stands. They expect the president to place the national interest above politics; yet they also expect him or her to be a skilled politician. They wish for an open administration, with few secrets; yet they admire the control and efficiency that openness can destroy. Finally, Americans want the president to be able to relate to the average person; yet they also want him to exhibit the dignity of a world leader and the exemplary personal conduct of a moral leader.[3]

In fairness, some of these seemingly contradictory expectations are perfectly sensible. The public realizes that how the president behaves should depend on the situation: Sometimes the president should compromise; at other times he should not. The voters' ideas about qualifications for the presidency are not so much contradictory as imprecise.

Skills. A more useful approach to the question of qualifications is to recognize that there are several dimensions of presidential leadership, each with its own demands.[4] First, a president must have a broad strategic sense, the ability to see the big picture and set a viable course for his administration. With some justice, Bush belittled prattling about "the vision thing," as he called it. But a president must be able to set coherent, attainable policy goals and formulate general plans to attain these goals. Second, a president should have a reasonably strong grasp of the major policy issues in national government and especially in economic and foreign policy, the central arenas for presidential decision making. It is neither necessary nor even desirable that he be a "policy wonk," able to discourse knowledgeably and at length on specific issues. But the president should be sufficiently familiar with the substance of policy debates to avoid simplistic or formulaic thinking and to distinguish balanced, responsible advice from tendentious advocacy.

Third, presidents must be able to work with other policy makers, especially in Congress, and build coalitions to adopt their policies. To do so requires communication skills and a taste for exercising interpersonal influence.[5] (Remarkably, some presidents, such as Nixon and Carter, have had difficulty even asking other officials for their support.) It also requires tactical shrewdness and a refined understanding of the policymaking process, although these skills can be provided largely by the president's staff. Because other policy makers have their own stakes and independent sources of power, building coalitions often requires flexibility and a collaborative disposition. Fourth, a president must be able to speak persuasively to the public. Appealing "over the heads" of Congress and the rest of the Washington establishment is a central technique of modern presidential leadership. As Ronald Reagan demonstrated, the skills required for effective public appeals are much akin to those of acting.

Finally, a president must understand how to manage the White House and the executive branch to obtain the assistance needed in performing all the other tasks of leadership. Devising a broad strategy, making good policy decisions, forming coalitions to adopt policies, and persuading the public are all, in large part, a matter of getting subordinates to work effectively.

Experience. In parliamentary systems, the prime minister is prepared for leadership by years of rising through the party ranks, normally including service in the cabinet or shadow cabinet. Indeed, becoming prime minister is often a matter of moving to the head of the table at cabinet meetings. In the United States, however, no comparable training system exists. Success in waging a presidential campaign presumably guarantees some skills in mass communications. But none of the other dimensions of presidential leadership can be taken for granted.[6] Whether presidents have cultivated the relevant skills and have been tested in their performance of them depends on their prior careers. Inevitably, most presidents are quite new to crucial aspects of the job.

Most presidents have held one of three positions before becoming president or vice president: member of Congress, governor of a state, or high official in the executive branch, including the cabinet and military. In this century, only five presidents (William McKinley, William Howard Taft, Theodore Roosevelt, Franklin D. Roosevelt, and Bush) have held two of these positions, and none has held all three.[7] Each position has severe limitations from the standpoint of training presidents. A member of Congress manages an organization (an office staff and sometimes a committee staff) roughly the size of a large automobile dealership. Governors, especially of small states, do not participate in national policy making or deal with comparably complex policy processes. Nor do they manage an economy or make foreign policy. Executive branch officials have specialized responsibilities and modest exposure to the mass public; many have little involvement in the legislative process.

Perversely, the only job that provides well-rounded preparation for the presidency *is* the presidency. An emerging additional training ground may be the vice presidency—inasmuch as recent presidents have treated their vice presidents increasingly as partners or understudies, rather than as rivals.[8] An important consideration in judging candidate qualifications, therefore, is what kinds of political and governmental experience candidates have had and what skills of presidential leadership they have demonstrated.

Personality. Finally, personality or character—fundamental traits that precede specific experience or skills—may be important to presidential performance. But it is hard to say what traits matter. In 1972 political scientist James David Barber proposed a simple typology of personality that he claimed could explain important aspects of presidential performance.[9] In one of the most celebrated predictions in political science, Barber got Nixon right—using Nixon's "active-negative" personality to predict irrational and self-destructive tendencies before they were dramatically demonstrated in the Watergate crisis. Unfortunately, as Jeffrey Tulis has pointed out, Barber's scheme would also have warned against Abraham Lincoln, often considered the greatest American president, who was just as clearly an active-negative.[10] After reviewing the research on presidential personality and performance, psychologist Dean Simonton concluded that no single personality type was clearly best suited for the presidency. Instead, various traits have both advantages and disadvantages.[11]

The key to presidential personality may not be finding a candidate with the right personality type but recognizing the dangers of various specific flaws. Barber was convincing in describing extreme, if not pathological, rigidity on the part of Woodrow Wilson[12] (in the controversy over ratifying the League of Nations treaty), Herbert Hoover (in responding to the Great Depression), and Lyndon Johnson (in escalating the Vietnam War), in addition to Nixon's paranoid aggression. Other presidents have had other deficiencies. Reagan's simplistic, categorical thinking helped produce the huge budget deficits that have dominated American politics in the 1980s and 1990s. Clinton's lack of self-discipline contributed to the chaotic, inconsistent White House decision making that produced numerous gaffes, scandals, and political failures in his first two years as president.[13]

The case of Reagan, whose simplistic thinking may have been symptomatic of early Alzheimer's disease,[14] is a reminder that age and health are also relevant to presidential performance. Other things being equal, the nation certainly should prefer to avoid a president who is likely to die or suffer a disabling illness during his term of office.

A lesson of all this is that presidents can go wrong in so many ways that we cannot hope to identify and avoid all potentially harmful personality flaws and other limitations. Our political system will just have to work with flawed presidents. We should be able to expect, however, that the electoral process will filter out candidates who have glaring deficiencies in skills, experience, or personality—for example, a candidate with no experience in building coalitions and no disposition for working with political opponents. More generally, we should expect the campaign to expose the personal characteristics of the candidates that we have discussed—what can be called their *conventional qualifications* for the office—so that the voters can take them into account.

These expectations pertain especially to the nominating process. Leaving aside independent and third-party candidacies, it is the nomination of the major-party candidates that narrows the field of potential presidents from the hundreds or thousands of constitutionally eligible persons who would like to be president to just two. Any ability of the electoral process to filter out unsuitable candidates must inhere primarily in this stage. Although the candidates' qualifications should certainly be debated in the general election, for most voters the choice at that stage will be dominated by party and ideology.

Qualifications and the 1996 Campaign

In practical terms, the 1996 election came down to a choice between two candidates, Democrat Bill Clinton and Republican Bob Dole, both of whom had imposing qualifications for the presidency. The election of a qualified president was therefore guaranteed. That result, however, apparently reflected good luck more than any careful scrutiny of qualifications in the campaign.

Dole presented the voters with an impressive résumé for a potential president. He had served twenty-eight years as a senator, two as Republican National Committee chair, and twelve as the Republican leader in the Senate. He had also been chair of the Senate Finance Committee. In these capacities, he had been centrally involved in the major issues facing the nation, especially the budget and taxes, and had worked closely with several presidents. Dole was widely praised as a responsible and effective Senate leader.

Largely by virtue of having spent the previous four years learning the job, sometimes painfully, Bill Clinton also had substantial credentials by 1996. A small-state governor who had been active in the national Democratic Party, Clinton had shown impressive political talents in the 1992 campaign. He had been an informed, articulate, and persuasive communicator, especially on domestic policy. During his first two years in office, however, Clinton demonstrated striking deficiencies of leadership and management skills. As Fred Greenstein wrote, somewhat delicately, Clinton's presidential style was "very much a work in progress." [15] Paul Quirk and Joseph Hinchliffe wrote, with less tact:

> The reason that Clinton was an apparent political failure after two years—with well under 50 percent public approval and a stunning defeat for his party in the midterm elections—was mainly his own deficiency as a political leader. . . . His first two years in office were dominated by a series of mistakes and manifestations of mismanagement. . . . At bottom, Clinton's troubles seem to derive from a few key personal shortcomings: in particular, an apparent tendency to cut corners on matters of personal and professional ethics and a lack of awareness or concern about the requirements of effective decision making and management in the White House. [16]

By 1996, however, Clinton had learned a great deal from his mistakes. He had strengthened the White House staff and submitted himself to orderly processes for decision making. He had begun to take foreign policy seriously, acting effectively in crises in Haiti and Bosnia. In contrast with the erratic, seemingly accidental positioning of his first two years, Clinton had staked out a moderate position on domestic issues and maintained it consistently. In the high-stakes 1995 budget negotiations, he had outmaneuvered House Speaker Newt Gingrich, Dole, and the Republican Congress, regaining popularity in the process. Through trial by fire, Clinton had become what he had not been in 1993: a competent president.

The strongly credentialed major-party nominees of 1996 do not indicate, however, an electoral process that rigorously tests presidential qualifications. Rather, Dole and Clinton happened to be the early front-runners—the result of past campaigns and, in Clinton's case, incumbency—and that status alone carried them far toward nomination. Indeed, Clinton had no serious opposition for the Democratic nomination. Dole bested several rivals for the Republican nomination, but the battle among them had little to do with qualifications.

The 1996 Republican primaries were marked by the strong candidacies of two presidential aspirants with doubtful qualifications for the office: political commentator Patrick Buchanan and magazine publisher Steve Forbes. Neither candidate had held an elective or high appointive office. Buchanan had been a White House speechwriter in two administrations, a good vantage point for learning about the presidency. But Democrats and Republicans alike worried about his harsh rhetoric, dogmatism, and extreme views on issues like abortion, immigration, and trade. His characteristic outlook was angry defiance. A Buchanan presidency would have threatened to polarize American politics and paralyze the federal government. Forbes, campaigning on a radical proposal for a flat tax, was a single-issue candidate. He demonstrated little substantive knowledge about most domestic and foreign issues and had no experience in building political coalitions or making public policy.

Buchanan and Forbes won more votes than other Republicans whose conventional qualifications were far stronger. These included Indiana senator Richard Lugar, a former chair of the Senate Foreign Relations Committee; Lamar Alexander, a former Tennessee governor and cabinet member; and Pete Wilson, a former senator and the current governor of California—all respected, experienced leaders in the mainstream of the Republican Party. Buchanan finished a strong second in the Iowa caucuses and upset Dole in the New Hampshire primary; Forbes won the Delaware and Arizona primaries. They were the only rivals to last much beyond Dole's sweep of eight primaries on March 5.

Dole, meanwhile, made little use of his extensive governmental experience in the campaign. To the contrary, he eventually resigned his seat in the Senate, hoping to put his connection with Washington out of voters' minds. It is unclear, therefore, that Dole's strong qualifications for the presidency played much of a role in his nomination.

The general election campaign featured one major theme concerning qualifications for the presidency—Dole's sustained attack, with assistance from third-party candidate Ross Perot, on Clinton's "character." Dole accused Clinton of legal or moral violations in connection with campaign contributions from Indonesian banking interests, the Whitewater scandal, the FBI files scandal, the White House travel office scandal, conflict-of-interest violations by Clinton appointees, and Clinton's alleged laxity about smoking marijuana—the latter the focus of a major Dole television advertisement. "I'll tell you one thing," Dole told a New Jersey audience, "I'll keep my word and I'll behave myself in the White House." [17] Perot ended his campaign by highlighting the scandals in the Clinton administration. He warned that Clinton "faced huge moral, ethical, and criminal problems" and predicted, "We are going to have a second Watergate and a constitutional crisis in 1997." [18]

Partly because Clinton did not deign to answer such charges, however, there was virtually no discussion of their actual merit. How likely was it that Clinton or his staff had acted illegally or immorally in the various matters?[19] How clear and serious were any such violations? And how crucial is this aspect of character to the presidency? Voters were neither enlightened nor induced to reflect on any of these questions.

Meanwhile, Dole and Perot mostly ignored aspects of Clinton's personality that had clear bearing on his performance as president. As Graham Wilson put it, "President Clinton vacillates . . . partly because he cannot make up his own mind and partly because he wants to please the last group to have spoken to him." [20] The result, during the first two years of his presidency, was an administration characterized by "indecision, uncertainty, and delay." [21] In our view, it would have been pertinent to debate whether, despite Clinton's improved performance in 1995 and 1996, these weaknesses were likely to reemerge in a second term.

Finally, the campaign essentially overlooked the obvious and significant issue of Dole's age. How likely was it that a seventy-three-year old male could work at a stressful job for four years without a major interruption or loss of capability caused by illness? In view of those risks, how satisfactory are the constitutional provisions for dealing with a president's death or disability? Clinton did not raise these issues, probably because doing so would have appeared mean-spirited. Here too, the voters were neither enlightened nor induced to reflect on an important aspect of presidential qualifications.

Commitments

The election campaign establishes the commitments that the president-elect will bring into office. The president's chances for success in governing will depend partly on whether those commitments, made in the heat of the campaign, still make sense, substantively and politically, after the election.

Varieties of Commitment

Political cynics like to suggest that campaign promises are made to be broken and have virtually no significance after the election. In fact, presidents work hard to fulfill most of the promises that they made during the campaign.[22] Looking at the presidencies from John F. Kennedy through Reagan's first term, Jeff Fishel found that presidents, on average, submitted legislation or signed executive orders consistent with roughly two-thirds of their campaign promises. Even the lowest-scoring president, Reagan, acted on more than half of his 1980 promises (including some of the most dramatic and important ones).[23]

Presidential candidates make commitments partly by promising specific actions, such as Carter's 1976 pledge to create a Department of Education and Reagan's 1980 vow to cut income taxes by 30 percent. They also make promises, implicitly, by attacking the proposals, past actions, or alleged intentions of the opposing candidate, as in Johnson's devastating attack in 1964 on Republican candidate Barry Goldwater's plan to abolish Social Security; the promise implicit in such attacks is to act differently. In either case, it is politically costly for presidents to go back on their word, and they try hard to avoid doing so.

Presidential promise making and promise keeping are generally constructive for popular control of government—which is the whole point of democratic elections. They give voters some confidence that what they see in a candidate is what they will get if they elect him or her as president. Moreover, the winner's promises sometimes have a larger effect. If a presidential candidate campaigns largely on issues and wins the election by a comfortable margin, his promises become his "mandate": It is widely assumed in the

Washington community that the voters have endorsed those promises.[24] Johnson's landslide victory in 1964, for example, was viewed as a mandate for his Great Society programs.

Very often, however, the effect of such promises is less benign, reflecting the voters' lack of sophistication and the superficiality of campaign debate. In pursuit of votes, a candidate may make promises that serve the needs of the campaign but that are problematic, at best, from the standpoint of governing. Such promises may exploit the voters' limited information or appeal to their emotions, stereotypes, or wishful thinking. These campaign-driven, sound-bite promises may call for policies that in all likelihood are not feasible, would have unacceptable costs, or would accomplish little while distracting attention from meaningful solutions. After the election, a president who has made such promises will face pressure to make good on them. He may fail to deliver, may use precious time and political support in pointless efforts, or, still worse, may deliver on the promises and harm the country.

Such problems do not arise from mere puffery—claims that are so vague or obviously hyperbolic that they have no specific implications. Nixon's famous promise to "bring us together" or Kennedy's vow to "get the country moving again" created no constraints on their actions as president.

Nor can we identify misleading promises with anything approaching perfect objectivity. Judging from discussion among informed, especially nonpartisan commentators, however, we can array campaign claims, very roughly, on a continuum from the unexceptionable to the almost completely unbelievable. Virtually everyone now understands that Reagan's 1980 campaign promise to balance the budget while cutting taxes 30 percent and raising defense spending was little more than a fantasy. So was Bush's 1988 promise to reduce the deficit with no new taxes. In much the same way, Democrats have demagogued on entitlement programs and environmental protection. In the 1990s major policy proposals seem increasingly to reflect a sound-bite mentality: a two-year limit on welfare, "three strikes and you're out" for criminal sentencing, and the death penalty for a proliferating number of crimes.

To provide the basis for successful presidential governance, the candidates should impose some discipline on their claims and promises and keep them reasonably connected with reality. And the campaign debate and media coverage should provide enough scrutiny of the candidates' positions to induce such discretion or, failing that, to help the voters discount the exaggerations.[25] Put simply, there should not be a vast gulf between the rhetoric of the campaign and the realities of governing.

Commitments and the 1996 Campaign

By far the largest and most discussed policy commitment of the 1996 campaign was Dole's proposal, announced shortly before the Republican convention, "to reduce taxes 15 percent across-the-board for every taxpayer in America." [26] Dole also promised to balance the budget by the year 2000 "without touching Social Security or Medicare" and without cutting defense.[27] The proposal followed in the tradition of Republican radical supply-side economics, which Dole had conscientiously resisted for fifteen years. But unlike Reagan's and Bush's antitax appeals in the 1980s, Dole's invocation of supply-side doctrine was ineffective for his campaign.

Like the Reagan tax cut, Dole's proposal was treated roughly by professional economists. To be sure, the Dole campaign lined up endorsements from a number of economists, including conservative Nobel prize-winner Milton Friedman. But in a survey of sixty university macroeconomists, the *Economist* magazine found that only 22 percent supported Dole's plan. Forty-six percent preferred Clinton's targeted tax cuts, and 32 percent opposed both.[28] Most experts believed that Dole's plan would reverse the trend of the preceding four years, in which time the annual budget deficit declined by 63 percent, from $290 billion in 1992 to $107 billion in 1996, the smallest inflation-adjusted deficit since 1974.[29]

In the televised presidential debates, Clinton cited the *Economist* survey to attack Dole's proposal. He warned that Dole's plan would "blow a hole in the budget deficit." Although misstated (if the deficit is bad, blowing a hole in it should be good), that warning became a constant refrain of the Clinton campaign.

For reasons that are not entirely clear, the voters, unlike in the past, shared the economists' and Democrats' skepticism and never warmed to Dole's proposals. Only 11 percent of the voters named taxes as the issue that mattered most in deciding their vote, fewer than chose "economy/jobs," "Medicare/Social Security," or "education." Just 30 percent agreed that "Bob Dole would be able to reduce the federal budget deficit and cut taxes by 15 percent at the same time." Of the two-thirds of voters who disagreed, 66 percent voted for Clinton.[30]

It is unlikely that the voters in 1996, compared with voters in other recent elections, had become more attentive to campaign debate or more sophisticated about economics. Instead, they may at long last have become more concerned about the budget deficit. "Forget the damn tax cut," a midwestern factory manager said, "We should use that money to get rid of the deficit." [31] They may also have been unwilling to suppress their doubts for the benefit of a candidate whom, for other reasons, they did not like very much anyway.

Clinton's campaign commitments had some of the same difficulties as Dole's, although on a lesser scale. Clinton offered the voters what he called "targeted" tax cuts, such as a tax credit to help pay for college tuition.[32] At the same time, he promised to balance the budget by 2002. With attention focused on Dole's plan, Clinton's escaped much scrutiny. But it was hardly more clear how his tax cuts would be paid for. The budget deficit, after falling throughout Clinton's first term, was projected to rebound to $171 billion in 1997 and then rise steadily to $285 billion in 2002.[33] Clinton's budget-balancing plan assumed $50 billion of additional tax revenues over the next six years. Even targeted tax cuts would make such an accomplishment more difficult.[34]

Clinton's most problematic commitment, however, stemmed from his repeated, effective attacks on the efforts by Dole and the congressional Republicans in 1995 to slow the growth of costs in the Medicare program. "You work your whole life and hope for a secure retirement," a Clinton television advertisement said. "That's why it's so wrong that Dole and Gingrich tried to slash Medicare $270 billion."[35]

Unfortunately for Clinton's position, the Medicare trust fund, which in recent years has covered the deficit between Medicare premiums and expenses, is expected to be exhausted in 2001. Medicare expenses, moreover, have been growing at an annual rate of 9–10 percent. With 38 million Medicare beneficiaries, the looming insolvency of the Medicare trust fund is likely to be the major issue of Clinton's second term. And after resorting to what Republicans called the "Mediscare" strategy, Clinton may be severely constrained in his ability to deal with it. As Senate majority leader Trent Lott said after the election,

> On Medicare [President Clinton] has been irresponsible. He has misled the people, he has misinformed them, he has been disingenuous. . . . And I think he needs to admit that Republicans were not so far off base, and in fact we're probably right.[36]

Such admissions come hard, however, even from a safely reelected president.

Support

The results of presidential and especially congressional elections go far toward determining whether the president will have political support for his or her policies. Such support is crucial to the president's chances for policy success. In particular, a "presidency of achievement," such as those of Wilson, Franklin Roosevelt, Johnson, or Reagan, depends on a highly supportive political environment.[37]

Support for a president's policies is less critical for his popular success, however. Clinton staged a political comeback in 1995 and 1996 largely by opposing the aggressive conservatives who controlled Congress. Nor is such support essential for success in governing. In fact, the government often works fairly well when the president and Congress are controlled by different parties.[38] Provided that the two parties are reasonably disposed to cooperate, presidents may negotiate with an opposition-party Congress to deal effectively with national problems even if they cannot enact their own preferences.[39]

Elections and the Sources of Support

Elections affect support for the president's policies in several ways. Most important, they determine the partisan and ideological balance in Congress.

As considerable research demonstrates, presidential influence in Congress depends more on that balance than on any presidential characteristics such as popularity or leadership skill.[40]

In one important study, Jon Bond and Richard Fleisher divide the members of Congress into four groups on the basis of their party and ideology.[41] Members of the president's party who largely share his ideology (for example, liberal Democrats for a liberal Democratic president) form the president's political base and are most likely to vote with him. From these members, presidents from Dwight D. Eisenhower to Reagan received annual rates of support on roll-call votes from 63 to 90 percent in the House and from 71 to 81 percent in the Senate. Opposition-party members who are ideologically opposed to the president (for example, conservative Republicans for a liberal Democratic president) form the opposition political base. From these members, presidents from Eisenhower through Reagan received support levels from 23 to 45 percent in the House and from 25 to 42 percent in the Senate. Members who were partially allied with the president, sharing either his partisanship or his ideology but not both, supported the president's positions at rates closer to 50 percent.[42] Other things being equal, a president whose political base dominates Congress will have a far better chance to pass his bills than one who faces a dominant opposition base.

The effects of the composition of Congress on the president's influence were highly evident during Clinton's first term. In 1993 and 1994, when he enjoyed Democratic majorities in both the House and the Senate, Clinton got his way more than 85 percent of the time in each house on roll-call votes on which he took a position. After the loss of both houses to the Republicans in the 1994 midterm elections, his success rate dropped precipitously. In 1995 Clinton won only 26 percent of the roll calls in the House, the lowest success rate on record, and 49 percent in the Senate. As both Clinton and congressional Republicans moved toward the center in 1996, Clinton had more success, winning 53 percent of the important votes in the House and 58 percent in the Senate; but these success rates were still low by historical standards, even for presidents who faced Congresses controlled by the opposition party.[43]

In addition, the congressional campaigns are an important barometer of national opinion on the president's policies and the role of government. The campaigns of the nearly one thousand congressional candidates constitute a massive and highly visible test of which issues and themes have force in the current climate of opinion. If, for example, Democratic congressional candidates constantly stress their association with the Democratic nominee for president, campaign on his or her policies, and are elected along with the presidential nominee in large numbers, the results are taken as powerful evidence of national support for the president's agenda. If, on the other hand, Democratic congressional candidates avoid speaking their standard bearer's name and they campaign largely on Republican themes, their strategy indicates that the Democrats have lost or surrendered in the philosophical battle.[44]

To a lesser degree, how a president is elected also affects congressional support for his agenda. One important aspect of the president's manner of election, discussed above, is whether he campaigned primarily on issues. Another is the effect of the campaign on what Richard Neustadt called the president's reputation and prestige.[45] Presidents who have suffered effective attacks on their character or competence, endured embarrassing gaffes and scandals, and been viewed by many voters as the lesser of two evils will have diminished ability to rally support. In Clinton's first term, for example, the questions that had been raised during the 1992 campaign about his avoiding service in Vietnam undermined his credibility as commander in chief. This lack of credibility helped defeat his effort to end the ban on homosexuals in the armed forces.

The most important aspect of the president's manner of election, at least in the short run, is the margin of victory. Winners of landslides are given credit for popularity and an ability to rally public support. They thus receive longer or more generous honeymoons in Congress. In 1981 Reagan's economic program derived powerful momentum from his late surge to overtake Carter and win by a ten percentage point margin in the popular vote. After the 1992 elections, Senate minority leader Dole pronounced Clinton's honeymoon, in effect, canceled—pointing out on election night and repeatedly afterward that a majority of the voters had rejected his candidacy.

The elections also shape the disposition of the two parties to collaborate in effecting policy change. If the opposing campaigns are ideologically divisive and feature brutal negative attacks, the parties are likely to carry the spirit of partisan warfare into government. If centrist strategies are more prominent and negative attacks more restrained, the potential for bipartisan cooperation is greater. The parties derive lessons about the rewards for confrontation or cooperation from how the voters respond to those strategies. In 1995 congressional Republicans adopted an exceptionally aggressive partisan posture partly because their obstruction of Clinton during his first two years had seemed to pay off in the 1994 congressional races.

The potential for bipartisanship also depends on what kinds of members are elected: moderates or ideologues. For some years, a gradual realignment of the party system has been weeding out the moderates—liberal Republicans and conservative Democrats—and thus shrinking the base for bipartisan coalitions.[46]

Elections can provide the necessary support for a successful presidency, therefore, in more than one way. To permit substantial policy achievements guided by the president's own agenda, the president should campaign on the issues, avoid significant damage to his image, and win the election by a large margin. Furthermore, congressional candidates of the president's party should link themselves with the president, campaign on the same issues, and win their elections in large numbers. To permit governing success through negotiation and compromise, the parties should avoid polarizing, highly ideological campaigns and vicious negative attacks, the campaigns should expose and penalize confrontationist tactics, and the voters should send a healthy number of moderates to Congress.

Support and the 1996 Election

Although Clinton won a second term as president by a comfortable margin, the campaigns and results of the 1996 elections offer him no prospect of achieving easy policy successes or even of defining the agenda for Congress. The elections produced somewhat favorable short-term conditions for bipartisan cooperation, giving Clinton an apparent opportunity for governing success. But they also revealed increasing long-term obstacles to such cooperation.

In terms of partisan composition, the 105th Congress should be at least as resistant to leadership by a Democratic president as the Republican 104th Congress, which fought pitched battles with Clinton over the budget, welfare, and other issues. The Republicans made a modest gain in the Senate elections. With the addition of seats in Alabama, Nebraska, and Arkansas, and the loss of only one seat, in South Dakota, they increased their Senate majority from fifty-three to fifty-five seats. They suffered a comparable loss in the House of Representatives, giving up nine seats. But they still maintained a nineteen-seat majority, with 227 Republican members. Because the rules of the House give more power to a narrow partisan majority than those of the Senate, the Republicans' House losses are less important than their Senate gains, and, on balance, the results should strengthen Republican control of Congress.

In addition to winning the congressional elections, the Republicans appear to have succeeded in changing the course of the political system. Few Democrats campaigned on promises of activist government, civil rights, or social and economic equality. The inner-city poor were hardly mentioned, except in regard to getting them off welfare. Democrats followed Republicans in promising low taxes, deregulation, and the shifting of responsibility from Washington to the states. Such campaigns reflected the public mood. A September 1996 poll found, for example, that 62 percent of the public believed the federal government did too much, while only 28 percent thought it should do more.[47]

The elections did not enhance Clinton's political standing or personal influence. He failed, by one percentage point, to win a majority of the popular vote. As a result, congressional opponents can claim (convincingly or not) to speak for the majority of Americans. In addition, the attacks on Clinton's ethics by Dole and Perot, along with a late-breaking scandal involving possible Democratic fund-raising violations, reinforced public doubts about his character. Such considerations had little effect on the vote. A week before the election, 54 percent of respondents to the CBS/*New York Times* poll said the ethics charges had not affected their voting plans at all, and only 8 percent said the charges had caused them to change their minds.[48] But the campaign left Clinton a decidedly untrusted president-elect. In the exit poll, only 41 percent of the voters said they trusted Clinton; 54 percent, some of whom nonetheless voted for him, said they did not.[49] If Clinton had won, say, 55 percent of the total vote (roughly his percentage of the two-party vote), and if most people who voted for him had a high regard for his character and leadership, members of Congress probably would show him more deference.

In effect, the main result of the 1996 elections was to reelect divided government. Far from being able to set the congressional agenda or pass a program of his own design, Clinton may have to rely for legislative influence on his ability to block action, either by vetoing or threatening to veto bills or by calling on Senate Democrats to use the filibuster. To achieve successes in governing, he will have to negotiate with the Republican Congress.

For the long term, the apparent trends in American electoral politics are distinctly unfavorable for bipartisan strategies. The 1996 elections produced a more ideologically polarized Congress. In the Senate, five retiring Republican moderates were replaced by conservatives; the Republican Senate majority thus has become not only a little larger but also a good deal more conservative.[50] Although the House Republicans lost seats, they did not drift toward the center. Five-sixths of the first-term Republicans, most of them avid supporters of the party's 1994 Contract with America, survived the election.[51]

The increase in ideological polarization in Congress that occurred in 1996 continued the trend of recent congressional elections and reflected, at bottom, the long-term realignment of the American party system. Moderately liberal Republicans in the Northeast are being replaced by even more liberal Democrats. Moderately conservative Democrats in the South are being replaced by even more conservative Republicans. In some districts dominated by racial or ethnic minorities, liberal Democrats are being replaced by very liberal Democrats. As a result, the political base for bipartisan policy making is shrinking.

Nevertheless, for the immediate future and perhaps for all of Clinton's second term, strong forces are pushing the president and the congressional Republicans toward working together. Clinton campaigned on a mostly conservative platform. He endorsed a reduction in the capital gains tax, signed a tough welfare reform bill, and pressed the television industry to adopt a voluntary ratings system for its programs. As the Dole campaign found to its dismay in June, the Clinton-Gore Web site already was displaying slogans that the Republican nominee had intended to champion: "strengthen America's families," "take back our streets from crime, gangs, and drugs," and "making government work better and cost less."[52]

For their part, the Republicans have learned from painful experience the virtues of moderation and cooperation. The public blamed them for repeatedly shutting down the government during the 1995 budget stalemate. The Democrats and their allies, such as labor unions, scored in the 1996 campaign by attacking radical Republican "Newtoids" and their schemes to cut

Medicare, Medicaid, education, and the environment. For a time, it appeared
that the Republicans might pay heavily for their overreaching. A June 1996
Washington Post poll found that public support for congressional Republicans had fallen to 38 percent—far below their 53 percent of the national vote
in 1994 and low enough to threaten a debacle in November.[53] Although the
party's vote rebounded to 50 percent on election day, Republicans will be
more leery of adopting extreme positions and confrontationist tactics for the
near future.

After the elections, the talk at both ends of Pennsylvania Avenue was
about bipartisanship. Gingrich went as far as to cede the initiative in setting
the national agenda to the White House, a remarkable reversal, even if merely rhetorical, from 1995. "We ought to work with him and give him a chance
to lead in the direction he campaigned on, and if he sticks to the things he
campaigned on, we should be able to find some common ground," Gingrich
said.[54] Senate majority leader Lott granted that "the President is sort of enti-
tled to the first at-bat."[55] In a more tangible sign of the new Republican posture, Sen. Alfonse D'Amato announced that he would not resume the Whitewater hearings. Clinton welcomed the Republican overtures and vowed to
name one or more Republicans to his new cabinet, a vow he fulfilled by
appointing retiring Republican senator William Cohen as secretary of
defense.

The Prospects for Presidential Governance

The 1996 elections went a long way toward defining the circumstances
of Clinton's second term. In what they revealed about electoral politics in this
era, the elections also have implications for future presidencies.

The prospects for effective presidential governance during the second
term are reasonably favorable. In Clinton, the voters selected a person who,
despite widely discussed and significant shortcomings, has considerable credentials for the job. (Much the same could have been said about Dole if he
had won.) Clinton has some extraordinary skills, especially in understanding
domestic policy and in communicating with the public. He also has shown
some glaring deficiencies—especially in staffing and managing the White
House and implementing a consistent political strategy. But by the end of his
first term, Clinton appeared to have learned a great deal and had largely
overcome his difficulties in those areas. That much of the public doubts his
personal integrity, owing to a variety of scandals and accusations of miscon-
duct, is certainly a liability. But it is not likely to affect the quality of his decisions or to undermine seriously the performance of government during his
administration. With the exception of the Medicare issue, where his campaign posturing may constrain his actions, Clinton largely avoided reckless
commitments that would have made it difficult to govern responsibly.

The elections did not give Clinton a strong mandate or automatic congressional support for his policies. They kept Congress solidly under Repub-

lican control. But they at least provided possibilities of bipartisan support for the centrist-conservative agenda that Clinton has pursued since 1994. Just as the 1994 elections drove Clinton and the Democrats toward the center, the 1996 elections, which highlighted the massive unpopularity of the confrontationist Gingrich, may drive Republicans to the same place.

At the same time, however, the indications from the 1996 elections about the functioning of the electoral process have troubling implications for future presidents. On the bright side, the campaign produced evidence of reduced and even negative voter response to substantively dubious campaign promises. The voters clearly rejected extravagant antitax rhetoric for the first time since Reagan introduced radical supply-side economics into presidential politics in the 1980 campaign. But this development should not inspire much confidence about the likelihood of avoiding reckless campaign-driven commitments in the future. The seeming reversal of fortune for antitax rhetoric was suspiciously dramatic. Conceivably, the public has become more sophisticated in evaluating campaign promises. Alternatively, after fifteen years of national anxiety about budget deficits, the public may have become more skeptical, specifically, about plans to cut taxes or increase spending. But it is also possible that voters rejected Dole's tax-cut proposal because they had already rejected his candidacy. If the last explanation is principally correct, the next presidential candidate to overlook budget realities by promising massive tax cuts or benefit increases may be more successful.

Moreover, difficulties for presidents and national policy making inhere in the trend toward increasing ideological polarization of Congress—the replacement of moderates by hard-line liberals and conservatives. In the near term, these difficulties are mitigated by the fact that both parties have had recent sad experience with voter rejection of ideologically extreme or confrontational positions. Nevertheless, the trend is apparently toward more severe partisan and ideological conflict. If it continues, future presidents will have ever greater difficulty avoiding deadlock. Even though most Americans are ideologically moderate, it will be especially difficult to build a working coalition for a centrist program.[56]

Finally, the 1996 elections demonstrated that the voters have a remarkably high tolerance for presidential candidates who, by any conventional or historical criteria, lack crucial qualifications for the presidency. Both parties nominated early front-runners who despite weaknesses were, by such criteria, highly qualified. But it is not evident that their qualifications, such as extensive experience and demonstrated capabilities in coalition building, played a role in their nominations. Dole tried to distance himself from his Washington experience, resigning from the Senate to become "just a man."

More important, voters in the Republican primaries quickly dispatched several conventionally well-qualified candidates—governors and senators from the mainstream of the party—and elevated a pair of inexperienced, confrontationist, and ideologically extreme candidates, Buchanan and Forbes, to the rank of Dole's principal challengers. Similar tastes had been evident in the widespread voter support for Perot's independent candidacy in 1992. We began with the aphorism that as presidents are elected, so will they govern. We conclude that in view of how presidents are elected in the current era, they are likely to have increasing trouble governing responsibly. We may soon have a president who has no experience in government, holds extreme and uninformed views about public policy, and has neither skills nor the taste for coalition building. That president may see his or her mission as carrying out campaign promises that could not withstand rational scrutiny. The president's institutional partner in this venture, Congress, may be consumed with partisan and ideological warfare and unable to supply the missing moderation and responsibility.

Notes

1. Donald R. Kinder, Mark D. Peters, Robert P. Abelson, and Susan T. Fiske, "Presidential Prototypes," *Political Behavior* 2 (1980): 315–337. The Kinder et al. study relied on a 1979 survey by the Center for Political Studies at the University of Michigan. Respondents in the national survey were given eight good traits, eight bad traits, eight good behaviors, and eight bad behaviors for an ideal president and were asked to choose four from each category that were most important for a president to have or not to have. In a second section they were asked how well four presidential candidates fulfilled each of the thirty-two attributes. Interestingly, Kinder et al. found no evidence that voters use these presidential prototypes in making voting decisions, but voters did appear to use them in assessing incumbent performance. See also Stephen J. Wayne, "Great Expectations: What People Want from Presidents," in *Rethinking the Presidency,* ed. Thomas E. Cronin (Boston: Little, Brown, 1982).
2. Kinder et al., "Presidential Prototypes," 333.
3. George C. Edwards and Stephen J. Wayne, *Presidential Leadership: Politics and Policy Making* (New York: St. Martin's, 1990), 100–102.
4. See Erwin C. Hargrove and Michael Nelson, *Presidents, Politics, and Policy* (Baltimore: Johns Hopkins University Press, 1984), and Paul J. Quirk, "Presidential Competence," in *The Presidency and the Political System,* 4th ed., ed. Michael Nelson (Washington, D.C.: CQ Press, 1995).
5. Barbara Kellerman, *The Political Presidency* (New York: Oxford University Press, 1984).
6. Richard Rose, "Learning to Govern or Learning to Campaign?" in *Presidential Selection,* ed. Alexander Heard and Michael Nelson (Durham, N.C.: Duke University Press, 1987).
7. Michael Nelson, "Who Vies for President?" in *Presidential Selection.*
8. See David Broder, "Al Gore: A Close Second," *Washington Post National Weekly Edition,* September 2–8, 1996, 6–7.
9. James David Barber. *The Presidential Character* (Englewood Cliffs, N.J.: Prentice-Hall, 1972).
10. Jeffrey Tulis, "On Presidential Character," in *The Presidency in the Constitutional Order,* ed. Jeffrey Tulis and Joseph M. Bessette (Baton Rouge: Louisiana State University Press, 1977), 287.
11. Dean K. Simonton, *Why Presidents Succeed: A Political Psychology of Leadership* (New Haven: Yale University Press, 1987), 230–232. Although there is some evidence that a president's motivation (generally conceived as the desire for

power, achievement, or affiliation) influences his behavior, no clearly preferable motivation has been established. David Winter and Abigail Stewart, for instance, found that desire for power, a trait most Americans express concern over, is strongly correlated with greater presidential success. The only two traits that do seem to be desirable are open-mindedness and intellectual sophistication. See David G. Winter and Abigail J. Stewart, "Content Analysis as a Technique for Assessing Political Leaders," in *A Psychological Examination of Political Leaders,* ed. Margaret G. Hermann (New York: Free Press, 1977), 28–62.

12. See also Alexander L. George and Juliette L. George, *Woodrow Wilson and Colonel House* (New York: Day, 1956).
13. Elizabeth Drew, *On the Edge: The Clinton Presidency* (New York: Simon and Schuster, 1994).
14. Reagan exhibited striking deficiencies of memory and factual knowledge as early as the 1980 campaign and throughout his presidency. By the end of his second term his increasingly severe lapses provoked press speculation that he was becoming senile. By the mid-1990s, Reagan was unable to make public appearances because he was suffering from advanced Alzheimer's disease. Because the course of Alzheimer's disease can be twenty years or more, it is very possible that Reagan's forgetfulness and simplistic thinking were caused by the disease throughout his presidency.
15. Fred Greenstein, "The Presidential Leadership Style of Bill Clinton: An Early Appraisal," *Political Science Quarterly* 108 (1993–1994): 598–599.
16. Paul J. Quirk and Joseph Hinchliffe, "Domestic Policy: The Trials of a Centrist Democrat," in *The Clinton Presidency: First Appraisals,* ed. Colin Campbell and Bert A. Rockman (Chatham, N.J.: Chatham House, 1995), 284–285.
17. Quoted in Katherine Q. Seelve, "Ethics Pushed in Challenger's Four-Day Tour," *New York Times,* November 3, 1996, 1.
18. Quoted in Ernest Tollerson, "Perot Sees Moral Problems for Clinton in '97," *New York Times,* October 25, 1996, A10; and "Perot to Spend Millions on TV Commercials," *New York Times,* November 3, 1996, 21.
19. Many of the criticisms of Clinton's character have been "based on hearsay or shaky evidence from sources with axes to grind." Betty Glad, "Judging Presidential Character" (Paper delivered at the annual meeting of the American Political Science Association, San Francisco, August 31, 1996).
20. Graham K. Wilson, "The Clinton Administration and Interest Groups," in *The Clinton Presidency: First Appraisals,* 212–233.
21. Bert Rockman, "Leadership Style and the Clinton Presidency," in *The Clinton Presidency: First Appraisals,* 325–362.
22. Jeff Fishel, *Presidents and Promises* (Washington, D.C.: CQ Press, 1985).
23. Ibid., 38–39.
24. John H. Aldrich, "Presidential Selection," in *Researching the Presidency: Vital Questions, New Approaches* (Pittsburgh: University of Pittsburgh Press, 1993), 23–68.
25. On the limitations of media coverage, see Thomas E. Patterson, *Out of Order* (New York: Random House, 1994).
26. The quote is from Dole's acceptance speech, Republican National Convention, August 15, 1996, reprinted in *Congressional Quarterly Weekly Report,* August 17, 1996, 2346–2350.
27. Remarks by Bob Dole to the Economic Conference of the Republican Governors' Association, Detroit, Mich., October 21, 1996. Federal Clearing House, 1996.
28. "Economists for Clinton," *Economist,* October 5, 1996. The *Economist* randomly selected sixty macroeconomists from fifteen of the top universities in the United States, of whom 70 percent responded.

29. In constant dollars, the 1996 deficit is the smallest since 1981. Alison Mitchel, "Clinton Hails Drop in Deficit, Declaring 'America's Awake'," *New York Times,* October 29, 1996.
30. These data were obtained from the PoliticsNow Web site *(http://www.politicsnow.com).*
31. Quoted in David E. Sanger, "Dole's Tax Message Heard, Not Heeded, in Midwest City," *New York Times,* September 18, 1996, A1.
32. John F. Harris, "Smack Dab in the Middle," *Washington Post National Weekly Edition,* November 4–10, 1996, 11.
33. Andrew Mollison, "Cutting the Deficit: Gains vs. Risks; Both Major Plans Are Full of Pitfalls, Experts Caution," *Atlanta Journal and Constitution,* October 31, 1996, A14.
34. David E. Sanger, "Drop Is Not Only Stunning, but Also a Mystery," *New York Times,* October 29, 1996, A10.
35. Presidential campaign press materials, Federal Document Clearing House, 1996.
36. Jerry Gray, "Bipartisan Mood Starting to Fade on Potent Issues," *New York Times,* November 11, 1996, A1, A8.
37. The term is from Hargrove and Nelson, *Presidents, Politics, and Policy.*
38. David Mayhew, *Divided We Govern* (New Haven: Yale University Press, 1992); Paul J. Quirk and Bruce Nesmith, "Divided Government and Policymaking: Negotiating the Laws," in *The Presidency and the Political System,* 531–554.
39. Charles O. Jones, *The Presidency in a Separated System* (Washington, D.C.: Brookings Institution, 1994).
40. Jon R. Bond and Richard Fleisher, *The President in the Legislative Arena* (Chicago: University of Chicago Press, 1990); George Edwards, *At the Margins: Presidential Leadership of Congress* (New Haven: Yale University Press, 1989); Mark Peterson, *Legislating Together* (Cambridge: Harvard University Press, 1996).
41. Bond and Fleisher, *The President in the Legislative Arena,* 44–45.
42. Ibid., 90, 93.
43. Jon Healey, "Clinton Success Rate Declined to a Record Low in 1995," *Congressional Quarterly Weekly Report,* January 27, 1996, 193–198; Carroll J. Doherty, "Clinton's Big Comeback Shown in Vote Score," *Congressional Quarterly Weekly Report,* December 21, 1996, 3427–3430.
44. For a fuller discussion of systemic influences on presidential performance, see Stephen Skowronek, *The Politics Presidents Make: Leadership from John Adams to George Bush* (Cambridge: Belknap Press, Harvard University Press, 1993), and *Presidents, Politics, and Policy.*
45. See Richard Neustadt, *Presidential Power* (New York: Wiley, 1960); Richard Neustadt, *Presidential Power and the Modern Presidents: The Politics of Leadership from Roosevelt to Reagan* (New York: Free Press, 1990). Neustadt's emphasis on the president's personal attributes has been seriously challenged since 1960, at least with respect to leadership of Congress. See the works cited in note 40.
46. Joseph Cooper and Garry Young, "Partisanship, Bipartisanship, and Crosspartisanship in Congress Since the New Deal," in *Congress Reconsidered,* 6th ed., ed. Lawrence C. Dodd and Bruce I. Oppenheimer (Washington, D.C.: CQ Press, 1997), 246–273.
47. James A. Barnes, "Planting the Seeds," *National Journal,* November 9, 1996, 2404. Although the public has rarely been friendly toward the federal government in general, these findings certainly indicate a conservative mood.
48. Richard L. Berke, "After a Long Trip, Election Arithmetic Has Gone Nowhere," *New York Times,* November 4, 1996, A1, A12.

49. Of those voters who thought issues mattered more, 70 percent voted for Clinton. Of those who thought character mattered more, 71 percent voted for Dole. Data are from Voter News Service exit polls, as reported in *National Journal*, November 9, 1996, 2408.
50. Retiring moderates were Dole and Nancy Kassebaum of Kansas, Alan Simpson of Wyoming, Hank Brown of Colorado, and Mark Hatfield of Oregon. Richard E. Cohen, "A Lott of Change," *National Journal*, November 9, 1996, 2439.
51. James Brooke, "Despite Narrow Victory, Republican Is Unbowed," *New York Times*, November 11, 1996, A8.
52. *Newsweek*, Special election issue, November 18, 1996, 81.
53. *Washington Post National Weekly Edition*, June 24–30, 1996, 12.
54. Quoted in Francis X. Clines, "Gingrich, Role as House Leader Intact, Offers Clinton an Olive Branch," *New York Times*, November 7, 1996.
55. Quoted in Adam Clymer, "Top Republicans Say They Seek 'Common Ground' with Clinton," *New York Times*, November 7, 1996.
56. Cooper and Young, "Partisanship, Bipartisanship, and Crosspartisanship in Congress Since the New Deal," in *Congress Reconsidered*, 6th ed.

7

The 105th Congress:
Unprecedented and Unsurprising

Gary C. Jacobson

After the upheavals of 1992 and 1994, the elections of 1996 look positively mundane. Democrat Bill Clinton, the incumbent president, won reelection by a comfortable margin, while the Republicans retained control of the House of Representatives (with a slightly smaller majority than before) and the Senate (with a slightly larger majority). After dumping a sitting Republican president in 1992 and ending the Democrats' forty-year reign in the House in 1994, voters in 1996 simply endorsed the status quo. But from a historical perspective, the results of the 1996 elections are anything but mundane. Indeed, they are totally unprecedented. While opting for the status quo, American voters did something they have never done before. From Thomas Jefferson in 1800 to William Jefferson Clinton in 1996, voters have elected twenty-six Democrats as president. Clinton is the first who did not bring a Democratic majority into the House with him, and he is only the third (after Andrew Jackson in 1832 and Grover Cleveland in 1884) whose party did not win a Senate majority as well.

The idea that the Democrats could win the White House by eight million votes without winning control of Congress would have been unthinkable only a few years ago. Yet by the time it happened, few informed political observers were surprised. That the 1996 election results were both unprecedented and unsurprising shows how profoundly the balance of partisan competition in congressional elections has changed. The purpose of this chapter is to use the 1996 House and Senate elections to illuminate this historic transformation and to consider what it may portend for electoral politics through the rest of the century.

Prelude: The 1994 Elections and the 104th Congress

The key to understanding what happened in 1996 lies in understanding what happened two years earlier, when Republicans took control of both houses of Congress for the first time in four decades. That victory, and the uses the Republican majority sought to make of it, were the dominant forces shaping the 1996 elections for both president and Congress. On the presidential side, the Republican Congress contributed mightily to Clinton's political revival and ultimate victory. To be sure, Clinton benefited in 1996 from a strong economy and relative international calm. But he also suffered from

widespread public doubts about his integrity, and peace and prosperity had
not helped the Democrats in 1994. The strong economy may have been necessary for his reelection, but it was not sufficient. Clinton coasted to victory
only because the Republican majorities elected in 1994 allowed him to rede-
fine his presidency, although, ironically, in a way that ultimately helped the
Republicans to retain control of Congress.

The conventional wisdom is that the House Republicans overplayed
their hand in 1995, opening the way to Clinton's political resurrection. In
this case, the conventional wisdom has it exactly right. Inspired by their historic triumph in 1994 and heady success in acting on every item in their
Contract with America within the promised first hundred days of the 104th
Congress, House Republicans, led by Speaker Newt Gingrich, took on the
federal budget. Pushing for radical changes simultaneously on many fronts,
they sought to slash or terminate numerous government programs and agencies, including some with potent constituencies, to achieve their professed
goal of balancing the budget by 2002, while reducing taxes by some $240
billion.

Clinton met the Republican challenge deftly. He agreed to accept in
principle those of the Republicans' goals that were popular (a balanced budget, a smaller federal government), while attacking the Republicans on the
means they chose to pursue them (cuts in Medicare spending for the elderly
and those with disabilities, Medicaid for recipients of welfare benefits, school
lunches, student loans, and environmental protection), which were far less
popular. In adopting this strategy, Clinton followed the political logic that
has driven budget politics since the early 1980s. The fundamental reality
shaping recent budget politics is that majorities of Americans want mutually
incompatible things from government: low taxes, a balanced budget, and
generous middle-class entitlements programs (such as Social Security,
Medicare, and tax deductions for mortgage payments and college tuition).
Incompatible preferences are not confined to budgets; Americans also want
a government that is smaller and less intrusive than it is now but that
nonetheless protects their health, safety, physical environment, and economic well-being. But conflicting goals emerge most conspicuously in fights over
the budget.

The public favors a balanced budget but not the sacrifices it takes to get
one: cuts in middle-class entitlements, higher taxes, or both. Thus every time
political leaders get serious about the deficit, they invite electoral punishment. Republican president George Bush and his party were badly damaged
when he went back on his "no new taxes" pledge in 1990 to attack the
deficit.[1] Clinton and his party were punished in 1994 for his 1993 deficit-
reduction package.[2] In 1995 it was the congressional Republicans' turn. To
carry out their promise of reducing taxes and the deficit at the same time,
they had to make drastic cuts in government spending. Well aware that balancing the budget is a popular idea but that the sacrifices it takes to do so
are not, Republicans proposed a budget that would impose as much of the

cost as possible on people who usually vote Democratic (if, indeed, they vote at all), most notably beneficiaries of welfare, housing, and job training programs. According to a report by the Democratic staff of Congress's Joint Economic Committee, fully half the spending cuts in the Republican plan to balance the budget by 2002 were to be borne by families in the poorest fifth of the population, with 75 percent coming from the poorest two-fifths.[3] The difficulty, from the Republicans' perspective, was that not nearly enough savings could be squeezed out of programs for poor people and other Democratic constituencies to cut taxes and balance the budget; they had to take on middle-class entitlements as well. Clinton and the Democrats had faced a kindred dilemma in 1993; politically feasible tax increases for corporations and the rich could not provide enough revenue to move the budget toward balance, so they had to cut middle-class entitlements and raise middle-class taxes.

In 1995 Medicare spending was the obvious target for cuts because of its explosive growth. But Medicare was also a dangerous target because of its huge cohort of politically active beneficiaries. When House Republicans put a $270 billion reduction in the future growth of Medicare funding in the same budget with a $240 billion tax cut plan that offered the largest benefits to the wealthiest taxpayers, Clinton seized the opportunity to cast himself as the protector of Medicare (and other programs) against cutbacks to finance tax breaks for the rich. When Republican leaders threatened to shut down the government in late 1995, expecting to force Clinton to sign their budget, he held firm. The Republicans' rhetoric (Gingrich had told the Public Securities Association, "I don't care what the price is. I don't care if we have no executive offices, no bonds for 60 days."[4]) helped Clinton to paint them as extremists, and the Republican Congress took most of the blame for the two shutdowns that occurred when the government's spending authority lapsed late in 1995. Republicans were left looking irresponsible and, in Gingrich's case, petulant,[5] as hundreds of thousands of government employees went without paychecks during the holiday season.

Clinton won the political standoff hands down. The public took his side in the budget wars by decisive margins,[6] and his firmness helped him shed the reputation he had developed for spinelessness. Public ratings of Congress and Gingrich turned sharply downward, as Figures 7-1 and 7-2 demonstrate. The figures show that, although at any given time different polls produced diverse evaluations of both Congress and Gingrich, they were unanimous in finding a major shift against the Republican Congress and its chief symbol at the end of 1995, with far more respondents disapproving of them after the budget impasse than approving.[7] At the same time, Clinton's approval ratings rose, and he assumed a lead over Republican presidential candidate Bob Dole that he was never to lose in any of the hundreds of horse-race polls taken after the showdown. By the time Congress relented and let the government go back to work in January 1996, the presidential election was effectively decided. Clinton's only challenge was to avoid mistakes, and he did so, keeping an iron

Figure 7–1 Net Disapproval of the 104th Congress (1995–1997)

Disapproval rating

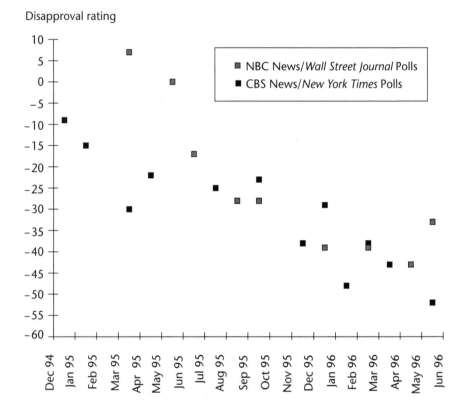

Note: The net disapproval is the percent of respondents who approve of the 104th Congress minus those who disapprove of it.

grip on the centrist ground the Republicans had ceded him by backing welfare reform, opposing gay marriages, and advocating the V-chip and school uniforms.

Clearly, the Republicans had misread their mandate, mistakenly assuming that public support for the goal—smaller, cheaper government—also meant public support for the means—cutbacks in specific programs and regulations. Clinton was able to exploit the Republicans' misreading, and his vow to protect "Medicare, Medicaid, education, and the environment" became the mantra of his victorious reelection campaign. But the Republican defeat on the budget raises the question that animates the remainder of this chapter: If the Republican Congress's mistakes reelected Clinton, why did they not also cost the party its control of Congress?

Figure 7–2 Net Disapproval of Speaker Gingrich, December 1994–
June 1996

Disapproval rating

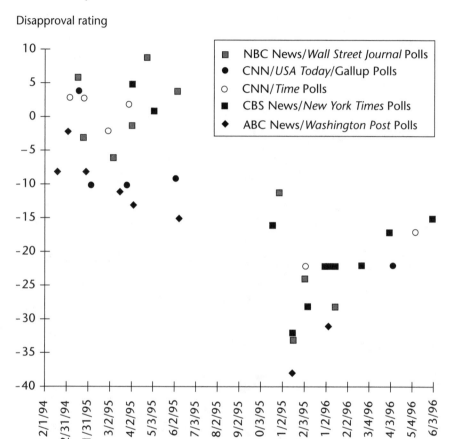

Note: The net disapproval is the percent of respondents who approve of Gingrich minus
those who disapprove of him.

The 1996 Congressional Results

Despite Clinton's easy reelection, Republican candidates did remarkably
well in the congressional elections. Table 7-1 summarizes the results in House
elections since 1992, and Table 7-2 does the same for Senate elections. On
election day 1996, Republicans lost only nine House seats. Moreover,
because five Democratic opportunists in the House had switched to the
Republican side of the aisle after the 1994 election and Republicans enjoyed
a net gain in special elections that were held during the 104th Congress, the
party ended up with only three fewer House seats in 1996 than it had won

Table 7-1   Membership Changes in the House, 103d to 105th
Congresses

Congress	Republicans	Democrats	Independents
103d			
Elected in 1992	176	258	1
104th			
Elected in 1994	230	204	1
At time of 1996 election	236	198	1
105th			
Elected in 1996	227[a]	207[b]	1
Change from 1992	+51	−51	0
Change from 1994	−3	+3	0
Change on election day 1996	−9	+9	0

[a] In the 105th Congress, 195 Republican incumbents were reelected to the House and 18 were defeated; 32 Republican freshmen were elected.

[b] In the 105th Congress, 165 Democratic incumbents were reelected to the House and 3 were defeated; 42 Democratic freshmen were elected.

Table 7-2   Membership Changes in the Senate, 103d to 105th
Congresses

Congress	Republicans	Democrats
103d (elected in 1992)	43	57
104th (elected in 1994)	53	47
105th (elected in 1996)	55[a]	45[b]
Change from 1992	+12	−12
Change from 1994	+2	−2

[a] In the 105th Congress, 12 Republican incumbents were reelected to the Senate and 1 was defeated; 9 Republican freshmen were elected.

[b] In the 105th Congress, 7 Democratic incumbents were reelected to the Senate and none were defeated; 6 freshmen were elected.

in 1994. Republicans did even better in the Senate, adding two new seats to the ten they had picked up in 1994. (See Table 7-3 for Senate election results by state.) Unlike Clinton, congressional Democrats enjoyed little in the way of a rebound from their 1994 debacle. Why did the Democrats do so poor-

Table 7-3   Senate Election Results by State, 1996

State	Vote total	Percent of two-party vote[a]
Alabama		
Roger Bedford (D)	681,651	46.4
Jeff Sessions (R)	786,436	53.6
Alaska		
Theresa Nangle Obermeyer (D)	23,977	11.9
*Ted Stevens (R)	177,893	88.1
Arkansas		
Winston Bryant (D)	400,241	47.3
Tim Hutchinson (R)	445,942	52.7
Colorado		
Tom Strickland (D)	677,600	47.5
Wayne Allard (R)	750,325	52.5
Delaware		
Raymond J. Clatworthy (R)	105,088	38.8
*Joseph R. Biden Jr. (D)	165,465	61.2
Georgia		
Guy Millner (R)	1,073,969	49.3
Max Cleland (D)	1,103,993	50.7
Idaho		
Walt Minnick (D)	198,422	41.2
*Larry E. Craig (R)	283,532	58.8
Illinois		
Al Salvi (R)	1,728,824	42.0
Richard J. Durbin (D)	2,384,028	58.0
Iowa		
Jim Ross Lightfoot (R)	571,807	47.4
*Tom Harkin (D)	634,166	52.6
Kansas		
Jill Docking (D)	461,344	44.6
Sam Brownback (R)	574,021	55.4
Sally Thompson (D)	362,380	35.7
Pat Roberts (R)	652,677	64.3
Kentucky		
Steven L. Beshear (D)	560,012	43.6
*Mitch McConnell (R)	724,794	56.4
Louisiana		
Louis "Woody" Jenkins (R)	847,157	49.8
Mary L. Landrieu (D)	852,945	50.2
Maine		
Joseph E. Brennan (D)	266,226	47.1
Susan Collins (R)	298,422	52.9
Massachusetts		
William F. Weld (R)	1,143,120	46.1
*John Kerry (D)	1,334,135	53.9
Michigan		
Ronna Romney (R)	1,500,106	40.6
*Carl Levin (D)	2,195,738	59.4

(Continued)

Table 7-3   (Continued)

State	Vote total	Percent of two-party vote[a]
Minnesota		
Rudy Boschwitz (R)	901,282	45.1
*Paul Wellstone (D)	1,098,493	54.9
Mississippi		
James W. "Bootie" Hunt (D)	240,647	27.8
*Thad Cochran (R)	624,154	72.2
Montana		
Dennis Rehberg (R)	182,111	47.4
*Max Baucus (D)	201,935	52.6
Nebraska		
Ben Nelson (D)	281,904	42.6
Chuck Hagel (R)	379,933	57.4
New Hampshire		
Dick Swett (D)	227,355	48.4
*Robert C. Smith (R)	242,257	51.6
New Jersey		
Dick Zimmer (R)	1,227,351	44.7
Robert G. Torricelli (D)	1,519,154	55.3
New Mexico		
Art Trujillo (D)	164,356	31.5
*Pete V. Domenici (R)	357,171	68.5
North Carolina		
Harvey B. Gantt (D)	1,173,875	46.6
*Jesse Helms (R)	1,345,833	53.4
Oklahoma		
Jim Boren (D)	474,162	41.4
*James M. Inhofe (R)	670,610	58.6
Oregon		
Tom Bruggere (D)	624,370	48.0
Gordon Smith (R)	677,336	52.0
Rhode Island		
Nancy J. Mayer (R)	127,368	35.6
Jack Reed (D)	230,676	64.4
South Carolina		
Elliott Close (D)	510,810	45.2
*Strom Thurmond (R)	619,739	54.8
South Dakota		
*Larry Pressler (R)	157,954	48.7
Tim Johnson (D)	166,533	51.3
Tennessee		
Houston Gordon (D)	654,937	37.5
*Fred Thompson (R)	1,091,554	62.5
Texas		
Victor M. Morales (D)	2,428,776	44.5
*Phil Gramm (R)	3,027,680	55.5
Virginia		
Mark Warner (D)	1,115,982	47.5
*John W. Warner (R)	1,235,744	52.5

Table 7-3 (*Continued*)

State	Vote total	Percent of two-party vote[a]
West Virginia		
Betty A. Burks (R)	139,088	23.4
*Jay Rockefeller (D)	456,526	76.6
Wyoming		
Kathy Karpan (D)	89,103	43.8
Mike Enzi (R)	114,116	56.2

Source: Congressional Quarterly.

Note: Asterisks indicate incumbents.

[a] Percent of two-party vote is the vote total for one major party candidate divided by the sum of the vote totals for both major party candidates in each Senate race.

ly? Part of the explanation lies in the electoral politics of divided government during good times, which I shall discuss later. More fundamental, however, were changes in the structure of electoral competition for congressional seats that were both revealed and magnified by the 1994 elections. Because both sets of circumstances were visibly in place well before 1996, the Democrats' failure to retake Congress was not surprising; indeed, it was predictable.[8]

The Structure of Competition for the House

The most important structural change in the balance of competition for control of the House was the reallocation of House seats that followed the 1990 census. The states in the South and West that gained seats were, on average, considerably more Republican in their voting habits than the states in the Northeast and Midwest that lost seats. The drawing of "majority-minority" districts also helped Republicans by packing overwhelmingly Democratic African American voters into minority districts, leaving neighboring districts relatively more Republican.[9] This change in the underlying competitive balance was easy to overlook in 1992, when Bush's dismal showing dragged down the entire Republican ticket; but even then the Republicans' pickup of ten House seats, despite their loss of the White House, signaled that the competitive balance between the parties had undergone a fundamental change. A regression analysis of post–World War II House election results indicates that, in elections since 1992, Republicans have won about 42 more House seats than they would have won under equivalent national conditions in the 1946–1990 period.[10] During that era, they won an average of 180 House seats; adding 42 seats gives them an approximate base of 222, a narrow majority very close to their current House strength of 227.

A second, related improvement in the Republicans' competitive position emerged from the 1994 election itself. Most of the seats the party added in 1994 were seats a Republican should have held in the first place. A serviceable measure of a district's partisan leanings can be computed by taking the average division of its two-party vote for president in 1988 and 1992.[11] Of the fifty-six districts newly taken by Republicans in 1994, thirty-seven (66 percent) had voted Republican, on average, in the two preceding presidential elections. Democrats took back only four of these thirty-seven seats (11 percent) in 1996, compared with six of the other nineteen (32 percent). Moreover, because Democrats still outnumbered Republicans in districts favoring the other party's presidential candidates (48 to 38), going into 1996, Democrats continued to hold the greater number of vulnerable House seats. In 1996 they lost seven of those seats, while Republicans were losing twelve of theirs.

The Democrats' problems were compounded by another legacy of 1994: the loss of majority control. Predictably, the insults of minority status prompted a voluntary exodus of Democrats from the House, giving Republicans a shot at open seats in Republican-leaning districts. As Table 7-4 shows, a higher number and proportion of Democrats than Republicans voluntarily left the House in 1996. As in 1994[12] a disproportionate share of the departing Democrats abandoned seats that had been voting Republican at the presidential level, particularly in the South; of the twelve such seats in 1996, the Democrats lost six. Revealingly, twenty-three of the twenty-eight retiring House Democrats announced their departures before the end of 1995, while a majority of Republican retirees (eleven of twenty-one) announced theirs in 1996. Strategic retirements inspired by the Republicans' seeming ascendancy during most of 1995 made it harder for Democrats to exploit the shift in public opinion away from the Republican Congress after the budget showdown.

Strategic responses to the new competitive environment worked to the Republicans' advantage in other ways as well. The Republican takeover of Congress transformed the campaign money market. Democrats no longer had the majority status and committee control to attract campaign contributions from business-oriented political action committees (PACs), which after 1994 were free to follow their Republican hearts as well as their pocketbooks in allocating donations. Not only did such PACs have less reason to contribute to incumbent Democrats, they also had less reason to worry about contributing against incumbent Democrats, whose ability to retaliate against interests that funded their opponents had diminished sharply.

The Republicans' fund-raising advantage was most pronounced in 1995. The National Republican Congressional Committee, for example, raised $25.9 million that year, an increase of 181 percent over the most recent comparable year, 1993. Although the Democratic Congressional Campaign

Table 7-4   Voluntary Retirement from the House, 1996

	Democrats		Republicans	
Sought reelection	168	(85.7%)	213	(91.0%)
Retired	21	(10.7%)	13	(5.6%)
Sought higher office	7	(3.6%)	8	(3.4%)
Total departures	28	(14.3%)	21	(9.0%)
Departures from:				
More vulnerable districts [a]	12		3	
Losses	6		3	
Less vulnerable districts	16		18	
Losses	3		1	
Total losses in open seats	9		4	

[a] More vulnerable districts are defined as those in which the average two-party district-level vote for the party's presidential candidates in 1988 and 1992 fell below 50 percent.

Committee also took in more in 1995 than in 1993 ($8.4 million compared with $6.7 million, for an increase of 25 percent), it was left very far behind.[13] Individually, the average House Republican raised $246,331 in 1995; the average House Democrat, $184,633.[14]

After the budget showdown, the Democrats' chances of retaking the House improved, and some contributors hedged their bets. Through October 16, Republican incumbents whose campaign-finance reports are available had raised 43 percent more than Democratic incumbents (an average of $661,000 compared with $463,000), but the Democrats, facing a less threatening electoral environment, may not have felt the need to raise as much money. Democratic challengers held a modest lead over Republican challengers in fund-raising for 1996 (receipts though October 16 averaged $228,000 for the Democrats reporting, compared with $196,000 for the Republicans),[15] but the gap was considerably smaller than one would expect in what was shaping up to be a good Democratic year.[16] The full effects of the new financial environment will probably not appear until 1998, when, because the president's party virtually always loses seats in midterm elections, the continuation of the Republicans' majority status will not be in doubt.[17]

Finally, the shock of 1994, the prospective imbalance in campaign funds, and the expectation that they were likely to be in the minority evidently made it more difficult for the Democrats to recruit high-quality candidates to take on incumbent Republicans. Quality candidates are crucial to a party's success because congressional elections remain largely candidate-centered events. A favorable national political climate does a party little good in districts where it fails to field a candidate with the skill and resources to take advantage of the climate. A simple but powerful measure of quality is experience in prior elective public office. In 1996 as in all postwar House elections, challengers who had previously won elective public office were far more successful than were those who had not. High quality, experienced Democratic challengers won 25.5 percent (twelve of forty-seven) of the contests they entered, whereas only 3.9 percent of the 158 political amateurs defeated the incumbent. (These are typical success rates for the two types of challengers during the postwar period.) Of course, experienced challengers are much more likely to run for seats that their party's candidate has a plausible chance to win, but, as is discussed later, their electoral superiority remains after other relevant electoral conditions are taken into account.[18]

The Democrats' problem in 1996 was that only 22.1 percent of their challengers had previous experience in elective office, a figure below their postwar average of 25.3 percent and not at all typical of the party in a good Democratic year. The Democrats needed to pick up at least nineteen seats to retake the House in 1996. In each of the five postwar elections in which they have added nineteen or more seats to their total, at least 31.2 percent of their challengers had served in elective office; the average for these elections (1948, 1958, 1964, 1974, and 1982) is 35.7 percent. If history is any guide, the Democrats did not have a sufficient number of high-quality challengers to retake the House in 1996. Indeed, the data in Table 7-1 show that even if strategic retirements had not cost them any open seats, they did not defeat enough Republican incumbents to win a majority. The signs of a Democratic revival in 1996 evidently came too late to bring out a class of challengers who were capable of taking back the House.

The Senate Contests

Retirements hurt the Democrats even more in Senate contests than in House races, and their troubles were compounded by the luck of the draw. Thirteen senators retired in 1996, the largest number of voluntary departures since 1914, when senators were first elected directly by voters. Eight of the thirteen were Democrats, four of them from the South. The timing of their retirement announcements again suggests strategic withdrawal; all eight of the Democrats, but only one of the Republicans, announced their retirements by November, 1995. Republicans won three of the seats left open by departing Democrats, two in the South (Alabama and Arkansas) and one in Nebraska, a state won handily by Dole. Republican senator Larry Pressler of South Dakota was the only incumbent defeated in the general election, and his was the only Republican Senate seat lost in 1996.

Democrats were also unlucky in the class of Senate seats up for reelection in 1996. As in 1992, Senate and presidential outcomes tended to match,

Table 7-5   The Relationship Between Senate and Presidential Election Results, 1996

	States won by presidential candidate	
Senate winner	Dole	Clinton
Republican	14	7
Democrat[a]	3	10
Total contests	17	17

[a] $X^2 = 6.10$, $p < 05$.

although more so in states won by Dole than in states won by Clinton. As Table 7-5 indicates, Republicans won fourteen of the seventeen seats at stake in states won by Dole, while Democrats won only ten of the seventeen seats at stake in states won by Clinton. The Republicans' good fortune was that states won by Dole were more likely to have Senate contests than those won by Clinton. Only three of Dole's nineteen states lacked a Senate race in 1996, compared with fourteen of Clinton's thirty-one states. By the luck of the draw, the Democrats were poorly positioned to take advantage of whatever help Clinton's victory might have provided their Senate candidates.

The Campaigns

Strategic career decisions taken by prospective Democratic congressional candidates, along with the other structural shifts in the balance of competition for seats, clearly made it hard for the Democrats to exploit Clinton's victory. But just how exploitable was Clinton's victory? Democrats and their supporters in labor, women's, and environmental groups certainly sought, like Clinton, to portray the Republicans in Congress as a gang of irresponsible extremists in thrall to Gingrich. But their efforts, although demonstrably effective, fell short of delivering Congress back to the Democrats.

Why was an anticongressional Republican stance so helpful to Clinton not equally helpful to congressional Democrats? The reasons are several. First, many potentially vulnerable House Republicans did what Democrats had routinely done to hold on to seats against contrary national tides during their forty years of control: they ran as independent champions of local district interests. Republicans took Congress in 1994 by nationalizing the election, acting in lock step on the agenda outlined in the Contract with America during the first few months of 1995. Had they stuck together throughout the 104th Congress, the 1996 congressional elections might have become a referendum on their collective performance as a party. That is certainly what the Democrats tried to make it after the Republicans moved from the popular generalities of the contract to the much less popular specifics of their "revolutionary" budget.

In the end, however, the Republicans' brief flirtation with responsible party government succumbed to the desire of individual members to win reelection and of the party as a whole to keep its majority. After the budget debacle, Republicans with moderate constituencies bolted the party on such issues as repealing the assault weapons ban, weakening endangered species protection, and raising the minimum wage.[19] As challengers sought to fuse vulnerable Republican incumbents to Gingrich with TV ads that digitally morphed their faces into his, the Republicans responded by highlighting the votes on which they had parted from Gingrich, a few reportedly padding their records of independence by voting against the Speaker on routine matters of House administration. Gingrich himself encouraged members to run against him if doing so would help their campaigns.[20] The Contract with America, so prominent in 1994 and 1995, was conspicuous by its absence from most of the Republican incumbents' 1996 campaigns.

The Republicans' tactical retreat culminated in the passage of spending measures and welfare and health insurance reforms acceptable to Clinton in the spring and summer of 1996. These popular actions strengthened Clinton's record and thus his candidacy. But they did the same for congressional Republicans, both as achievements in their own right and as counters to charges of extremism and intransigence.

Such charges were, of course, crucial elements in the Democrats' campaign to retake Congress. They also were grist for the independent campaigns against Republican incumbents financed by labor, environmental, and women's groups that were a notable feature of the 1996 House elections. The AFL-CIO, an umbrella group for organized labor, made the most extensive effort, mounting a $35 million campaign beginning more than a year before the election to attack the positions on Medicare and other issues taken by Republican members of the House. Because they kept their majority, Republican leaders have argued that labor reaped nothing from its investment.[21] The reality is otherwise. Although the AFL-CIO campaigns were insufficient by themselves to defeat enough Republican incumbents to return control of the House to the Democrats, they actually had a substantial effect on the elections.

Table 7-6 presents some data on the AFL-CIO campaign and its results. The table divides Republican incumbents into three categories, depending on whether or not they were targeted by labor and, if so, whether they were also the target of a voter video guide, the unions' heaviest campaign weapon.[22] It also distinguishes freshmen from more senior Republican incumbents. The table reveals that targeted incumbents, freshmen or otherwise, lost much more frequently than those who were not targeted. Twelve of the forty-four freshmen who were targeted lost, while every one of the twenty-seven who were not targeted won reelection. Senior Republicans were much less likely to be targets (14 percent, compared with 62 percent of freshmen), but they

Table 7-6   The Fates of House Republicans Targeted by AFL-CIO
Advertisements

House Republicans	Freshmen	Nonfreshmen	Total
Not targeted by AFL-CIO	27	122	149
Losers	0	2	2
Percent losers	0.0%	1.6%	1.3%
Target of at least one advertisement	23	17	40
Losers	5	2	7
Percent losers	21.7%	11.8%	17.5%
Target of voter video guide	21	3	24
Losers	7	2	9
Percent losers	33.3%	66.7%	37.5%
Statistical significance[a]	p = .006	p < .001	p < .001

[a] From analysis of variance of differences across categories of AFL-CIO targeting.

were only slightly less likely to lose when they were (20 percent compared with 27 percent).

Of course, the AFL-CIO concentrated its efforts on Republicans whom they considered vulnerable, so its relative success could be spurious. Table 7-7 reports the results of regression equations designed to test this possibility. The equations estimate the effect of the AFL-CIO's campaigns on the share of votes won by Republican incumbents, taking into account other relevant electoral factors, including the partisan inclinations of the district (measured by the district-level presidential vote), the share of the vote won by the Republican candidate in 1994, the presence or absence of an experienced challenger, and the incumbent's level of support for the Contract with America.

The results show that, other things being equal, AFL-CIO targets did substantially worse than untargeted Republican incumbents on election day, particularly if they were freshmen. For example, taking other electoral circumstances into account, the coefficient in the second equation indicates that the vote for Republican freshmen who were targets of AFL-CIO video campaigns was typically about eight percentage points lower than the vote for freshmen who were not targeted. (The equation further shows that experienced Democratic challengers outperformed their party's inexperienced challengers and that district voting habits had their expected strong effect on electoral results.)

The equations in Table 7-7 also estimate the effects of a Republican incumbent's level of support for the Contract with America (measured as the percentage of times the member sided with the party on votes pertaining to

Table 7-7   The Effects of Labor Targeting and the Contract with America on the Vote for Republican Incumbents in the 1996 House Elections

Variables	All Republicans	Freshmen Republicans
Intercept	27.30***	58.72
	(9.72)	(30.61)
Republican's vote in 1994[a]	.39***	.22
	(.06)	(.16)
Average Republican presidential vote, 1988–1992[b]	.31***	.36**
	(.07)	(.13)
Experienced challenger[c]	−2.35**	−2.66*
	(.88)	(1.29)
AFL-CIO target[d]	−2.95***	−6.33***
	(1.00)	(1.55)
AFL-CIO target—video[e]	−5.23***	−8.03***
	(1.28)	(1.68)
Support for Contract[f]	−.07*	−.30
	(.09)	(.29)
Adjusted R^2	.66	.60
Number of Cases	174	69

Note: The dependent variable is the percentage of the two-party vote won by the Republican incumbent; standard errors are in parentheses.

[a] Republican candidate's share of the two-party vote in the district in 1994.

[b] Average share of the two-party vote won by George Bush in 1988 and 1992 in the district.

[c] Democratic challenger has held elective public office.

[d] Republican incumbent was the target of at least one AFL-CIO advertisement.

[e] Districts where AFL-CIO ran voter video guides attacking the Republican incumbent.

[f] Percentage of votes in favor of items in the Republicans' Contract with America.

*p < .05

**p < .01

***p < .001

items in the contract). For all Republican incumbents, the relationship between support for the contract and electoral performance is negative—the higher the support, the lower the vote in 1996—but the estimated coefficient is small and does not come close to statistical significance. For Republican freshmen, the estimated effect is considerably larger (suggesting, for example, that the vote for those who supported the contract 95 percent rather than 100 percent of the time would be 1.5 points higher on election day), but again the standard error of the coefficient is so large that it falls well short of statistical significance. On the whole, ignoring the contract during the 1996 campaign was probably a wise tactical choice for Republican incumbents, but loyalty to the contract was not a significant electoral liability.

The evidence, then, is that labor's independent campaigns against Republican incumbents did help Democratic challengers, and quite substantially. For most, however, the help was insufficient to boost them over the 50 percent line. This was most clearly the case in districts without experienced Democratic challengers. Against incumbents targeted by the AFL-CIO, Democrats won 48 percent (twelve of twenty-five) of the districts where they fielded an experienced challenger, but only 10 percent (four of thirty-nine) where they did not. As noted earlier, help from outside the district, in whatever form it arrives, is much more effective if a quality challenger is available to exploit it. Finally, this analysis suggests that without labor's help, the Democrats would have done even worse; if we subtract the additional vote for Democratic challengers opposing Republican freshmen attributed by the equation to the AFL-CIO's campaign, only two of the twelve victorious Democrats would still be predicted to win more than 50 percent of the vote.[23] Because they show every indication of being effective, independent campaigns of the sort waged by the AFL-CIO in 1996 are likely to assume a larger role in future congressional contests, particularly if campaign finance reforms are enacted that restrict the flow of funds to the candidates themselves.

The 1996 Election in Historical Context

The closest historical precedent for the Republican triumph of 1994 was 1946, the most recent election in which the Republicans won control of Congress at midterm with a Democrat in the White House. Democrats hoped, and Republicans feared, that the precedent for 1996 would be 1948, when Harry Truman's political resurrection swept the Democrats back into control of Congress. Unfortunately for the Democrats, the historical model for 1996 was 1984, when Ronald Reagan, the Republican president, rode to easy reelection on a tide of good economic news while his party was picking up only fourteen seats in the House and losing three in the Senate.

Both Reagan and Clinton ran upbeat campaigns extolling a strong economy and popular policy successes. Both drew upon extraordinary political skills to extend their personal appeal beyond their party's normal electoral

Table 7-8 Congressional Results When Presidents Are Elected to
Second Full Terms

Year	President	Vote	House	Senate
1956	Eisenhower (R)	57.7%	2 D	1 D
1972	Nixon (R)	61.8%	12 R	2 D
1984	Reagan (R)	59.2%	14 R	2 D
1996	Clinton (D)	54.5%	9 D	2 R

Note: *D* refers to Democrats, *R* to Republicans.

base. Both won easy reelection. But neither of their campaigns offered much
leverage to their congressional challengers. If times are good and the president deserves another term, why replace incumbents of the majority party in
Congress, who plausibly can claim a share of the credit for peace, prosperity, and progress? Other status-quo presidential elections under divided government—Dwight D. Eisenhower's reelection in 1956 and Richard M.
Nixon's reelection in 1972—offer confirming examples. As Table 7-8 shows,
every postwar president reelected to a second full term has had remarkably
short coattails. All four saw their party lose seats in the Senate, and the
largest pickup in the House was Reagan's paltry fourteen seats in 1984.

    In 1996 the difficulty for Democratic congressional challengers was
amplified by the very strategy that revived Clinton's presidency. By accepting
so many of the Republicans' goals—agreeing to balance the budget by 2002,
declaring that "the era of big government is over," signing a bill to end welfare entitlements that had been part of the social safety net since the New
Deal, opposing gay marriages, and supporting prayer in school—Clinton
took command of the political center. But by campaigning on a record indistinguishable from that of a moderate Republican, he gave voters little reason
to elect more Democrats to Congress. The contrast with Truman's reelection
campaign, a spirited partisan defense of the New Deal, could hardly be more
stark.

    Clinton, of course, faced a very different political environment in 1996
than Truman did in 1948. Truman had a natural Democratic majority to
rally; now the parties are evenly matched. The New Deal policies that Truman defended enjoyed broad public support; now the Republican themes of
lower taxes and smaller government hold sway. Clinton won reelection by
adapting to a more conservative political environment in much the same way
that moderate and conservative Democrats had won congressional seats in
areas unfriendly to their party for years. Such a strategy acknowledges political reality but does nothing to alter it.

    Clinton helped congressional Republicans in other ways as well. He
saved them from themselves by thwarting their efforts in 1995 and bringing

them back toward the political center in 1996. His firm opposition to unpopular budget cuts, assaults on environmental regulation and the Department of Education, and kindred Republican proposals in 1995 forced the Republicans to rein in their most extreme impulses and alerted them to the political danger lurking in revolutionary rhetoric and radical policy changes. His maneuvering toward consensus on budget decisions and on issues such as welfare reform, minimum wage, and health insurance portability gave Republicans a chance to look responsible and effective.

Moreover, the aura of scandal around the administration and widespread doubts about Clinton's personal character offered voters an additional reason to leave the Republicans in a position to keep an eye on him. Indeed, there is some evidence that the revelations late in the campaign of foreign contributions to the Democratic National Committee moved many late-deciding voters into the Republican column, reducing Clinton's margin of victory and thereby impeding the Democrats' effort to retake the House.[24] In addition, despite the implied affront to Dole, Republican leaders did not hesitate to make the near certainty of Clinton's reelection an argument for voting Republican for Congress. Whether or not many voters deliberately balanced their vote for Clinton with one for a Republican congressional candidate, the public was pleased with the final equilibrium. A majority of respondents to a Pew Research poll conducted immediately after the election said they were happy with Clinton's reelection (53 percent, compared with 42 percent who said they were unhappy), but an even larger majority—65 percent—said they were happy that the Republicans had retained control of Congress (only 27 percent were unhappy).[25]

1998 and Beyond

The 1996 elections leave no doubt that the balance of competition for congressional seats has shifted sharply toward the Republicans in the 1990s. The narrow House majority now held by the Republicans approximates their current "natural" strength in House elections and constitutes a decisive break from the solid Democratic majorities of the previous four decades. Although the House, like the Senate, is now up for grabs by either party, Republicans probably enjoy a small advantage in both.

The biggest changes have occurred in the South, where the decades-long realignment of white voters from Democratic to Republican allegiance has increasingly registered at the congressional level. Figures 7-3 and 7-4 show this regional transformation in House representation during the postwar period. Republican representation in the South has grown from almost nothing to a 57 percent majority, with the steepest growth in the 1990s. In their 1994 sweep, Republicans picked up seats in the same proportion outside the South as in it; in 1996 Republicans continued to add southern seats even as they were losing ground elsewhere. Republicans have further opportunities

Figure 7–3 Republican House Victories, 1946–1996, by Region

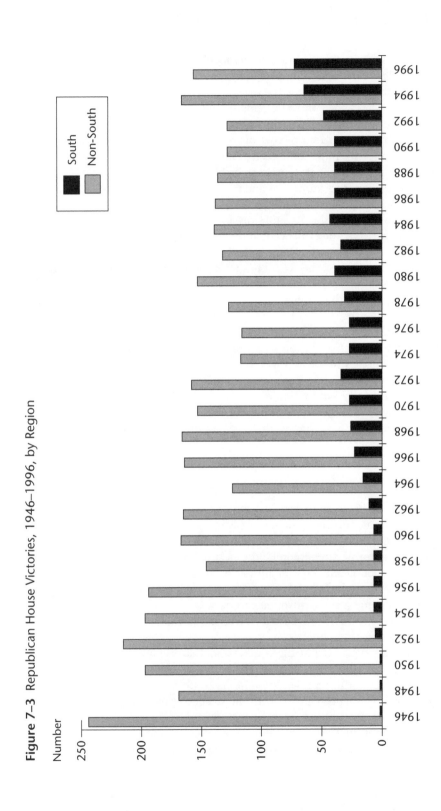

Figure 7–4 Republican House Victories, 1946–1996, by Region

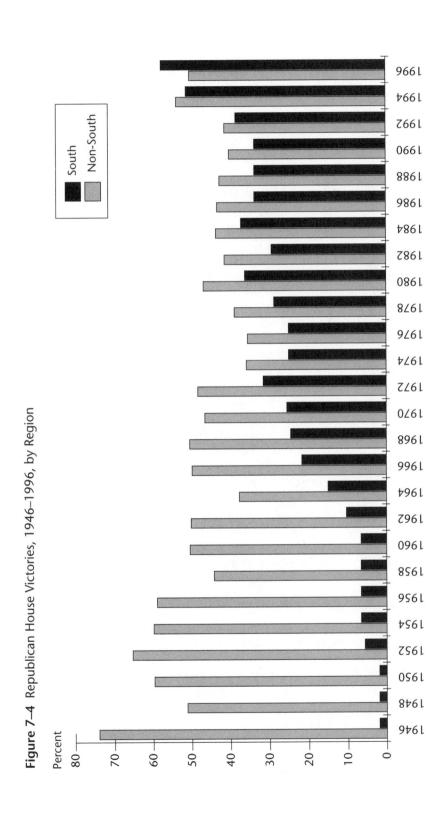

even after these gains, because Democratic members still hold more than a dozen southern districts where their party has been running well behind the Republicans at the presidential level.

Southern Republican gains in the Senate have been even more spectacular. As late as 1960, the party held none of the twenty-two seats in the states of the old Confederacy. As recently as 1990, they held only seven of these seats. After gains in 1992, 1994, and 1996, they now hold fifteen seats and are poised to pick up more in 1998. The Republican advances in the South have been only partly offset by losses elsewhere, notably in the Northeast and Midwest.

In sum, the Republican Party is on its way to building the kind of strong congressional base in the South that once gave the Democrats a formidable head start in the battle to control the House and Senate. But a Republican Party that speaks with a heavy southern accent, ideologically as well as literally, may continue to have trouble winning presidential elections. The social and economic conservatism espoused by congressional leaders such as Gingrich (Speaker—Georgia), Trent Lott (Senate majority leader—Mississippi), Dick Armey (House majority leader—Texas), Tom DeLay (House majority whip—Texas), Robert Livingston (chair of House Appropriations Committee—Louisiana), and Jesse Helms (Chair of Senate Foreign Relations Committee—North Carolina) is of limited appeal to moderates, especially among educated women. The 1996 elections moved the congressional wing of the party even further to the right; not just the three who replaced Democrats, but every one of the nine newly elected Republican senators is more conservative than the senator he or she replaced. Republicans may find themselves in the same bind Democrats were in during the 1970s and 1980s, when the drift of their party's image toward the ideological left continually handicapped Democratic presidential candidates.

At the congressional level, by contrast, the near-term Republican future looks rosy. As noted earlier, the most regular occurrence in American political history is the loss of House seats in midterm elections by the president's party, which means the Republicans can count on strengthening their grip on the House in 1998. And although the opposition party does not invariably pick up Senate seats, a review of the lineup of seats up for election in 1998 suggests that Republican opportunities for gain outnumber those of Democrats, especially if several older Southern Democrats (Dale Bumpers, Arkansas, 71; Ernest Hollings, South Carolina, 75; Wendell Ford, Kentucky, 72) decide to call it quits. Speculating beyond 1998 is riskier—no one who has witnessed the reversals of fortune that beset Bush, Clinton, or the congressional Republicans in recent years should feel confident about any prediction. But if our recent experience with electoral politics under divided government is any guide, the Democrats will have a very difficult time winning control of Congress as long as a Democrat sits in the White House. Their best opportunity will come if and when the voters become disenchanted with the next Republican administration.

Bill Clinton and the 105th Congress

Clinton is certain to face a Republican majority in Congress for the rest of his presidency. For him, the peril is obvious: perpetual congressional probing of his administration, his family, and himself. Less obvious, although equally noteworthy, are the potential advantages. Controlling Congress, the Republicans cannot avoid sharing the responsibility for governing. The strategy of reflexive opposition and obstruction that is always effective against narrow Democratic majorities and that served Republicans so well during Clinton's first two years is not an option. Republicans will certainly try to make Clinton take the lead on specifying the cuts (most particularly in the growth of Medicare) necessary to fulfill his promise to balance the budget by 2002, for the clearest lesson of budget politics is that whoever goes first with specific proposals loses politically. But Republicans will have to share responsibility for whatever cuts are enacted, because nothing can be enacted without their votes. The voters have left Clinton and the congressional Republicans no choice but to work together if either side wants to build any record of accomplishment. If the wave of investigations subsides (by no means a certainty), Clinton may find that governing as a centrist in compulsory harness with a Republican Congress gives him more scope for achievement than would governing with a narrow, predictably fractious Democratic majority.

Notes

1. Gary C. Jacobson, "Deficit Cutting Politics and Congressional Elections," *Political Science Quarterly* 108 (fall 1993): 375–402.
2. Gary C. Jacobson, "The 1994 House Elections in Perspective," in *Midterm: The Elections of 1994 in Context*, ed. Philip A. Klinkner (Boulder, Colo.: Westview Press, 1996), 1–20.
3. Elizabeth Shogren, "GOP Budget Plans Would Put Burden on the Poor," *Los Angeles Times*, October 29, 1995, A1.
4. George Hager, "GOP Ready to Take Debt Limit to the Brink and Beyond," *Congressional Quarterly Weekly Report*, September 23, 1995, 2865.
5. Gingrich admitted that he had forced the shutdown partly because he felt snubbed by Clinton during a trip on *Air Force One* to attend the funeral of Israeli prime minister Yitzhak Rabin; Clinton had not talked about the budget with Gingrich or Bob Dole, then Senate majority leader, on the trip and made them exit from the rear of the plane when it landed in the United States. See Jackie Koszczuk, "'Train Wreck' Engineered by GOP Batters Party and House Speaker," *Congressional Quarterly Weekly Report*, November 18, 1995, 3506.
6. Gary C. Jacobson, "Divided Government and the 1994 Elections," in *Divided Government: Change, Continuity, and the Constitutional Order*, ed. Peter A. Galderisi with Roberta Hertzberg and Peter McNamara (Lanham, Md.: Rowman and Littlefield, 1996), 79.
7. The data for Figures 7-1 and 7-2 are from charts published on the World Wide Web by PoliticsNow *(http://www.politicsnow.com)* during the 1996 campaign.
8. And predicted; see Gary C. Jacobson and Thomas P. Kim, "After 1994: The New Politics of Congressional Elections" (Paper presented at the annual meeting of the Midwest Political Science Association, Chicago, April 18–20, 1996).

9. Kevin A. Hill, "Does the Creation of Majority Black Districts Aid Republicans? An Analysis of the 1992 Congressional Elections in Eight Southern States," *Journal of Politics* 57 (May 1995): 384–401.
10. A standard regression model of Democratic House victories in postwar elections as a function of the economy's performance (measured as the change in real income per capita in the election year) and presidential approval (percent approving of the president's performance in the last Gallup Poll prior to the election), conditional on which party controls the presidency, shows a sharp and significant increase in Republican House representation after 1990. The equation is:

    Democratic House seats = 352.8 – 183.9 (Democratic administration) + 3.20 (change in real income per capita) + 1.52 (presidential approval) – 40.05 (year > 1990).

    All coefficients are significant at $p < .05$ or better; the post-1990 dummy is significant at $p < .001$; the adjusted $R^2 = .68$. If the post-1990 variable is replaced with variables representing the individual years, the coefficients are –34 (1992), –47 (1994), and –44 (1996).
11. The data are from Michael Barone and Grant Ujifusa, *The Almanac of American Politics, 1994* (Washington, D.C.: National Journal, 1993).
12. Jacobson, "1994 House Elections," 10.
13. "New Highs in Fundraising for House Majority GOP," *Congressional Quarterly Weekly Report*, March 16, 1996, 726.
14. John Wang, "Building a Dream House," *Washington Post*, National Weekly Edition, March 25–31, 1996, 11.
15. From Federal Election Commission data made available over the Internet by PoliticsNow *(http://www.politicsnow.com)*.
16. Gary C. Jacobson, *The Politics of Congressional Elections*, 4th ed. (New York: Longman, 1997), 137.
17. Only once in the thirty-five midterm elections held since the Civil War has the president's party not lost seats: in 1934, when the nation was in the midst of the New Deal realignment.
18. Gary C. Jacobson, "Strategic Politicians and the Dynamics of House Elections, 1946–86," *American Political Science Review* 83 (September 1989): 773–793.
19. Jonathan D. Salant, "House Republicans Stray from 'Contract' Terms," *Congressional Quarterly Weekly Report*, July 6, 1996, 1929–1933.
20. Jackie Koszczuk, "For Embattled GOP Leadership, a Season of Discontent," *Congressional Quarterly Weekly Report*, July 20, 1996, 2023.
21. Robin Toner, "GOP Leaders Declare Victory over Labor," *New York Times*, November 7, 1996, B3.
22. The information is from "Labor Targets," *Congressional Quarterly Weekly Report*, October 26, 1996, 3084.
23. Labor reaped one other benefit from its campaign: When the bill to raise the minimum wage came up for final passage in the House, 58 percent of the targeted Republicans, but only 36 percent of those not targeted, voted to raise the minimum wage. In an earlier crucial vote on the bill, the respective figures were 37 percent and 15 percent.
24. According to the national exit poll, voters who made their decision in the last few days before the election went for Dole over Clinton, 40 percent to 35 percent. See *Los Angeles Times*, November 7, 1996, A22. An additional 1 percent of the vote would have put the Democratic candidate over 50 percent in eleven House districts; an additional 2 percent would have put the Democrat over 50 percent in twenty-two districts.
25. Reported in *Hotline*, November 15, 1996.

8

Conclusion: Valence Voters, Valence Victors

John J. DiIulio Jr.

A rguably, the most revealing public opinion surveys of the 1996 election
season were the ones in which voters were asked whether they would
rather have Bill Clinton or Bob Dole "responsible for raising [their] children"
if "something happened to you or your spouse." A clear majority favored
Clinton. But when asked, "Who would you rather have your child grow up
to be more like?" a clear majority favored Dole.[1]

An electorate that would prefer its children to be brought up by Clinton
in order to have them turn out like Dole is an electorate that defies easy
explanations or predictions. And, as the different viewpoints presented in this
volume attest, it is bound to give even the best political scientists, strategists,
and pundits fits.

In Chapter 3, Michael Nelson observes that politics in this country has
experienced "weather-like turbulence during the last third of the twentieth
century." Still, he reassures us, "underlying the stormy political weather have
been steadier, more slowly changing elements in the political climate of the
contemporary era." But do political meteorologists—with or without Ph.D.s,
campaign experience, syndicated columns, or television contracts—really
understand either the many sudden changes in political weather or the more
glacial changes in political climate? I think the answer is clearly "no." Let me
begin to explain my answer, and to offer a conceptual way out of our interpretive morass, by reviewing a few of the recent, uninspiring attempts to
explain recent elections.

The Failure of Expert Opinion

In the 1992 campaign—if one follows the polls—there were days on
which Ross Perot, who was on no one's presidential radar screen in 1990,
could well have been elected president. Even after several well-publicized
bouts of bizarre behavior, Perot won nearly a fifth of the popular vote—far
more than most analysts, including students of third-party candidacies,
thought likely. President George Bush's approval ratings were sky high in
1991 after the Persian Gulf War. Several leading Democrats had stayed out
of the race because they thought the president was unbeatable—a judgment
widely shared at the time by many, perhaps most, leading experts, pollsters,
and commentators. Yet Clinton won with a plurality and began his first term

with 258 fellow Democrats in the House of Representatives and 57 fellow Democrats in the Senate. The period of divided government was over, and, as some experts hoped, others feared, and nearly all predicted, the new Democratic president was in for a good old-fashioned first-term political honeymoon.

But there was no honeymoon. Then, in the 1994 midterm elections, the first Republican majority in forty years was elected to Congress. Nobody predicted a Republican victory until some preelection polls preordained it. Most of the election-interpretation establishment—the overlapping circles of academics, campaign strategists, pollsters, and journalists who study, write, publish, and pontificate about what decides elections and what elections tell us about American politics and culture—had greeted the Republicans' idea of "nationalizing" congressional elections through the Contract with America as if it were a bad political joke. After all, congressional elections were notoriously local affairs. But when, unexpectedly, 230 Republicans were elected to the House and 53 Republicans were elected to the Senate, the laughing stopped and the instant expert commentary and analysis on the "earthquake election" of 1994 began.

Angry White Males

Never mind that had as few as twenty thousand votes in just thirteen congressional districts switched from Republican to Democratic, the Speaker of the 103d Congress would have been Speaker of the 104th: Democrat Tom Foley, not Republican Newt Gingrich. From many different quarters, the instant conventional electoral wisdom was that Gingrich had been carried to the Speaker's chair on the shoulders of a new, powerful, and suddenly growing bloc of voters—namely, "angry white males." These voters, the experts and their media mouthpieces intoned, were angry about many things, chief among them government affirmative action policies that favored African Americans and women over economically strapped white men.

The angry white male interpretation of the 1994 elections took off like a media rocket, slowed down hardly at all by the gravitational pull of highly contradictory and easy-to-locate data. Jack Citrin, however, examined the phenomenon in relation to national and state survey findings. He discovered that, nationally, between 1986 and 1994 men and women, blacks and whites, Democrats, independents, and Republicans had all become less supportive of certain affirmative action policies than they had been in the past. Blacks were more in favor of such policies than were whites, but the divide between blacks and whites did not widen between 1986 and 1994. Moreover, differences between white males and females had diminished. In 1986, for example, 66 percent of white males were strongly opposed to racial preferences in hiring, compared with 58 percent of white females; in 1994 the gap had narrowed to 70 percent and 67 percent, respectively. And Citrin found no statistically significant difference between white males and white females concerning preferential treatment based on sex. "The angry white male," he concluded, was an interpretive "straw man."[2]

Soccer Moms

By 1996 the angry white males had disappeared as quickly as they had appeared, replaced by "soccer moms"—the pundits' term for white, married, suburban women with children. These moms, it was widely predicted, would decide the presidential race by supporting Clinton over Dole in big numbers, not least of all because they ostensibly favored Clinton's pro-choice views over Dole's pro-life stands. And the prediction—or so one keeps hearing— came true. A typical postelection example comes from *Newsweek* magazine: "It was married white suburban women—some of whose children play soc- cer—who held the balance of power in 1996," for they "voted 49 to 42 (almost Clinton's exact overall margin) for the president."[3]

Voting at the winner's "exact electoral margin" hardly makes a group the winner's electoral catapult. As Table 3-3 of this volume shows, African Americans went for Clinton over Dole 84 to 12, Hispanics by 72 to 21, and gay, lesbian, and bisexual voters by 66 to 23. These and other groups such as Catholic voters, not white suburban women with or without soccer-playing children, held the balance of power in 1996 and tipped the election Clinton's way. Married people favored Dole over Clinton by 46 to 44, whites favored him by 46 to 43. "Soccer moms" themselves favored Republicans for Con- gress by 55 to 45. And the moms, like the rest of the electorate, were actual- ly closer to Dole's (and many congressional Republicans') position on abor- tion (namely, to keep abortion legal but limited to first- and second-trimester cases involving rape, incest, or danger to the life of the mother) than to Clin- ton's (and many congressional Democrats') pro-choice position.[4] Further- more, pro-choice presidential candidates such as California governor Pete Wilson and Pennsylvania senator Arlen Specter had dropped like flies in the Republican primaries, and pro-choice Republicans lost convincingly to pro- choice Democrats in a number of key races (for example, Republican gover- nor William Weld's unexpectedly large defeat by incumbent Senate Democrat John Kerry in the Massachusetts Senate election).

Stupid Voters?

If the angry white male was the electoral-interpretation establishment's favorite straw man of the 1994 elections, while the soccer mom was its dar- ling of the 1996 elections, what's next? "Dewey defeats Truman," the pre- maturely released headline in the 1948 election, was an understandable mis- take. But the unloosing of one baseless interpretation of America's electoral politics and culture after another is a situation that is out of control. It is symptomatic of two underlying problems: first, the experts have little to offer in the way of analytically tested and historically informed knowledge, and, second, very little of whatever sound conceptual and empirical knowledge they do possess ever manages to insinuate itself into the contemporary discourse on campaigns, elections, and political culture.

If you doubt my argument, take heed of a point made by V. O. Key in his classic work *The Responsible Electorate* (1966). As Key famously argued, "Voters are not fools." In his analysis of voters who switched parties from one presidential election to the next, he found that most of them switched in a direction perfectly consistent with their own beliefs and interests. His pioneering research painted "an image of an electorate moved by concern about central and relevant questions of public policy, of governmental performance, and of executive personality."[5]

In the three decades since Key wrote, the best empirical studies of political participation in the United States have confirmed that average Americans are capable of figuring out their own values and needs in relation to electoral politics and policy choices. Virtually all the evidence shows that the American people are not easily duped by high-paid media spin doctors or political consultants. Most voters can filter out bogus information and smell a rat in candidate's clothing. As summarized by Edward S. Greenberg and Benjamin I. Page, "recent research has indicated that Americans' collective policy preferences react rather sensibly to events, to changing circumstances, to new information, so that we can speak of a 'rational public.'"[6]

The voters-are-not-fools research literature includes works such as Morris Fiorina's *Retrospective Voting in American National Elections* (1981), which demonstrated that the voters can learn much of what they need to know to reach a rational decision simply by monitoring the performance of those in power.[7] The literature also includes a small library of specialized articles, including a 1995 study, published in the *American Political Science Review*, which found that "over time people forget most of the campaign information they are exposed to but are nonetheless able to later recollect their summary affective evaluation of candidates" and use it "to inform their preferences and vote choice."[8]

I do not mean to suggest either that every jot and tittle of empirical evidence is consistent with the "rational public" thesis, that "retrospective voting" is a completely uncontested concept, or that one should not utter a word about the meaning and significance of election outcomes until one has read the relevant articles in the latest editions of the *American Political Science Review* (surely a "cruel and unusual punishment" if inflicted on any non–card carrying social scientist).

But I do mean to suggest that, even as the essential validity of Key's optimistic understanding of the American voter has been supported by most of the best subsequent scholarship, it has been almost completely ignored in most of the commentary, analysis, and opinion put out by election interpreters. Most of the experts still write and talk as if the best science of the subject had found that voters were indeed fools. A typical if unusually explicit preelection 1996 example appeared in a syndicated *Washington Post* column that castigated Americans as "dolts who bellow at their government" but cannot even name their senators. "Such blathering ignorance ought to be condemned."[9]

Actually, "blathering ignorance" of basic political facts is not particularly relevant to the integrity and health of the democratic process. But you would never know this from the "expert" ideas about campaigns and elections that most Americans read or hear—and that most electoral scholars, with their fifteen minutes of fame in the media's election-cycle spotlight, seem more interested in reinforcing and repeating than in corralling and correcting. Metaphorically speaking, the problem is not that the emperors of electoral commentary have no clothes. It is that nobody much cares for or even pays attention to their best fashions.

The Need for Interpretation

No refuge from this problem of misleading or faulty pronouncements can be found in the maxim "If you can't say something profound, say something commonplace." It is true, for example, that in 1996 Clinton won in part because he was an incumbent running during a time of peace and relative prosperity. Likewise, it is true that by election day most Americans disliked Newt Gingrich, and many regarded him, fairly or not, as an extremist, a view that benefited Clinton. No one can much doubt that a number of idiosyncratic events—the 1995 Oklahoma City bombing and Colin Powell's decision not to run for president, to cite just two examples—played out in ways that helped clear Clinton's path back to the Oval Office. And no one much doubts that some issues (for example, the economy, education, and Social Security) helped Clinton more than Dole, while others (for example, the deficit, taxes, crime and drugs) helped Dole more.

But such "expert" observations are as trite as they are true. They explain little and predict almost nothing. With respect to the 1996 elections, they do not even begin to help us understand the "volatility of public opinion" referred to by Harold Stanley in Chapter 2; or the fact, as noted by Nelson in Chapter 1, that the American people gave "every sign of being disengaged from the elections of 1996" and were utterly bored by it all; or the effects of the "personalized, politicized, self-interested" campaign coverage described by Matthew Robert Kerbel in Chapter 4. They do not explain why, as Paul J. Quirk and Sean Matheson discuss in Chapter 6, major campaign and policy proposals increasingly reflect a "sound-bite mentality" and require presidents to cultivate skills "much akin to those of acting;" or why, as Gary Jacobson notes in Chapter 7, predicting the political complexion of Congress and legislative-executive relations beyond 1998 is risky given the quick reversals of fortune that beset Bush, Clinton, and congressional Republicans in recent years.

Revisiting the Valence Framework

Nor do such trite but true observations help us to answer the question posed by Jean Bethke Elshtain and Christopher Beem in Chapter 5 and echoed in every other chapter: "Are we moving from presidential elections as political events to elections as collective Rorschach tests?" Or, in a version of essentially the same question stimulated by Nelson's Chapter 1, why was Clinton able both to garner support with words about the future that were "shrouded in the empty, gauzy rhetoric" of building a bridge to the twenty-first century and to win through "the mostly nonpartisan vacuousness of the reelection campaign"?

In Nelson's volume on the 1992 elections, Donald E. Stokes and I argued that the conceptual key to understanding contemporary campaigns and elections is to recognize that they tend not to be dominated by "position issues," which are specific issues such as raising tariffs (yea or nay) and cutting welfare entitlements (for or against) on which the rival parties or candidates reach out for the support of the electorate by taking different positions on policy questions that divide the electorate. Instead, modern elections are mostly about "valence issues"—that is, issues on which the voters distinguish parties and candidates not by their real or perceived differences on position issues but by the degree to which they are linked in the voters' minds with conditions, symbols, or goals that are almost universally approved of or disapproved of by the electorate, such as economic prosperity, public corruption, and resolute leadership:

> The economy is a prime example of a valence issue. . . . We do not have one party advocating economic prosperity and the other advocating economic bad times. There is no constituency for economic distress. . . . The issue of economic prosperity acquires its power from the fact that the parties or candidates may be very unequally linked in the public's mind with the universally approved condition of good times and the universally disapproved condition of bad times. The difference between electoral success and disaster may turn on each party's ability to strengthen or weaken these perceptual bonds, or valences, in the public's mind.[10]

As we argued then, national elections have always involved a mix of both position politics and valence politics, and they still do. But the "structure of valence issues, which allows successful candidates to soar to great heights and unsuccessful ones to plummet to great depths, explains the fluidity of contemporary politics."[11] The valence framework is owed entirely to Stokes's path-breaking work, including his coauthored 1960 classic *The American Voter,* and the articles in which he explored the concept's explanatory power as well as its normative implications.[12]

As every chapter in this book indicates to one degree or another, the Clinton campaign of 1996 was run almost purely in valence terms. Examples are the "Mediscare" strategy discussed by Quirk and Matheson, the administration's savvy media wrap on the government shutdowns in late 1995 and early 1996, and what Stanley calls Gingrich's "display of personal peevishness" on *Air Force One*.

Clinton's "strategy of triangulation and acting presidential," which Nelson describes in Chapter 3, was a valence strategy par excellence. Likewise, Kerbel notes the administration's effort to counter the public's belief that Clinton had lied about Whitewater with the notion that "the press was making too much of the story." This was, in effect, a conscious campaign effort to neutralize one negative valence (the president is not truthful) with another (the press is not fair).

As several contributors to this volume observe, voters viewed Dole—who, in reality, was as physically vigorous during the campaign as any average man in his forties—as "old," "wooden," and worse. This judgment was no accident. The Clinton campaign took measured valence swipes at Dole's age and health, thanking him for his "long, long" record of public service while contrasting his "bridge to the past" with the baby boomer incumbent's "bridge to the future."

The Dole campaign responded, albeit belatedly and weakly, with valence appeals of its own. Dole and his staff characterized Clinton as generally untrustworthy, up to his neck in corruption scandals, and morally indifferent to teenage drug addiction. But Dole's valence missiles were never fully launched. Take the Republican National Committee's mistaken decision in 1995 to let the president run unanswered what were essentially valence–armor building ads depicting the president as tough on crime and in favor of "family values." Add to it the Dole camp's money shortages at several critical junctures during the campaign (which prevented it from running countervailing valence ads when and where they might do the most good), and you have what are almost certainly two important determinants of the outcome. Not even on the seemingly ready-made issue of Clinton's veto of a bill outlawing partial-birth abortion—a procedure in which the doctor forces scissors into the base of the skull of a partially delivered fetus and suctions out its brains—did the Dole campaign wage a well-conceived valence strike.

Elshtain and Beem are right when they argue that many issues of importance to voters were not debated in 1996: "they were at best ignored and often were the focus of demagogy—campaign finance reform, the future of entitlements, the condition of the inner city." But the point needs to be generalized: even the position issues that were debated were debated in the context of a valence war of words and symbols. For example, Dole's specific, at times almost policy-wonkish arguments in favor of changes in how Washington finances Medicare and Medicaid were met not by opposing Clinton campaign white papers but by a barrage of valence attacks questioning Dole's compassion for needy children, the sick, and the elderly and linking Dole to Gingrich's supposed extremism on social issues.

How, precisely, can we measure the intensity and pervasiveness of the valence politics of 1996? That I cannot say; I leave this difficult question to others. Of this much, however, I am certain: unless the election-interpretation establishment begins to think, talk, research, and write in a way that takes full advantage of the valence framework, we will continue to meet angry white males, soccer moms, stupid voters, and other creatures with mythical electoral power and importance in the election commentary of 2000 and beyond.

It is increasingly clear that, save for the conceptual insights and organizing power of the valence framework, we are living in a political age that is more complicated, harder to explain, tougher to understand, and more difficult to predict than the experts would like to admit, either to themselves or to the rest of us. We are not all Stokesians now, but we should become so, and soon.

Notes

1. *American Enterprise,* November/December 1996, 102, reporting data from Princeton Survey Research Associates and the *Washington Post.*
2. Jack Citrin, "The Angry White Male Is a Straw Man," *Public Affairs Report* 37 (January 1996): 1.
3. Jonathan Alter, *Newsweek,* December 30, 1996/January 6, 1997, 32.
4. CBS News/*New York Times* polls, as reported in the *New York Times,* August 12 and 26, 1996.
5. V. O. Key, *The Responsible Electorate* (Cambridge: Belknap Press, Harvard University Press, 1966), 5.
6. Edward S. Greenberg and Benjamin I. Page, *The Struggle for Democracy,* 2d ed. (New York: HarperCollins, 1994), 156.
7. Morris P. Fiorina, *Retrospective Voting in American National Elections* (New Haven: Yale University Press, 1981).
8. Milton Lodge, Marco R. Steenbergen, and Shawn Brau, "The Responsive Voter: Campaign Information and the Dynamics of Candidate Evaluation," *American Political Science Review* 89 (June 1995): 309.
9. Richard Cohen, "Ignorant, Apathetic, and Smug," *Washington Post,* February 2, 1996, A19.
10. Donald E. Stokes and John J. DiIulio Jr., "The Setting: Valence Politics in Modern Elections," in *The Elections of 1992,* ed. Michael Nelson (Washington, D.C.: CQ Press, 1993), 7–8.
11. Ibid., 18.
12. For a summary, see Donald E. Stokes, "Valence Politics," in *Electoral Politics,* ed. Dennis Kavanaugh (Oxford: Clarendon Press, 1992), 141–164.

Index

Page references followed by italic *t*, *f*, or *n* indicate tables, figures, or notes, respectively.